NE능률 영어교과서

대한민국 고등학생 10명 중
4.7 명이 보는 교과서

영어 고등 교과서 점유율 1위
(7차, 2007 개정, 2009 개정, 2015 개정)

리딩튜터

그동안 판매된
리딩튜터 1,900만 부
차곡차곡 쌓으면 19만 미터

에베레스트
21 배 높이

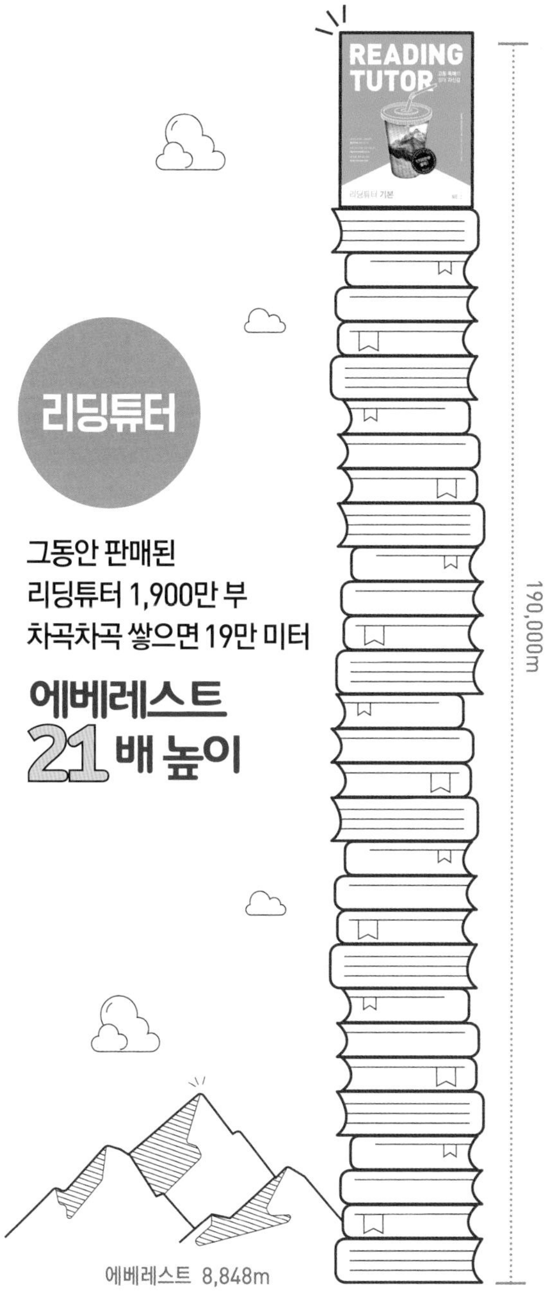

능률보카

그동안 판매된
능률VOCA 1,100만 부

대한민국 박스오피스
천만명을 넘은 영화
단 28개

그래머존

그동안 판매된 450만 부의 그래머존을 바닥에 쭉 ~ 깔면
1000km 서울-부산 왕복가능

중학

천문장 LEVEL 2

지은이	NE능률 영어교육연구소
선임연구원	김지현
연구원	장경아, 가민아, 오보은
영문교열	Angela Lan, Curtis Thompson, Keeran Murphy
디자인	민유화, 안훈정, 오솔길
맥편집	한서기획
Photo Credits	www.shutterstock.com

Let's grow together

NE능률이 미래를 창조합니다.

건강한 배움의 고객가치를 제공하겠다는 꿈을 실현하기 위해
40년이 넘는 시간 동안 열심히 달려왔습니다.

앞으로도 끊임없는 연구와 노력을 통해
당연한 것을 멈추지 않고

고객, 기업, 직원 모두가 함께 성장하는 NE능률이 되겠습니다.

NE 능률

Grammar Inside Level 1
[2021 개정]
NELT

중학

천문장

「구문이 독해로 연결되는 해석 공식」

LEVEL 2

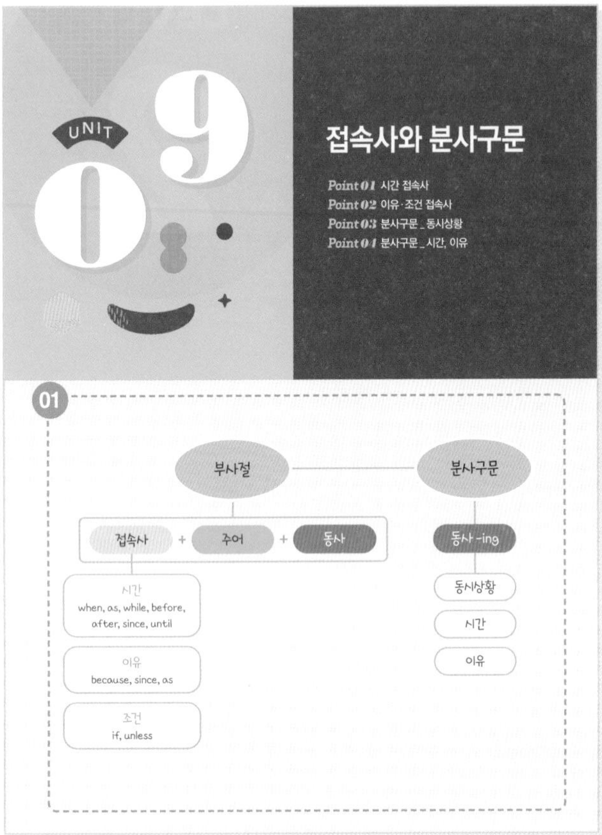

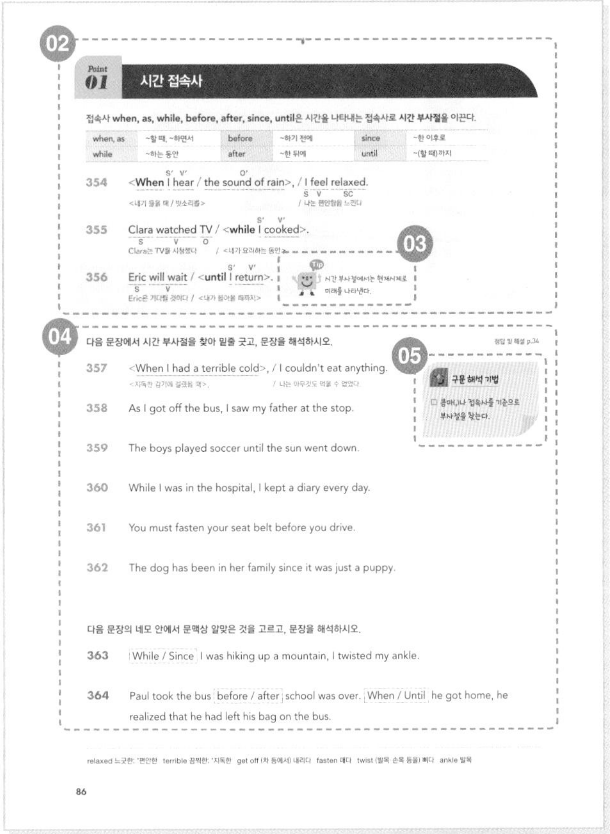

02

Point 01 시간 접속사

접속사 **when, as, while, before, after, since, until**은 시간을 나타내는 접속사로 **시간 부사절**을 이끈다.

when, as	~할 때, ~하면서	before	~하기 전에	since	~한 이후로
while	~하는 동안	after	~한 뒤에	until	~(할 때)까지

354 <**When** I hear / the sound of rain>, / I feel relaxed.
<내가 들을 때 / 빗소리를> / 나는 편안함을 느낀다

355 Clara watched TV / <**while** I cooked>.
Clara는 TV를 시청했다 / <내가 요리하는 동안>

356 Eric will wait / <**until** I return>.
Eric은 기다릴 것이다 / <내가 돌아올 때까지>

03 Tip 시간 부사절에서는 현재시제로 미래를 나타낸다.

04 다음 문장에서 시간 부사절을 찾아 밑줄 긋고, 문장을 해석하시오. 정답 및 해설 p.34

357 <When I had a terrible cold>, / I couldn't eat anything.
<지독한 감기에 걸렸을 때>, / 나는 아무것도 먹을 수 없었다

358 As I got off the bus, I saw my father at the stop.

359 The boys played soccer until the sun went down.

360 While I was in the hospital, I kept a diary every day.

361 You must fasten your seat belt before you drive.

362 The dog has been in her family since it was just a puppy.

05 구문 해석 기법
□ 콤마(,)나 접속사를 기준으로 부사절을 찾는다.

다음 문장의 네모 안에서 문맥상 알맞은 것을 고르고, 문장을 해석하시오.

363 While / Since I was hiking up a mountain, I twisted my ankle.

364 Paul took the bus before / after school was over. When / Until he got home, he realized that he had left his bag on the bus.

relaxed 느긋한; *편안한 terrible 끔찍한; *지독한 get off (차 등에서) 내리다 fasten 매다 twist (발목·손목 등을) 삐다 ankle 발목

86

01 한눈에 들어오는 구문 도식

학습 Point를 확인하고
문장 구조를 한눈에 이해할 수 있게 구성하였습니다.

02 이해하기 쉽게 설명한 학습 Point

중학 학년별 필수 구문을 세분화한 학습 Point를
제시하고, 끊어 읽기와 직독직해를 통해 영어 문장 구조를
쉽게 이해할 수 있게 하였습니다.

03 Tip

구문을 이해하는 데 도움이 되는 문법 사항을 간략히
정리하였습니다.

04 확인 문제

학습한 Point를 바로 적용해 보는 문장별 확인 문제로
두 단계 점검이 가능하도록 구성하였습니다.

05 구문 해석 기법

학습 Point와 관련하여 독해에 유용한
해석 기법을 제공하였습니다.

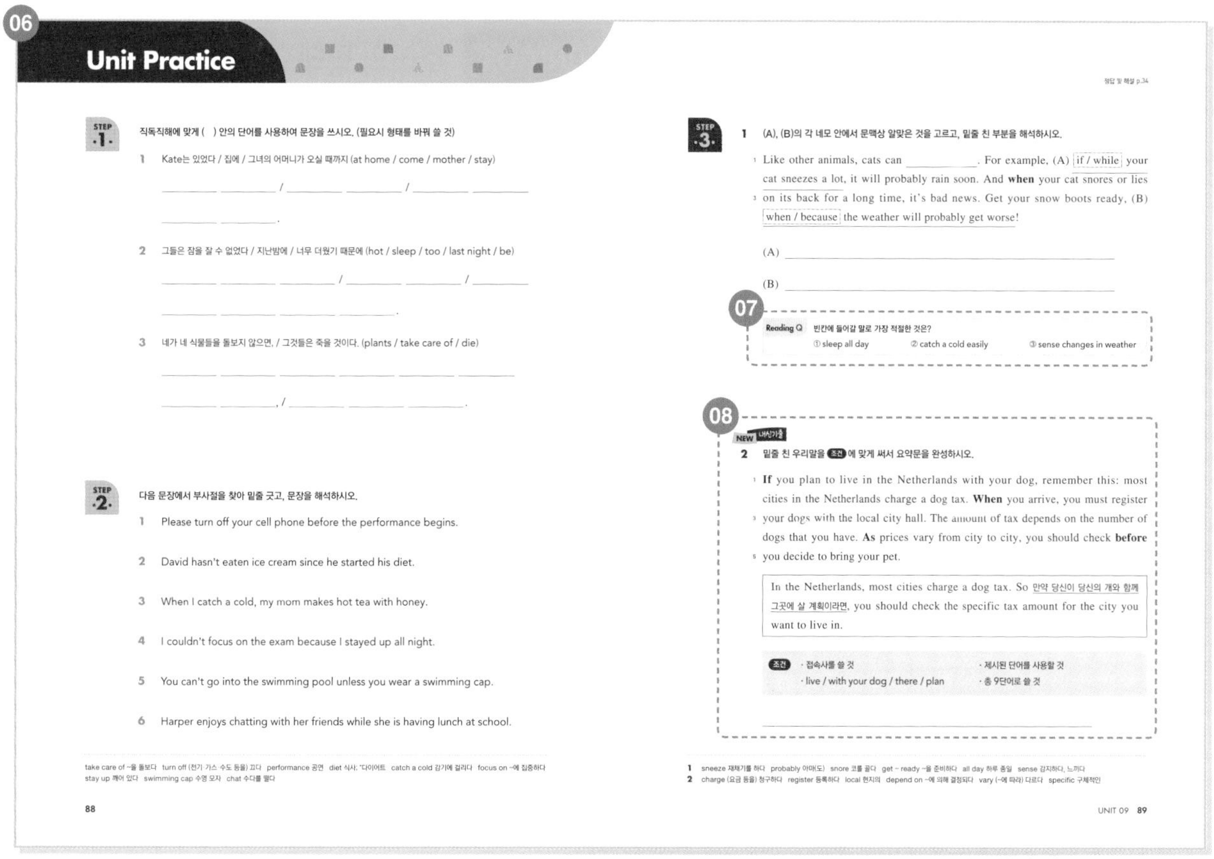

06

Unit Practice

정답 및 해설 p.34

STEP 1 직독직해에 맞게 ( ) 안의 단어를 사용하여 문장을 쓰시오. (필요시 형태를 바꿔 쓸 것)

1 Kate는 있었다 / 집에 / 그녀의 어머니가 오실 때까지 (at home / come / mother / stay)

2 그들은 잠을 잘 수 없었다 / 지난밤에 / 너무 더웠기 때문에 (hot / sleep / too / last night / be)

3 네가 네 식물들을 돌보지 않으면, / 그것들은 죽을 것이다. (plants / take care of / die)

STEP 2 다음 문장에서 부사절을 찾아 밑줄 긋고, 문장을 해석하시오.

1 Please turn off your cell phone before the performance begins.

2 David hasn't eaten ice cream since he started his diet.

3 When I catch a cold, my mom makes hot tea with honey.

4 I couldn't focus on the exam because I stayed up all night.

5 You can't go into the swimming pool unless you wear a swimming cap.

6 Harper enjoys chatting with her friends while she is having lunch at school.

take care of ~을 돌보다 turn off (전기·가스·수도 등을) 끄다 performance 공연 diet 식사; 다이어트 catch a cold 감기에 걸리다 focus on ~에 집중하다 stay up 깨어 있다 swimming cap 수영 모자 chat 수다를 떨다

88

STEP 3 1 (A), (B)의 각 네모 안에서 문맥상 알맞은 것을 고르고, 밑줄 친 부분을 해석하시오.

Like other animals, cats can ________. For example, (A) if / while your cat sneezes a lot, it will probably rain soon. And when your cat snores or lies on its back for a long time, it's bad news. Get your snow boots ready, (B) when / because the weather will probably get worse!

(A)

(B)

07

Reading Q 빈칸에 들어갈 말로 가장 적절한 것은?
① sleep all day ② catch a cold easily ③ sense changes in weather

08

NEW 내신기출

2 밑줄 친 우리말을 조건에 맞게 써서 요약문을 완성하시오.

If you plan to live in the Netherlands with your dog, remember this: most cities in the Netherlands charge a dog tax. When you arrive, you must register your dogs with the local city hall. The amount of tax depends on the number of dogs that you have. As prices vary from city to city, you should check before you decide to bring your pet.

In the Netherlands, most cities charge a dog tax. So 만약 당신이 당신의 개와 함께 그곳에 살 계획이라면, you should check the specific tax amount for the city you want to live in.

조건 · 접속사를 쓸 것 · 제시된 단어를 사용할 것
· live / with your dog / there / plan · 총 9단어로 쓸 것

1 sneeze 재채기를 하다 probably 아마도 snore 코를 골다 get ~ ready ~을 준비하다 all day 하루 종일 sense 감지하다, 느끼다
2 charge (요금 등을) 청구하다 register 등록하다 local 현지의 depend on ~에 의해 결정되다 vary (~에 따라) 다르다 specific 구체적인

UNIT 09 89

06 Unit Practice

학습 Point에 대한 통합 학습 3단계로 구성하였으며,
앞에서 배운 문장을 반복함으로써 구문에 익숙해지게 하였습니다.

- STEP 1 우리말 직독직해 영작하기
- STEP 2 문장 구조를 파악하고 해석하기
- STEP 3 지문 속에서 학습 Point 적용하기

07 Reading Q

내용 확인 문제를 통해 지문 이해를 높일 수 있게 하였습니다.

08 NEW 내신기출

최신 내신 기출 유형을 반영한 서술형 문제를 통해
내신 실전 감각을 기를 수 있게 하였습니다.

09 Wrap Up

구문 도식과 주요 예문을 반복 학습함으로써
학습 Point를 정리할 수 있게 하였습니다.

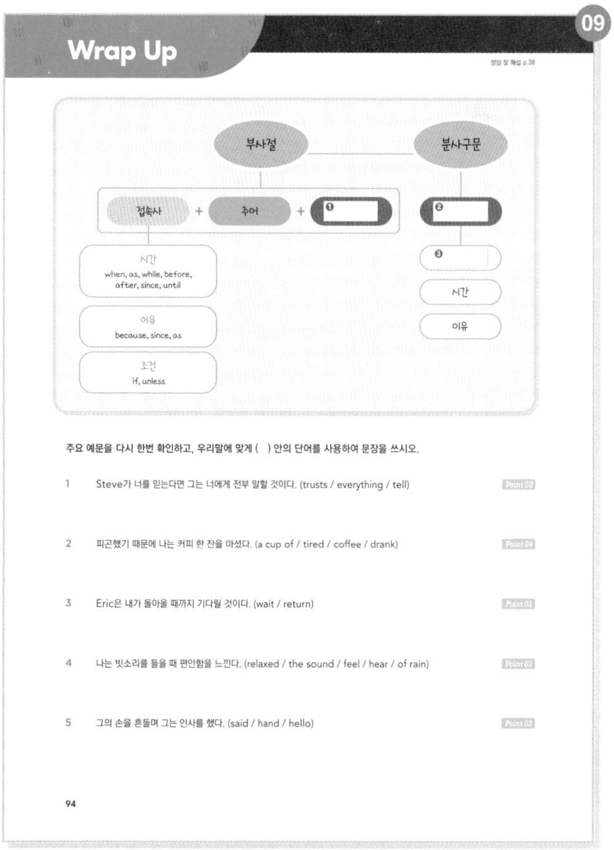

09

Wrap Up

정답 및 해설 p.38

주요 예문을 다시 한번 확인하고, 우리말에 맞게 ( ) 안의 단어를 사용하여 문장을 쓰시오.

1 Steve가 너를 믿는다면 그는 너에게 전부 말할 것이다. (trusts / everything / tell)

2 피곤했기 때문에 나는 커피 한 잔을 마셨다. (a cup of / tired / coffee / drank)

3 Eric은 내가 돌아올 때까지 기다릴 것이다. (wait / return)

4 나는 빗소리를 들을 때 편안함을 느낀다. (relaxed / the sound / feel / hear / of rain)

5 그의 손을 흔들며 그는 인사를 했다. (said / hand / hello)

94

목차

이 책에 쓰인 표기법

표기법	뜻	표기법	뜻	표기법	뜻
S	주어	SC	주격보어	S', V' 등	종속절의 주어·동사 등
V	동사	OC	목적격보어	( )	생략된 어구
O	목적어	M	수식어(구)	/	끊어 읽기
IO	간접목적어	to-v	to부정사	//	등위절과 등위절의 구분
DO	직접목적어	v-ing	동명사, 분사	{[< >]}	구나 종속절의 구분

끊어 읽기는 구문 이해를 돕기 위해 의미 단위로 끊어 읽는 하나의 장치이다. 따라서 무조건 끊어 읽거나 너무 많이 끊어 읽을 필요는 없으며 자신의 독해 호흡에 따라 끊어 읽도록 한다.

UNIT 01

주어의 형태

Point 01 명사와 대명사
Point 02 동명사와 to부정사
Point 03 that절과 의문사절
Point 04 가주어와 비인칭 주어

주어

- 명사(구)
- 대명사
- 동명사(구)
- to부정사(구)
- that절
- 의문사절
- 가주어 it
  - + 진주어 to부정사(구)
  - + 진주어 that절
- 비인칭 주어 it

Point 01

명사와 대명사

주어는 '**누가/무엇이**'에 해당하며, 동사가 나타내는 **동작·상태의 주체**이다. **명사(구)**나 **대명사**가 주어로 쓰일 수 있다.

001 **Giraffes** have / purple tongues.
S V O
기린은 가지고 있다 / 보라색 혀를

002 **They** arrived / at the station / at seven.
S V M_1 M_2
그들은 도착했다 / 역에 / 7시에

003 **The ending <of this novel>** / is really interesting.
S V SC
결말은 <이 소설의> / 정말 흥미롭다

다음 문장에서 주어를 찾아 밑줄 긋고, 문장을 해석하시오.

정답 및 해설 p.1

004 My stomach hurts / a lot.
나의 배가 아프다 / 많이

005 Sweet desserts have lots of sugar.

006 He writes a letter to me every week.

007 The airplane from London just landed at the airport.

008 Some famous painters visited this art museum yesterday.

009 Olivia invited her friends to her house. She will have a party tomorrow.

다음 문장의 네모 안에서 어법상 알맞은 것을 고르고, 문장을 해석하시오.

010 The causes of the accident [is / are] not clear. The police are looking for clues.

011 Jake and his mother went to the restaurant. He ordered pasta and [she / they] ordered a steak.

tongue 혀 stomach 위, 배 dessert 디저트, 후식 land 착륙하다 art museum 미술관 cause 원인 accident 사고 clear 분명한; *확실한 look for 찾다 clue 단서 order 명령하다; *주문하다

Point 02 동명사와 to부정사

동명사(v-ing)나 **to부정사(to-v)**가 주어로 쓰일 수 있으며, 동명사(구), to부정사(구) 주어는 **단수 취급**한다.
• 동명사와 to부정사의 **부정형**은 **동명사나 to부정사 바로 앞에 not/never**를 붙여 나타낸다.

012 **Eating breakfast** / is good / for teenagers.
S / V SC / M
아침을 먹는 것은 / 좋다 / 십 대들에게

013 **To see** / is to believe.
S / V SC
보는 것이 / 믿는 것이다. (백문이 불여일견)

014 **Not apologizing** <for your mistake> / wasn't wise.
S / V SC
사과하지 않은 것은 <네 잘못에 대해> / 현명하지 못했다

다음 문장에서 주어를 찾아 밑줄 긋고, 문장을 해석하시오. 정답 및 해설 p.1

015 Traveling alone / is sometimes dangerous.
혼자 여행하는 것은 / 때때로 위험하다.

016 Lying on this sofa relaxes me.

017 To break a promise destroys trust.

018 Becoming an astronaut was my dream long ago.

019 Never forgetting to say "thank you" shows respect for others.

020 Cooking delicious meals gives her great pleasure.

> **구문 해석 기법**
> □ 문장 맨 앞의 동명사나 to부정사부터 동사 바로 앞까지가 주어이며, '~하는 것은[하기는]'으로 해석한다.

다음 문장의 네모 안에서 어법상 알맞은 것을 고르고, 문장을 해석하시오.

021 [To accept not / Not to accept] the invitation would be rude.

022 [Listen / Listening] to music relieves stress. To take a walk for a few minutes also [help / helps].

apologize for ~에 대해 사과하다 alone 혼자 lie 누워 있다 destroy 무너뜨리다, 파괴하다 trust 신뢰 astronaut 우주 비행사 respect 존경; *존중 pleasure 즐거움 accept 받아들이다 invitation 초대 rude 무례한 relieve 덜어 주다 take a walk 산책하다

Unit Practice

STEP 1

직독직해에 맞게 ( ) 안의 단어를 사용하여 문장을 쓰시오. (필요시 형태를 바꿔 쓸 것)

1 Chloe는 통화 중이었다 / 그때 (talk / at that time / be / on the phone)

______ ______ ______ ______ ______ ______ /

______ ______ ______.

2 규칙적으로 운동을 하는 것은 / 너의 건강에 좋다. (good for / be / regularly / exercise / health)

______ ______ ______ / ______ ______ ______

______ ______.

3 새로운 언어를 배우는 것은 / 도전적이지만 흥미진진하다. (challenging / learn / but / a new language / exciting / be)

______ ______ ______ ______ / ______ ______

______ ______.

STEP 2

다음 문장에서 주어를 모두 찾아 밑줄 긋고, 문장을 해석하시오.

1 To talk loudly during a movie is annoying.

2 The sound of the bell surprised the students.

3 To become the president of a large company is my life goal.

4 Spending time with family on weekends is important to him.

5 Doing volunteer work provides valuable experience for children.

6 Teenagers love to take photos, and they also love sharing them on social media.

regularly 규칙적으로 challenging 도전적인 exciting 흥미진진한 annoying 짜증스러운 surprise 놀라게 하다 president 대통령; *회장 company 회사 goal 목표 volunteer work 자원봉사 provide 제공하다 valuable 소중한 share 공유하다

STEP 3

1 밑줄 친 (A), (B)에서 주어에 [ ], 동사에 동그라미 하고, 주어를 해석하시오.

King cake is a traditional French cake with an interesting custom. **A small doll** is inside the cake. After **someone** cuts the cake, **everyone** takes a piece. (A) Finding the doll inside your piece makes you "king" for the day. (B) Becoming the king allows you to make the rules all day. And **your friends and family** must follow your rules!

(A) ______________________________

(B) ______________________________

Reading Q 윗글의 주제로 가장 적절한 것은?

① the origin of king cake
② the custom of king cake
③ the way to make king cake

NEW 내신기출

2 밑줄 친 우리말을 조건에 맞게 쓰시오.

Salar de Uyuni is a huge salt desert in Bolivia. **It** is famous for its beautiful scenery. After **it** rains, **the water** forms a large but very thin salt lake. Like a huge mirror, **it** reflects the whole sky. 그 소금 호수 위를 걷는 것은 멋지다. **You** can see the sky under your feet. So **people** sometimes call this place "Heaven on Earth."

조건
· 동명사구를 주어로 쓸 것
· 제시된 단어를 사용할 것 (필요시 형태를 바꿔 쓸 것)
· on / wonderful / the salt lake / walk
· 총 7단어로 쓸 것

____

1 traditional 전통적인 custom 관습 inside ~의 안에 take 가지고 가다 piece 조각 all day 하루 종일 follow 따르다 origin 기원
2 huge 거대한 desert 사막 scenery 경관, 경치 form 형성하다 thin 얇은, 가느다란 reflect (물·거울 등에 상을) 비추다, 반사하다 whole 전체의

Point 03 that절과 의문사절

접속사 that이나 **의문사가 이끄는 절**은 **명사절**로, 문장에서 주어로 쓰일 수 있다.

that절 주어	That + 주어 + 동사 ~	의문사절 주어	의문사(+ 주어) + 동사 ~

023 <That(S) everyone(S′) has(V′) worries(O′)> / is(V) obvious(SC).
<모두가 고민을 가지고 있다는 것은> / 명백하다.

명사절 주어는 단수 취급하므로, 문장의 동사는 단수로 쓴다.

024 <When(S) he(S′) came(V′) / here(M′)> / is not(V) clear(SC).
<그가 언제 왔는지는 / 여기에> / 분명하지 않다

025 <Who(S, S′) found(V′) the answer(O′)> / doesn't matter(V).
<누가 정답을 찾았는지는> / 중요하지 않다.

다음 문장에서 주어를 모두 찾아 밑줄 긋고, 문장을 해석하시오.

정답 및 해설 p.3

026 <When she will visit us> / is not certain.
그녀가 언제 우리를 방문할지는 / 확실하지 않다.

027 That so many people died in the accident was shocking.

028 Where I hid my report card is a secret.

029 What she asked me to do is unclear.

030 That I passed the exam made my parents happy.

031 That he escaped from prison is big news. Who helped him is a mystery.

다음 문장의 네모 안에서 어법상 알맞은 것을 고르고, 문장을 해석하시오.

032 [That / Who] Bella was angry at him is clear. But [that / why] she was upset is uncertain.

033 It doesn't matter [that / what] the team won first prize. How [it became / became it] the best is the important thing.

worry 걱정하다; *걱정거리 obvious 명백한 clear 분명한 matter 문제; *중요하다 certain 확실한 accident 사고 shocking 충격적인
hide 숨기다(-hid-hidden) unclear 불확실한 escape 탈출하다 prison 감옥 big 큰; *심각한 upset 마음이 상한

Point 04 가주어와 비인칭 주어

긴 to부정사(구)나 that절이 주어인 경우, **진주어는 뒤로** 보내고 주어 자리에 **가주어 it**을 써서 「It ~ to-v/that절」의 형태로 쓴다. **비인칭 주어 it**은 **시간, 요일, 날짜, 날씨, 계절, 명암(밝고 어두움), 거리** 등을 나타낸다.

034 **It** is necessary / **to keep your promise**.
S(가주어) V SC S(진주어)
필요하다 / 네 약속을 지키는 것은

035 **It** was nice / <**that you gave up your seat** / **to the elderly woman**>.
S(가주어) V SC S(진주어) S′ V′ O′ M′
멋졌다 / <네가 네 자리를 양보한 것은 / 노부인께>

036 **It** is cold and dry / in winter.
비인칭 주어 V SC M
춥고 건조하다 / 겨울에는

다음 문장에서 주어를 모두 찾아 밑줄 긋고, 문장을 해석하시오. 정답 및 해설 p.3

037 It was seven o'clock / in the morning.
7시였다 / 오전

038 It is impossible to do everything well.

039 It is hard to imagine my life without a smartphone.

040 It made me sad that he forgot my birthday.

041 It is around 100 meters from here to my house.

042 It seems that my parents are sleeping deeply.

> **구문 해석 기법**
> - □ 가주어 it은 해석하지 않고, 진주어인 to부정사구나 that절을 '~하는 것은[하기는]'으로 해석한다.
> - □ 비인칭 주어 it은 따로 해석하지 않는다.

다음 문장의 네모 안에서 어법상 알맞은 것을 고르고, 문장을 해석하시오.

043 When you feel sick, [it / that] is helpful [to / that] take medicine and rest at home.

044 [It / That] is getting hotter every year. It is probably true [to / that] global warming is becoming a serious problem.

---

keep 유지하다; *약속을 지키다 give up 포기하다 elderly 연세가 드신 impossible 불가능한 imagine 상상하다 around 약, ~쯤 deeply 깊이 helpful 도움이 되는 take medicine 약을 먹다 rest 쉬다, 휴식을 취하다 probably 아마 global warming 지구 온난화

Unit Practice

STEP 1 직독직해에 맞게 ( ) 안의 단어를 사용하여 문장을 쓰시오. (필요시 형태를 바꿔 쓸 것)

1 흥미롭다 / 개가 꿈을 꿀 수 있다는 것은 (dogs / interesting / dream / can)

_____ _____ _____ / _____ _____ _____ _____.

2 오늘은 일요일이다, / 그리고 나는 나의 조부모님을 방문할 것이다. (and / grandparents / be / visit)

_____ _____ _____ _____, / _____ _____

_____ _____ _____ _____.

3 그녀가 언제 돌아올지는 / 여행에서 / 확실하지 않다 (will / from the trip / when / certain / be / get back)

_____ _____ _____ _____ _____ / _____

_____ _____ / _____ _____ _____.

STEP 2 다음 문장에서 주어를 모두 찾아 밑줄 긋고, 문장을 해석하시오.

1 Why he committed the crime is still unknown.

2 It is fun to try new foods from different cultures.

3 It was dark in the cave, and I was scared of the bats.

4 That they canceled the concert was disappointing.

5 What children watch on television affects their behavior.

6 It seems that you are a big fan of superhero movies.

commit (그릇된 일·범죄를) 저지르다 crime 범죄 still 아직 unknown 알려지지 않은 try 노력하다; *시도해 보다 culture 문화 cave 동굴 bat 박쥐 cancel 취소하다 affect 영향을 미치다

정답 및 해설 p.3

STEP 3

1 밑줄 친 (A), (B)에서 진주어를 찾아 [ ]로 묶고, 밑줄 친 부분을 해석하시오.

(A) It sounds unrealistic to make artificial eggs from beans. However, a company in the US can do this! Real eggs have harmful cholesterol. But artificial eggs don't have any. So **it** is healthier **to eat artificial ones**. Also, **it** doesn't cost much **to make them**. So (B) it is possible that these eggs will make baking cookies and bread cheaper.

*cholesterol 콜레스테롤

(A) ______________________________

(B) ______________________________

Reading Q 인공 달걀에 관한 윗글의 내용과 일치하지 않는 것은?

① 콩으로 만든다. ② 생산에 많은 비용이 들지 않는다.
③ 진짜 달걀을 먹는 것보다 건강에 해롭다.

NEW 내신기출

2 밑줄 친 우리말 (A), (B)에 맞게 보기 의 단어를 사용하여 각 문장을 쓰시오. (필요시 형태를 바꿔 쓸 것)

(A) 짧은 연필들을 쥐는 것은 어렵다. So most people just throw them away. However, one company makes special pencils. (B) 당신이 그것들을 어떻게 사용하는지는 간단하다. When they get short, plant them in some soil. The pencils have herb seeds inside. The seeds sprout and grow. **It** will make you happy **that you helped the earth**. And you can enjoy the herbs too!

보기 hold / hard / simple / short / use / it / how / pencils

(A) _____ _____ _____ _____ _____ _____ _____.

(B) _____ _____ _____ _____ _____ _____.

1 unrealistic 비현실적인 artificial 인공의 harmful 해로운 possible 가능한 bake (음식을) 굽다 cheap 싼, 돈이 적게 드는(-cheaper-cheapest)
2 throw away 버리다 plant (식물을) 심다 soil 땅, 흙 seed 씨앗 sprout 싹이 나다 hold (손으로) 잡다, 쥐다

Wrap Up

정답 및 해설 p.5

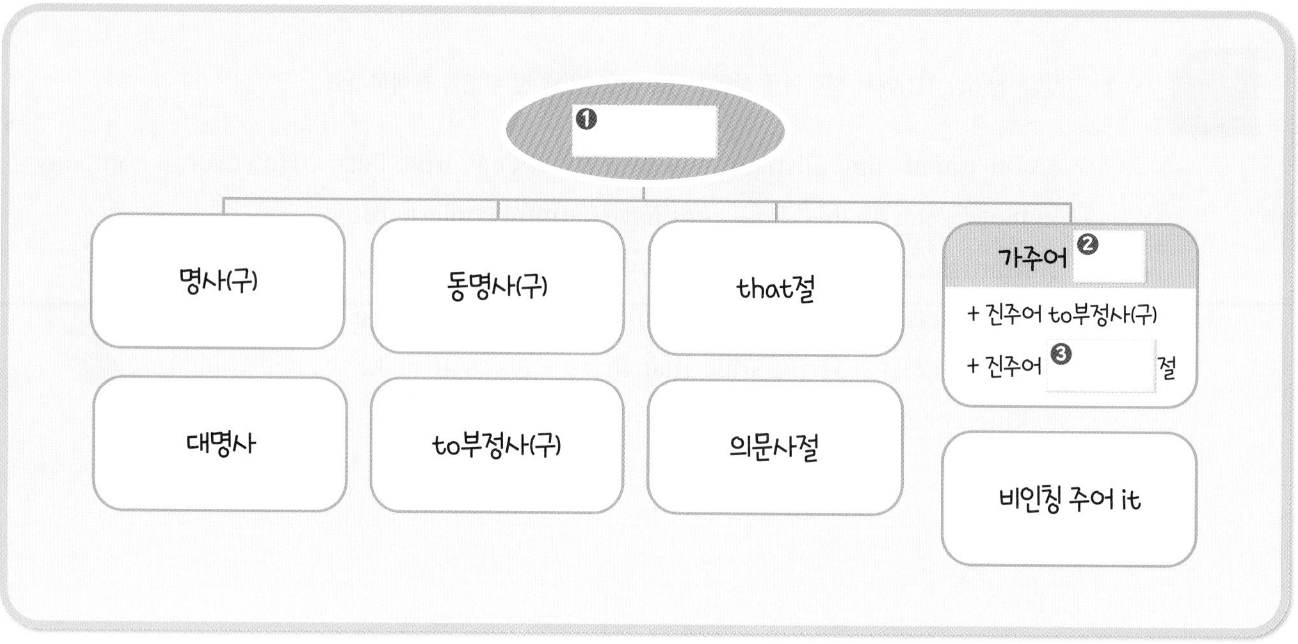

주요 예문을 다시 한번 확인하고, 우리말에 맞게 (   ) 안의 단어를 사용하여 문장을 쓰시오.

1 누가 정답을 찾았는지는 중요하지 않다. (matter / found / the answer) Point 03

2 아침을 먹는 것은 십 대들에게 좋다. (breakfast / for teenagers / good / eating) Point 02

3 네 약속을 지키는 것은 필요하다. (keep / necessary / promise / it) Point 04

4 이 소설의 결말은 정말 흥미롭다. (really / of this novel / interesting / the ending) Point 01

5 모두가 고민을 가지고 있다는 것은 명백하다. (worries / has / everyone / obvious / that) Point 03

6 네가 노부인께 네 자리를 양보한 것은 멋졌다. (gave up / nice / it / to the elderly woman / seat) Point 04

UNIT 02

목적어의 형태

Point 01 명사와 대명사
Point 02 동명사와 to부정사
Point 03 that절과 의문사절
Point 04 가목적어, 전치사의 목적어

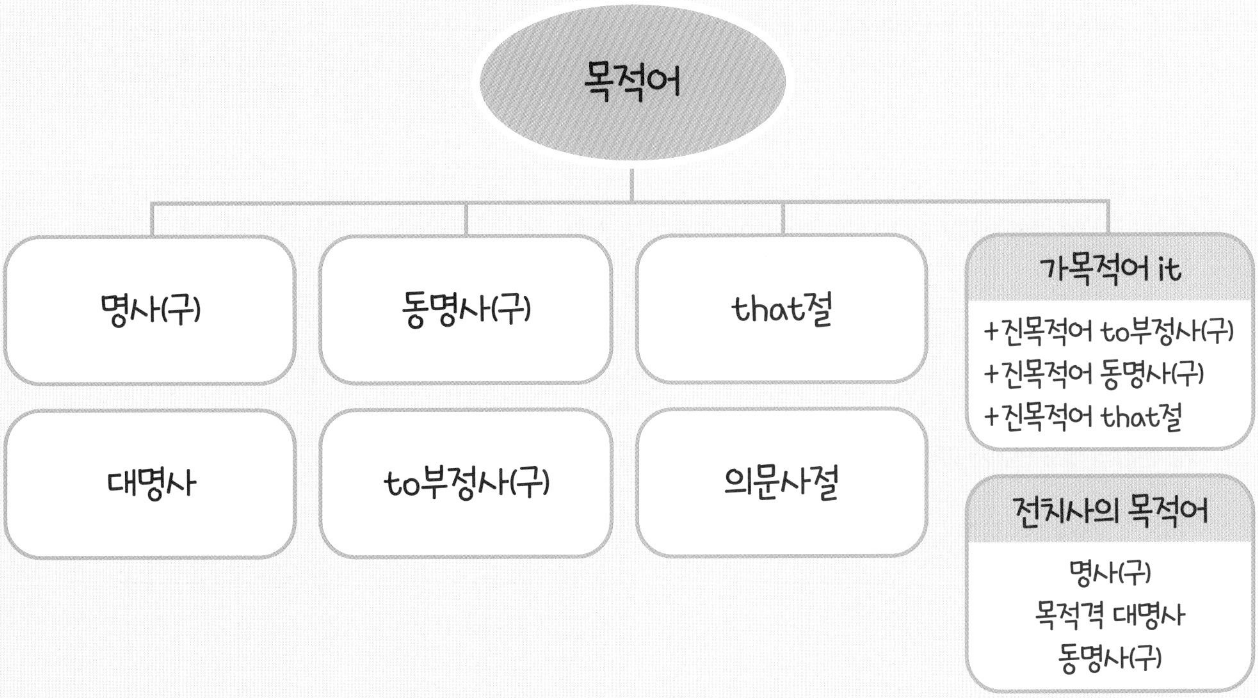

Point **01**

명사와 대명사

목적어는 **동사가 나타내는 동작의 대상**으로 **'무엇을/누구를'**에 해당하는 말로 **명사(구)**나 **대명사**가 쓰일 수 있다. 동사의 성격에 따라 두 개의 목적어가 필요한 경우도 있다.

S+V+O	S가 O를 V하다	S+V+IO+DO	S가 IO에게 DO를 V하다
S+V+O+OC	S는 O가 OC하게 V하다		

045 We passed / **the test.**
S V O
우리는 합격했다 / 그 시험을

046 Oliver didn't help / **them.**
S V O
Oliver는 돕지 않았다 / 그들을

047 I forgot / **the name <of the song>.**
S V O
나는 잊어버렸다 / 이름을 <그 노래의>

048 My aunt bought **me** / **a new bike.**
S V IO DO
우리 이모가 내게 사 주셨다 / 새 자전거를

다음 문장에서 목적어를 모두 찾아 밑줄 긋고, 문장을 해석하시오. 정답 및 해설 p.5

049 Eric likes / all kinds of films.
Eric은 좋아한다 / 모든 종류의 영화를

050 You don't have to do it now.

051 My dad cooked us pizza at home.

052 We made him our team captain.

053 We lost our way to the shopping mall.

054 After Clara solved the math problem, she raised her hand.

다음 문장의 네모 안에서 어법상 알맞은 것을 고르고, 문장을 해석하시오.

055 Ava sent [my / me] a text message after school.

056 I didn't drink coffee when I was young. Now I drink [it / them] every day.

pass 지나가다; *(시험에) 합격하다 captain 선장; *(스포츠 팀) 주장 lose 잃다(-lost-lost) solve (문제 등을) 해결하다, 풀다 raise 들어올리다

Point 02 동명사와 to부정사

동명사(v-ing)와 to부정사(to-v)는 목적어로 쓰일 수 있는데, 동사에 따라 동명사(구)나 to부정사(구)를 쓰거나 둘 다 쓴다.

동명사를 목적어로 쓰는 동사	avoid, enjoy, mind, practice, finish, give up, stop 등
to부정사를 목적어로 쓰는 동사	want, agree, need, choose, decide, expect, hope, learn 등
둘 다 목적어로 쓰는 동사	like, love, hate, start, begin, continue 등
목적어의 형태에 따라 의미가 달라지는 동사	remember, forget, try 등

057 Nell finished / **doing his homework**.
S V O
Nell은 끝냈다 / 그의 숙제를 하는 것을

058 We hope / **to see you** / **again**.
S V O
우리는 바란다 / 너를 보기를 / 다시

059 I remember / **calling him** / **yesterday**.
S V O
나는 기억한다 / 그에게 전화했던 것을 / 어제

060 I remembered / **to call him**.
S V O
나는 기억했다 / 그에게 전화할 것을

다음 문장에서 목적어를 찾아 밑줄 긋고, 문장을 해석하시오.

정답 및 해설 p.5

061 I expect / to go abroad / this summer.
나는 기대한다 / 외국에 가기를 / 이번 여름에

062 He began looking for a new job.

063 Leo always practices dancing.

064 My elder brother and I enjoy watching soccer matches.

065 She agreed to accept my suggestion.

066 I forgot to bring my history textbook.

구문 해석 기법

□ 「remember/forget+v-ing」는 '(과거에) ~했던 것을 기억하다/잊다', 「remember / forget+to-v」는 '(미래에) ~할 것을 기억하다/잊다'로 해석한다.

□ 「try+v-ing」는 '(시험 삼아) ~해 보다', 「try+to-v」는 '~하려고 노력하다'로 해석한다.

다음 문장의 네모 안에서 어법상 알맞은 것을 고르고, 문장을 해석하시오.

067 Henry wants [losing / to lose] weight. He avoids [eating / to eat] sweets these days.

068 I'm trying [to study / study] for my test. Do you mind [turning / to turn] down the volume?

---

go abroad 외국에 가다 match 성냥; *경기 suggestion 제안 textbook 교과서 lose weight 살을 빼다 sweet 단; *단것 these days 요즘에는

Unit Practice

STEP 1 **직독직해에 맞게 ( ) 안의 단어를 사용하여 문장을 쓰시오. (필요시 형태를 바꿔 쓸 것)**

1 나의 할아버지는 키우신다 / 소와 닭을 / 그의 농장에서 (cows / grandfather / chickens / raise / on his farm)

__________ __________ __________ / __________ __________ __________ /

__________ __________ __________.

2 Karen은 그를 알아보지 못했다 / 처음에는 (at first / recognize)

__________ __________ __________ __________ / __________ __________.

3 우리는 포기했다 / 지하철을 기다리는 것을 / 그리고 집으로 걸어갔다 (walk / give up / for the subway / home / wait)

__________ __________ __________ / __________ __________ __________

__________ / __________ __________ __________.

STEP 2 **다음 문장에서 목적어를 찾아 밑줄 긋고, 문장을 해석하시오.**

1 Don will introduce her to his family next month.

2 She will try making a cake by herself for the first time.

3 The dogs continued barking until late at night.

4 The athlete finished the marathon within three hours.

5 I learned to swim last year, but I still can't swim in the sea.

6 Diana is expecting to get a good grade on the midterm exam.

raise 들어올리다; *키우다 at first 처음에는 recognize 알아보다 home 집으로 introduce 소개하다 bark 짖다 athlete (운동)선수 marathon 마라톤 within 이내에 grade 등급; *성적 midterm exam 중간고사

STEP 3

1 밑줄 친 우리말에 맞게 ( ) 안의 단어를 배열하여 문장을 완성하시오. (필요시 형태를 바꿔 쓸 것)

In Baltimore, some schools enjoy **Meatless Monday**. 그 학교들에서는 월요일마다 모두가 고기 제품을 먹는 것을 멈춘다. Instead of meat, cafeteria workers provide **vegetables, fruits, and grains**. These are healthy foods with low fat. Also, they make **people** full on fewer calories. The schools expect **to reduce student health problems with Meatless Monday**.

At those schools, ______________________________ on Mondays.
(eat / stop / meat products / everyone)

Reading Q 윗글의 내용을 한 문장으로 요약하고자 한다. 빈칸 (A)와 (B)에 들어갈 말로 가장 적절한 것은?

With Meatless Monday, the schools can help their ___(A)___ to stay ___(B)___.

	(A)		(B)
①	workers	…	smart
②	students	…	healthy
③	animals	…	happy

NEW 내신기출

2 다음 중 어법상 어색한 부분이 있는 문장 2개를 찾아 바르게 고쳐 쓰시오. (고친 문장 전체를 쓸 것)

Do you want being a reporter? Then you should join the broadcasting club at school. You can learn to report news and to present feature stories. You should also practice to write about the things around you. Finally, you must work on your communication skills. This is important because reporters need to read, write, speak, and listen well.

*feature story 특집 기사

(1) ______________________________

(2) ______________________________

1 meatless 고기가 없는 cafeteria (학교·회사 등의) 구내식당 provide 제공하다 grain 곡물 fat 지방 full 가득 찬; *배부른 reduce 줄이다
2 reporter 기자(*v.* report 알리다; *보도하다) broadcasting club 방송부 present 주다; *제시하다 work on ~에 노력을 들이다

Point 03 that절과 의문사절

접속사 that이나 **의문사가 이끄는 절은 명사절**로, 문장에서 목적어로 쓰일 수 있다.

069 Kate believes / <**(that) James is innocent**>.
S V O (S′ V′ SC′)
Kate는 믿는다 / <James가 무죄라는 것을>

070 He thought / <**(that) you were** / **with Matt**>.
S V O (S′ V′ M′)
그는 생각했다 / <네가 있다고 / Matt와>

071 She asked / <**when they came back**>.
S V O (S′ V′)
그녀는 물었다 / <그들이 언제 돌아왔는지>

072 I didn't know / <**who lived there**>.
S V O (S′ V′ M′)
나는 몰랐다 / <누가 그곳에 사는지>

Tip
절 형태의 목적어를 자주 쓰는 동사
know, think, believe, imagine, guess, understand, say 등

다음 문장에서 목적어를 찾아 밑줄 긋고, 문장을 해석하시오.

정답 및 해설 p.7

073 I wonder / <where Sam is>.
나는 궁금하다 / <Sam이 어디에 있는지>

074 You didn't say what the answer was.

075 We all know cheating on exams is bad.

076 I don't understand why you must leave.

077 Hilary forgot how old the man was.

078 Sometimes I imagine that I can communicate with animals.

구문 해석 기법

☐ that절 목적어는 '~하다는 것을' 또는 '~라고'로 해석한다.

☐ 의문사절 목적어는 의문사에 따라 '무엇이/누가/언제/어디서/왜/어떻게 ~하는지(를)'로 해석한다.

다음 문장의 네모 안에서 어법상 알맞은 것을 고르고, 문장을 해석하시오.

079 Lisa doesn't believe [that / what] ghosts exist. She thinks the scary stories are fake.

080 Kevin forgot [that / when] Amy's birthday was. He thought [it was / was it] in May.

---

innocent 무죄인 imagine 상상하다 wonder 궁금(해)하다 cheat 속이다; *부정행위를 하다 sometimes 가끔씩 communicate 의사소통하다 exist 존재하다 fake 가짜의, 거짓된

Point 04 가목적어, 전치사의 목적어

길이가 긴 **to부정사(구)**나, **동명사(구)** 또는 **that절**이 **목적어**인 경우, 종종 **긴 진목적어는 뒤**로 보내고 문장의 목적어 자리에 **가목적어 it**을 쓴다. 한편, 전치사 뒤에는 **명사(구)**나 **목적격 대명사**, **동명사(구)**가 목적어로 올 수 있다.

081 I made **it** a goal / **to improve my English**.
S V O(가목적어) OC / O(진목적어)
나는 목표로 삼았다 / 내 영어 실력을 향상시키는 것을

082 I found **it** hard / **waking up early**.
S V O(가목적어) OC / O(진목적어)
나는 어렵다고 생각했다 / 일찍 일어나는 것이

083 They thought **it** strange / <**that he didn't come**>.
S V O(가목적어) OC / O(진목적어) S' V'
그들은 이상하다고 생각했다 / <그가 오지 않은 것이>

084 The pen fell / under **my desk**.
S V M
그 펜은 떨어졌다 / 내 책상 아래로

085 She stays healthy / by **exercising** / **every day**.
S V SC M
그녀는 건강을 유지한다 / 운동을 함으로써 / 매일

다음 문장에서 목적어를 모두 찾아 밑줄 긋고, 문장을 해석하시오.

정답 및 해설 p.7

086 Mom always takes care of me / <when I'm sick>.
엄마는 항상 나를 돌봐주신다 / <내가 아플 때>

087 He finds it difficult speaking in public.

088 Please keep it a secret that Luhan is my boyfriend.

089 The movie is about surviving on a desert island.

090 The traffic jam made it impossible to arrive on time.

> **구문 해석 기법**
> □ 진목적어인 to부정사구, 동명사구 또는 that절 내용을 가목적어 it 자리에 넣어 해석한다.

다음 문장의 네모 안에서 어법상 알맞은 것을 고르고, 문장을 해석하시오.

091 My parents consider it rude [leave / to leave] without saying goodbye.

092 We think [it / that] essential that we maintain a work-life balance.

improve 향상시키다 find 찾다; *~라고 생각하다[여기다](-found-found) stay (계속·그대로) 있다 take care of ~을 돌보다 in public 대중 앞에서 desert island 무인도 traffic jam 교통 체증 on time 제시간에 essential 필수적인 maintain 유지하다

Unit Practice

STEP 1 직독직해에 맞게 ( ) 안의 단어를 사용하여 문장을 쓰시오. (필요시 형태를 바꿔 쓸 것)

1 너는 말하지 않았다 / 정답이 무엇인지를 (the answer / say)

______ ______ ______ / ______ ______ ______ ______.

2 Monica는 깨달았다 / 정직이 최고의 수단임을 (the best policy / honesty / realize)

______ ______ / ______ ______ ______ ______

______ ______.

3 나는 싫증이 난다 / 교복을 입는 것에 (a school uniform / tired / wear / of)

______ ______ / ______ ______ ______ ______ ______.

STEP 2 다음 문장에서 목적어를 <u>모두</u> 찾아 밑줄 긋고, 문장을 해석하시오.

1 They believe you will pass the exam.

2 People thought it impossible to travel to space.

3 Colin considers it boring studying alone.

4 She agrees that saving money is important for the future.

5 He doesn't remember why he didn't pay the bills on time.

6 We are thinking of attending a music festival.

policy 정책; *수단, 방법 honesty 정직 realize 깨닫다 impossible 불가능한 space 공간; *우주 consider 생각하다, 여기다 save 구조하다; *저축하다
bill 청구서 attend 참석하다 festival 축제

STEP 3

1 밑줄 친 문장의 네모 안에서 어법상 알맞은 것을 고르고, 문장을 해석하시오.

In **the** (a) **past**, coffee plants only grew in **the wild** in **East Asia and Arabia**. According to **one story**, a young shepherd noticed [that / when] his animals behaved strangely after **eating coffee berries**. He decided to try some and thought **that they were** (b) **terrible**. Soon, coffee became popular throughout **Arabia**, and later it (c) spread to **Europe**.

*coffee berry 커피 열매

____

Reading Q 윗글의 밑줄 친 (a)~(c) 중에서 문맥상 낱말의 쓰임이 적절하지 않은 것은?
① (a)　② (b)　③ (c)

NEW 내신기출

2 밑줄 친 우리말을 조건 에 맞게 써서 문장을 완성하시오.

Shoes played an important role in **ancient Roman life**. The Romans knew **that shoes sent an important message**. 그들의 신발은 그들이 누구이며 그들이 얼마나 부유한지를 나타냈다. Also, Roman kids wore the same kind of **shoes** as **their parents**. Wearing a certain kind of **shoes** was a way of **saying**, "I'm a member of **this social class**."

조건
- 의문사절 목적어를 쓸 것
- 제시된 단어를 사용할 것 (필요시 형태를 바꿔 쓸 것)
- who / rich / be / how (필요시 두 번 사용 가능)

Their shoes expressed ________ ________ ________ and ________ ________ ________ ________.

1 wild 야생 according to ~에 따르면 shepherd 양치기 notice 알아차리다 behave 행동하다 throughout ~의 도처에 spread 퍼지다
2 play a role 역할을 하다 ancient 고대의 kind 종류 certain 틀림없는; *어떤, 특정한 social class 사회 계급 express 나타내다

정답 및 해설 p.9

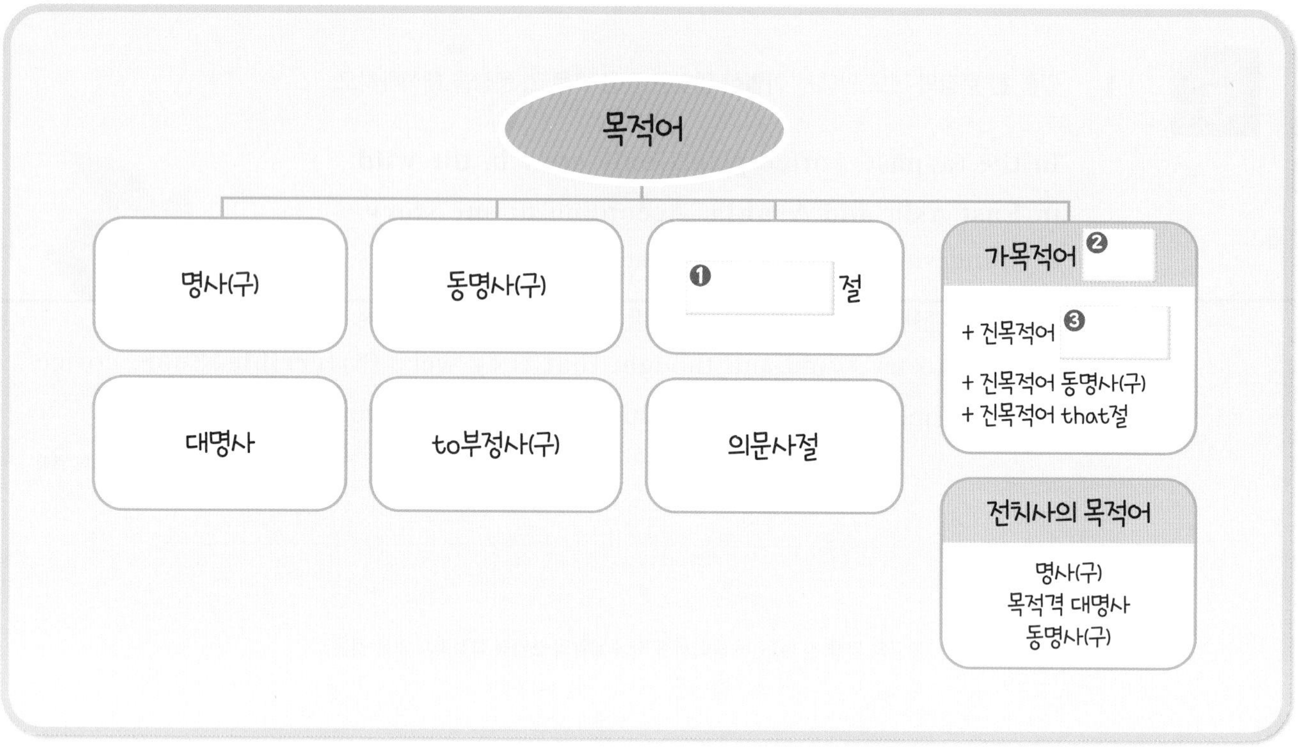

주요 예문을 다시 한번 확인하고, 우리말에 맞게 (　) 안의 단어를 사용하여 문장을 쓰시오.

1 그는 네가 Matt와 있다고 생각했다. (with Matt / thought) Point 03

2 나는 내 영어 실력을 향상시키는 것을 목표로 삼았다. (improve / it / made / English / a goal / to) Point 04

3 나는 어제 그에게 전화했던 것을 기억한다. (yesterday / remember) Point 02

4 Kate는 James가 무죄라는 것을 믿는다. (innocent / believes) Point 03

5 나는 그 노래의 이름을 잊어버렸다. (the name / forgot / of the song) Point 01

6 그녀는 매일 운동을 함으로써 건강을 유지한다. (by / healthy / every day / stays) Point 04

UNIT 03

보어의 형태

Point 01 주격보어 _ 명사, 형용사, 분사
Point 02 주격보어 _ 동명사와 to부정사
Point 03 목적격보어 _ 명사와 형용사
Point 04 목적격보어 _ to부정사와 동사원형

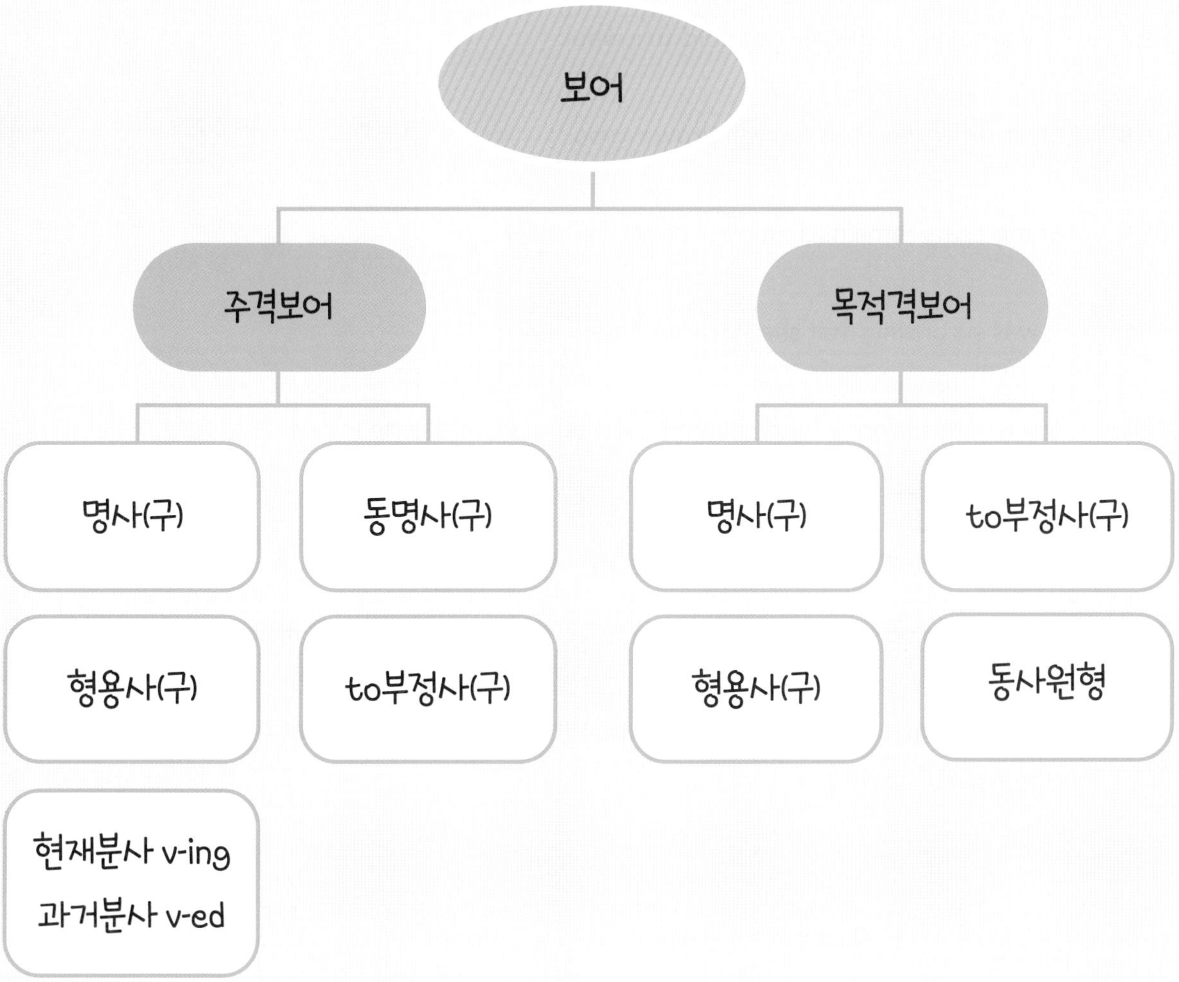

Point 01

주격보어_ 명사, 형용사, 분사

주격보어는 동사 뒤에서 **주어를 보충 설명해 주는 말**로, 의미상 '**주어 = 주격보어**'의 관계가 성립한다. 주격보어로 쓰인 **명사(구)**는 주어의 **신분이나 자격**을, **형용사(구)와 분사**는 주어의 **성질이나 상태**를 보충 설명한다.

주격보어를 쓰는 동사	상태 동사 (~이다, ~한 상태로 있다)	be, keep, stay, remain 등
	상태 변화 동사 (~이 되다)	become, grow, turn, get 등
	감각 동사 (~한[하게] 보이다/들리다/냄새 나다/맛이 나다/느끼다)	look, sound, smell, taste, feel 등

093 Smoking is **harmful**.
S V SC
흡연은 해롭다.

094 My older sister became **a dentist**.
S V SC
우리 언니는 치과 의사가 되었다.

095 Liam felt **exhausted** / after the long trip.
S V SC M
Liam은 기진맥진해졌다 / 긴 여행 뒤에

다음 문장에서 주격보어를 찾아 밑줄 긋고, 문장을 해석하시오.

정답 및 해설 p.9

096 All these books look boring.
이 책들은 모두 지루해 보인다.

097 The weather suddenly got cold this week.

098 Over time, the problem will grow worse.

099 Some seats remained empty during the show.

100 It was surprising that she became the winner.

101 My favorite food is fried chicken. It tastes and smells delicious.

> **구문 해석 기법**
>
> □ 동사의 의미에 따라 '~는 보어이다' 또는 '~는 보어하게 …하다'로 해석한다.
>
> □ 감정을 나타내는 동사의 현재분사는 '~한 (감정을 느끼게 하는)'으로, 과거분사는 '(~한 감정을 느끼게) 된'으로 해석한다.

다음 문장의 네모 안에서 어법상 알맞은 것을 고르고, 문장을 해석하시오.

102 The mission was [successful / successfully]. We felt [satisfying / satisfied] after we finished it.

103 Emma became [disappointing / disappointed] when she saw her quiz grade. She looks [sad / sadly] now.

dentist 치과 의사 smoking 흡연 harmful 해로운 exhaust 기진맥진하게 만들다 over time 시간이 흐르면서 seat 자리, 좌석 empty 빈
mission 임무 successful 성공적인 satisfy 만족시키다 disappoint 실망시키다 grade 품질; *성적

Point 02 주격보어 _ 동명사와 to부정사

동명사(v-ing)와 **to부정사(to-v)**도 주어의 성질이나 상태를 보충 설명하는 주격보어로 쓰일 수 있다. 이때 목적어나 수식어구가 붙으면 주격보어가 길어진다.

104 My favorite activity (S) is (V) / **riding a bicycle** (SC).
내가 가장 좋아하는 활동은 ~이다 / 자전거를 타는 것

105 His dream (S) is (V) / **to explore the whole world** (SC).
그의 꿈은 ~이다 / 전 세계를 탐험하는 것

106 Their goal (S) is (V) / **to win the final match** (SC).
그들의 목표는 ~이다 / 결승전에서 이기는 것

다음 문장에서 주격보어를 찾아 밑줄 긋고, 문장을 해석하시오.

정답 및 해설 p.9

구문 해석 기법

□ 동명사나 to부정사는 '~하는 것[하기]'로 해석한다.

107 Sandra's hobby is / collecting dolls.
Sandra의 취미는 ~이다 / 인형을 수집하는 것

108 Our decision was to cancel the party.

109 My father's job is writing fairy tales for children.

110 Nana's dream is to become a famous guitarist.

111 The purpose of the event is to raise money for charity.

112 I did volunteer work last weekend. My role was taking care of the elderly.

다음 문장의 네모 안에서 어법상 알맞은 것을 고르고, 문장을 해석하시오.

113 I love [travel / to travel]. My favorite thing about traveling is [meet / meeting] new people.

114 The first step to happiness is [be / being] kind to yourself. The next step is [connect / to connect] with others.

explore 탐험하다 whole 전체의 final match 결승전 collect 수집하다 decision 결정 cancel 취소하다 fairy tale 동화 event 사건; *행사 raise 들어 올리다; *(자금·사람 등을) 모으다 charity 자선 단체 role 역할 step 걸음; *단계 connect 연결되다; *관계를 가지다

Unit Practice

STEP 1 **직독직해에 맞게 ( ) 안의 단어를 사용하여 문장을 쓰시오. (필요시 형태를 바꿔 쓸 것)**

1 그들의 결정은 ~이었다 / 돈을 나누는 것 / 똑같이 (the money / decision / equally / divide)

_______ _______ _______ / _______ _______ _______

_______ / _______.

2 저 소설이 베스트셀러이다 / 올해의 (of this year/ that / a bestseller / novel)

_______ _______ _______ _______ _______ / _______

_______ _______.

3 그녀의 취미는 ~이다 / 그녀의 방을 꾸미는 것 / 직접 (hobby / room / herself / decorate)

_______ _______ _______ / _______ _______ _______ / _______.

STEP 2 **다음 문장에서 주격보어를 찾아 밑줄 긋고, 문장을 해석하시오.**

1 The song of the bird sounds beautiful.

2 The rules of the game are confusing.

3 I felt worried about my parents' medical test results.

4 Her main means of transportation is biking and walking.

5 The snowman became the movie's most popular character.

6 My plan is to read one book per month.

equally 똑같이 divide 나누다 decorate 장식하다, 꾸미다 confuse (사람을) 혼란시키다 medical 의학[의료]의 main 주된 means 수단, 방법 transportation 운송; *이동 (수단) character 성격; *(책·영화 등의) 등장인물

STEP 3

1 밑줄 친 (A), (B)에서 주격보어를 찾아 동그라미 하고, 문장을 해석하시오.

One morning, a hungry lion was hiding behind a dog. The __________ dog noticed this and shouted, "(A) That was one tasty lion! I should eat more lions." (B) The lion got scared and ran away. Then a squirrel told the lion about the dog's trick. The lion became **angry**. "Take me to the dog!" said the lion, and they ran back. But the dog was **ready** and shouted, "Where's that squirrel? I told him to bring me another lion!"

(A) ____

(B) ____

Reading Q 빈칸에 들어갈 말로 가장 적절한 것은?

① lazy ② clever ③ greedy

NEW 내신기출

2 밑줄 친 ①~④ 중 어법상 틀린 2개를 찾아 해당 번호를 쓰고 바르게 고쳐 쓰시오.

Charles M. Schulz was ① a shy boy and often received poor grades. But he had a dream. His goal was ② be a cartoonist. His dream came ③ truly with his cartoon *Peanuts*. Its main character, Charlie Brown, is **small and weak**. His personality is ④ different from most heroes. Schulz chose him because he wanted to draw a character like himself.

번호	적절하지 않은 단어	고쳐 쓴 단어

1 hide 숨다 notice 알아차리다 tasty 맛있는 run away 도망치다 squirrel 다람쥐 trick 속임수
2 shy 수줍음이 많은 receive 받다 cartoonist 만화가(*n*. cartoon 만화) come true 실현되다, 이루어지다 weak (연)약한 personality 성격

Point 03 목적격보어 _ 명사와 형용사

목적격보어는 목적어 뒤에서 **목적어를 보충 설명해 주는 말**이다. 목적격보어로서 **명사(구)**와 **형용사(구)**는 **목적어의 호칭**이나 **상태** 또는 **목적어에 대한 주어의 생각을 보충 설명**한다.

목적격보어를 쓰는 동사	호칭·선택을 나타내는 동사	call, name, elect 등
	상태를 나타내는 동사	make, get, keep, leave, turn 등
	생각을 나타내는 동사	consider, think, find 등

115 People call / her **a genius**.
S V O OC
사람들은 부른다 / 그녀를 천재라고

116 Smartphones make / our lives **more convenient**.
S V O OC
스마트폰은 만든다 / 우리의 삶을 더욱 편리하게

117 Alex considers / BTS **the world's best pop group**.
S V O OC
Alex는 여긴다 / BTS를 세계 최고의 팝 그룹이라고

다음 문장에서 목적격보어를 찾아 밑줄 긋고, 문장을 해석하시오.

정답 및 해설 p.11

118 The dye turned / his hair red.
그 염색약은 변하게 만들었다 / 그의 머리를 빨갛게

119 The drivers got their cars ready for the race.

120 Wendy thinks him an incredibly handsome man.

121 The chef named the special dish Pacific Delight.

122 Last night, my worries about the exam kept me awake.

123 A bad smell came out of my room. So I left the windows open.

> **구문 해석 기법**
> □ 명사나 형용사가 목적격보어로 쓰인 문장은 '목적어를 목적격보어라고[로/하다고/하게]'로 해석한다.

다음 문장의 네모 안에서 어법상 알맞은 것을 고르고, 문장을 해석하시오.

124 The town elected Nicole its [leader / leaders]. But the position made her [arrogant / arrogantly].

125 People find making a speech [difficult / difficulty]. But practice makes it [easy / easily].

elect 선출하다 convenient 편리한 dye 염색약 incredibly 대단히 pacific 태평양의 delight 기쁨 arrogant 오만한 make a speech 연설하다

Point 04

목적격보어 _ to부정사와 동사원형

목적격보어로서 **to부정사**와 **동사원형**은 **목적어의 행동을 보충 설명**하는 말이며, 동사에 따라 목적격보어의 형태가 다르다.

목적격보어의 형태	to부정사	want, ask, allow, order, tell, advise, expect, cause 등
	동사원형	사역동사(make, have, let), 지각동사(see, hear, notice, feel 등)
	to부정사, 동사원형	help

126 The teacher told / them **to be quiet**.
S V O OC
그 선생님은 말씀하셨다 / 그들에게 조용히 하라고

127 Iris felt / somebody **push her**.
S V O OC
Iris는 느꼈다 / 누군가가 그녀를 미는 것을

128 A kind man helped / me **(to) find the way**.
S V O OC
한 친절한 남자가 도와주었다 / 내가 길을 찾도록

다음 문장에서 목적격보어를 찾아 밑줄 긋고, 문장을 해석하시오.

정답 및 해설 p.11

129 He made / his girlfriend wait / for a long time.
그는 만들었다 / 그녀의 여자친구가 기다리게 / 오랫동안

130 This pill will help you feel better.

131 His boss doesn't let him go home early.

132 Amy noticed some raindrops fall down from the sky.

133 Our teacher advised us to study hard for the final exam.

134 I heard the phone ring. I asked my friend to answer it.

구문 해석 기법

□ to부정사나 동사원형이 목적격보어로 쓰인 문장은 '목적어가[에게] 목적격보어하는 것을[하도록]'로 해석한다.

다음 문장의 네모 안에서 어법상 알맞은 것을 고르고, 문장을 해석하시오.

135 Mom doesn't allow me [play / to play] computer games before dinner. She wants me [finish / to finish] my homework first.

136 Edwin saw a girl [say / to say] something to a dog. She ordered the dog [sit / to sit].

let ~하게 두다 push 밀다 pill 알약 raindrop 빗방울 final exam 기말고사 ring 반지; *(종 등이) 울리다 first 우선 order 명령하다

Unit Practice

STEP 1

직독직해에 맞게 ( ) 안의 단어를 사용하여 문장을 쓰시오. (필요시 형태를 바꿔 쓸 것)

1 너는 명령할 수 없다 / 나에게 내 꿈을 포기하라고 (can't / dream / order / give up)

__________ __________ __________ / __________ __________ __________

__________ __________ __________.

2 대부분의 사람들은 생각한다 / 그 영화의 제목이 꽤 특이하다고 (the movie's title / most / quite / people / consider / unique)

__________ __________ __________ / __________ __________ __________

__________ __________.

3 그 새로운 프로그램은 도와주었다 / 우리가 시간을 절약하도록 (time / the new program / save / help)

__________ __________ __________ __________ / __________ __________ __________.

STEP 2

다음 문장에서 목적격보어를 찾아 밑줄 긋고, 문장을 해석하시오.

1 Henry named his son Austin.

2 We found the dress on display beautiful.

3 I heard my father snore in the living room.

4 The hot soup caused me to burn my tongue.

5 My teacher expects us to learn from our mistakes.

6 Mom sometimes had me do the dishes after dinner.

unique 독특한 save (위험·재난 등에서) 구하다; *절약하다 name 이름을 지어주다 display 전시, 진열 snore 코를 골다 burn (불이) 타오르다; *데다 tongue 혀 do the dishes 설거지를 하다

STEP 3

1 밑줄 친 ①~④ 중 어법상 틀린 것을 모두 고르시오.

Some schools are replacing wooden chairs with rubber ball chairs. These ball chairs help kids ① learn better. On the balls, students must concentrate for balance. This makes their brains ② actively during class. Also, ball chairs let students ③ to have better posture. Best of all, students find the ball chairs ④ fun and comfortable.

Reading Q 윗글의 주제로 가장 적절한 것은?

① 고무공 의자를 제작하게 된 이유
② 고무공 의자의 긍정적인 효과
③ 고무공 의자의 위험성

NEW 내신기출

2 다음 글을 읽고 보기 에 제시된 단어만을 모두 한 번씩 사용하여 질문에 답하시오. (필요시 형태를 바꿔 쓸 것)

From time to time, the moon hides the sun during the daytime. The day becomes dark as night. You cannot see the sun for a while. People call this event **an eclipse**. Many years ago, people considered the sun **God**. They thought eclipses were signs of God's anger. They felt afraid of eclipses and thought them **unlucky**.

보기 people / them / consider / because / of God's anger / signs

Q. Why were people afraid of eclipses?

A. It's ______________________________.

1 replace 교체하다 rubber 고무(로 만든) concentrate 집중하다 balance 균형 posture 자세 best of all 무엇보다도
2 hide 감추다; *(보이지 않게) 가리다 daytime 낮 event 행사; *(일어난) 일, 현상 sign 징후 anger 분노 unlucky 불행한; *불길한

Wrap Up

정답 및 해설 p.13

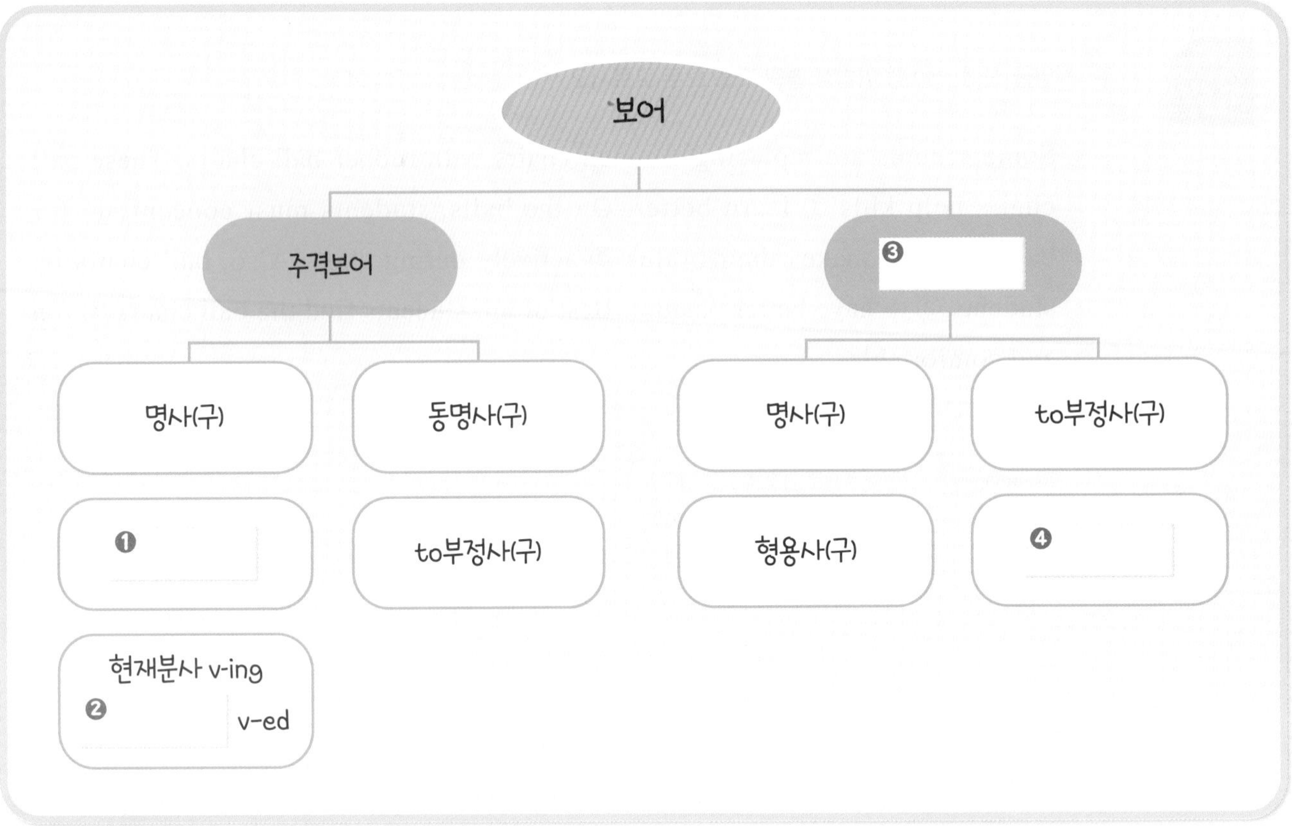

주요 예문을 다시 한번 확인하고, 우리말에 맞게 (   ) 안의 단어를 사용하여 문장을 쓰시오.

1 한 친절한 남자가 내가 길을 찾도록 도와주었다. (find / a kind man / helped / the way) Point 04

2 Liam은 긴 여행 뒤에 기진맥진해졌다. (exhausted / felt / after the long trip) Point 01

3 그의 꿈은 전 세계를 탐험하는 것이다. (the whole world / explore) Point 02

4 그 선생님은 그들에게 조용히 하라고 말씀하셨다. (told / the teacher / quiet / be) Point 04

5 사람들은 그녀를 천재라고 부른다. (a genius / call / people) Point 03

6 스마트폰은 우리의 삶을 더욱 편리하게 만든다. (make / convenient / smartphones / lives) Point 03

UNIT 04

시제와 수동태

Point 01 현재완료
Point 02 과거완료
Point 03 수동태의 개념
Point 04 수동태의 시제 표현

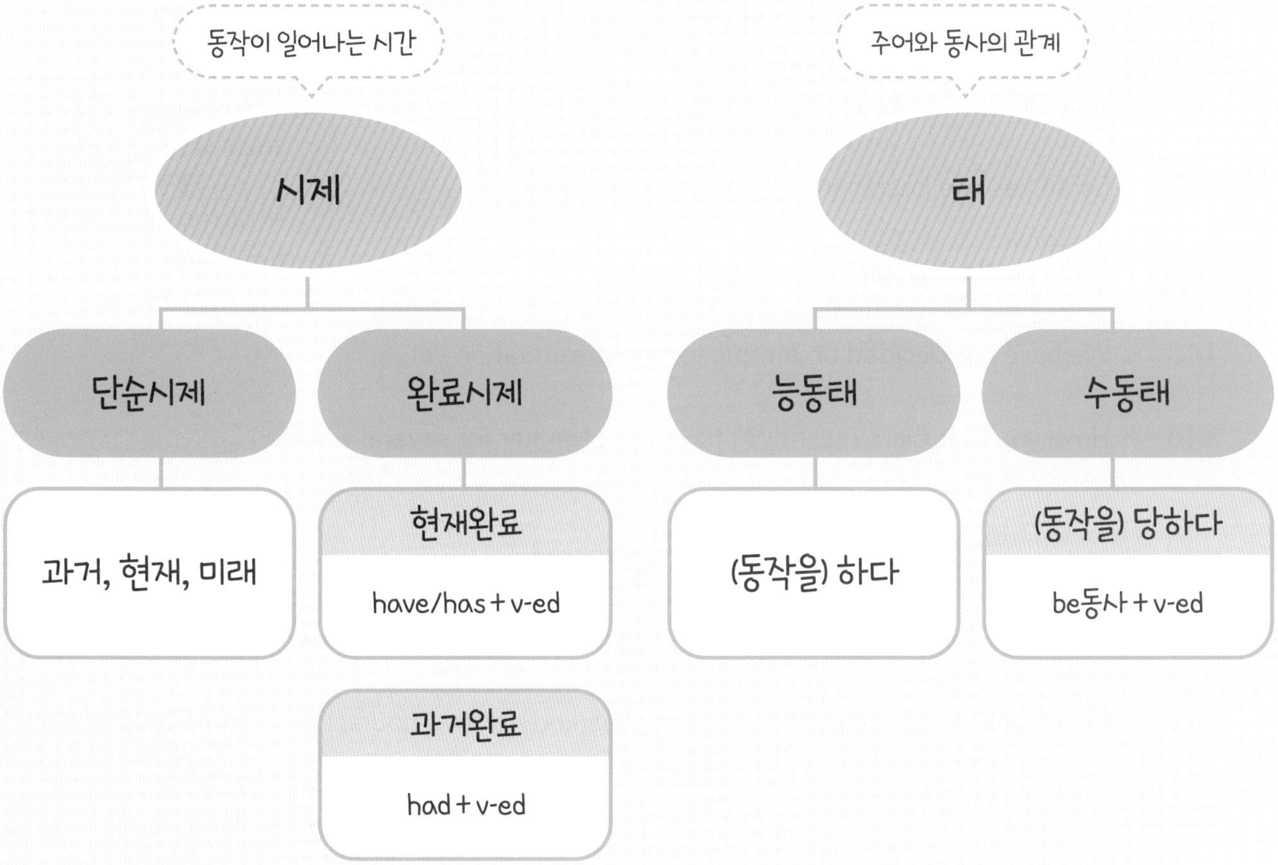

Point 01 현재완료

현재완료는 **과거에 시작된 일이 현재까지 영향을 미치는 상태**를 나타내며 **「have/has+과거분사(v-ed)」**로 표현한다.
현재완료 부정형은 「have/has not+과거분사(v-ed)」이다.

완료	(막) ~했다	yet(아직), just(막, 방금), already(이미)
경험	~한 적이 있다	ever(언젠가), never(한 번도 ~않다), before(전에), once(한 번)
계속	(지금까지 계속) ~해 왔다	since(~ 이후로), for(~ 동안)
결과	~했다 (그 결과 현재 ~한 상태이다)	

137 The car **has** already **broken down.** 완료
S V(M)
그 차는 이미 망가졌다.

138 We **have visited** Vietnam / once. 경험
S V O M
우리는 베트남을 방문한 적이 있다 / 한 번

139 I **have been listening to** music / for an hour. 계속
S V O M
나는 음악을 듣고 있다 / 한 시간 동안

140 Rachel **has gone** / to Germany. 결과
S V M
Rachel은 가 버렸다 / 독일로 (현재 그녀는 여기에 없다)

다음 문장에서 현재완료를 나타내는 동사에 밑줄 긋고, 문장을 해석하시오. 정답 및 해설 p.13

141 It has snowed a lot / this weekend.
눈이 많이 왔다 / 이번 주말에 <결과>

142 Jessica has already left the country.

143 Sarah has had heart surgery before.

144 My uncle has just arrived at the train station.

145 We have not decided on a topic for the presentation yet.

146 Have you met Clare recently? I have not seen her for several weeks.

> **구문 해석 기법**
> □ 현재완료 진행형 「have/has been+v-ing」는 과거에 시작된 동작/상태가 현재까지 계속되고 있음을 나타내며 **'~해 오고 있다'**로 해석한다.

다음 문장의 네모 안에서 어법상 알맞은 것을 고르고, 문장을 해석하시오.

147 Irene has [being / been] ill since last month. I hope she gets better soon.

148 My neighbor's dog has been [barking / barked] for two hours. I can't stand it anymore.

---

break down 고장 나다 surgery 수술 presentation 발표 recently 최근에 several (몇)몇의 ill 아픈 get better 좋아지다 stand 서다; *참다

Point 02 과거완료

과거완료는 **과거의 특정 시점 이전에 일어나 과거의 어느 시점까지 영향을 준 일**을 나타내며 「**had+과거분사(v-ed)**」로 표현한다. 과거완료 부정형은 「had not+과거분사(v-ed)」이다.

149 He **had left** / <when I got there>.
(S: He, V: had left; S′: I, V′: got, M′: there)
그는 떠나버렸다 / <내가 그곳에 갔을 때>

150 I watched the movie / <after it **had become** / a big hit>.
(S: I, V: watched, O: the movie; S′: it, V′: had become, SC′: a big hit)
나는 그 영화를 보았다 / <그것이 ~이 된 후 / 대단한 흥행>

151 Mom **had been working** / for ten years / <before I was born>.
(S: Mom, V: had been working, M: for ten years; S′: I, V′: was born)
엄마는 일해 오셨다 / 10년 동안 / <내가 태어나기 전에>

152 Its price **had not changed** / for a long time.
(S: Its price, V: had not changed, M: for a long time)
그것의 가격은 변하지 않았었다 / 오랫동안

다음 문장에서 과거완료를 나타내는 동사에 밑줄 긋고, 문장을 해석하시오.

정답 및 해설 p.14

153 I had not met Jane / until that day.
나는 Jane을 만난 적이 없었다 / 그날까지

154 Martin had not been on an airplane before.

155 He had been waiting for thirty minutes when I arrived.

156 David couldn't take notes because he had hurt his hands.

157 I had just finished taking a shower when my mother called me.

158 Sammy had been studying Chinese for a year before he went to China.

구문 해석 기법

□ 과거완료 진행형 「had been+v-ing」는 과거 어느 시점 이전에 시작된 동작 / 상태가 과거의 어느 시점까지 계속되고 있음을 나타내며 '~해 오고 있었다'로 해석한다.

다음 문장의 네모 안에서 어법상 알맞은 것을 고르고, 문장을 해석하시오.

159 I thought Matt [has / had] already had dinner. So I ate all the food on the table.

160 Alex and Jay had just [return / returned] home. They [have / had] traveled around Europe for three months.

hit 치다; *흥행 take notes 메모하다, 필기를 하다 hurt 다치게 하다(-hurt-hurt) take a shower 샤워를 하다 Chinese 중국어 return 돌아오다

Unit Practice

STEP 1

직독직해에 맞게 ( ) 안의 단어를 사용하여 문장을 쓰시오. (필요시 형태를 바꿔 쓸 것)

1 Dante는 말했다 / 그가 낮잠을 잤다고 / 3시간 동안 (take a nap / for three hours / say)

________ ________ / ________ ________ ________ ________

________ / ________ ________ ________.

2 Erica와 나는 가장 친한 친구이다 / 어린 시절부터 / 10년이 넘는 동안 (for over / childhood / be / best friends / since)

________ ________ ________ ________ ________ ________ ________ /

________ ________ / ________ ________ ________ ________.

3 나는 막 끝냈었다 / 샤워하는 것을 / 어머니가 나에게 전화하셨을 때 (call / take a shower / just / when / finish)

________ ________ ________ ________ / ________ ________

________ / ________ ________ ________ ________ ________.

STEP 2

다음 문장에서 완료시제를 나타내는 동사를 찾아 밑줄 긋고, 문장을 해석하시오.

1 She has moved to Seattle with her family.

2 Frankie had not driven his new car until yesterday.

3 I didn't know that he had been sick with the flu.

4 Grace has worn eyeglasses for reading since last year.

5 They have sold all the tickets for the concert.

6 He had been cleaning his room before his cousins came to his house.

take a nap 낮잠을 자다 childhood 어린 시절 just (정확히) 딱; *막 move 움직이다; *이사하다 flu 독감 sell 팔다(-sold-sold) clean 청소하다 cousin 사촌

STEP 3

1 **밑줄 친 ①~④ 중 어법상 틀린 것을 모두 고르시오.**

In 1945, an engineer ① was working with a radar system. Suddenly, he noticed that the candy bar in his pocket ② has melted. At that moment, he realized he ③ had discovered something special. He put some pieces of dry corn in front of the radar, and they quickly ④ had popped. This was the start of the microwave oven.

*radar 레이더

Reading Q 윗글의 주제로 가장 적절한 것은?
① 전자레인지 원리의 발견
② 레이더를 사용한 실험의 위험성
③ 전자레인지를 활용한 조리 방법

NEW 내신기출

2 **밑줄 친 우리말 (A), (B)를 조건에 맞게 써서 각 문장을 완성하시오.**

(A) Chuck Lamb은 2005년 이후로 색다른 직업을 가져왔다. His job is to act like a dead person in movies. (B) Lamb은 어려서부터 배우가 되는 것을 꿈꿨었다. However, he thought he didn't have the talent to be one. One day, he realized the easiest way to get on TV: to act as a corpse. Now he **has become** famous as a professional corpse.

*corpse 시체

조건
· 완료시제를 쓸 것
· 제시된 단어를 사용할 것 (필요시 형태를 바꿔 쓸 것)
· a strange job / dream of / become / have

(A) Chuck Lamb ________ ________ ________ ________ ________ since 2005.

(B) Since childhood, Lamb ________ ________ ________ ________ ________ ________.

1 suddenly 갑자기 notice 알아차리다 melt 녹다 realize 깨닫다 discover 발견하다 pop 펑 하고 터지다 microwave oven 전자레인지
2 act 행동하다; *연기하다 professional 전문적인 strange 이상한, 색다른 dream of ~을 꿈꾸다

Point 03 수동태의 개념

수동태는 **동작의 영향을 받는 대상에 초점**을 두고자 할 때 사용하며 「**주어(동작의 영향을 받는 대상)+be동사+과거분사(+by+행위자)**」로 표현한다. 수동태의 부정형은 「be동사+not+과거분사」로 쓴다.

• 행위자가 일반인(you, we, they 등)이거나 명확하지 않을 때, 또는 중요하지 않을 때는 생략한다.

161 This song **is played** / by a famous guitarist.
S V by+행위자
이 노래는 연주된다 / 유명한 기타 연주자에 의해

162 Many people **were killed** / during the war.
S V M
많은 사람들이 죽임을 당했다 / 전쟁 동안

163 This app **is not used** / by young people / these days.
S V by+행위자 M
이 앱은 사용되지 않는다 / 젊은 사람들에 의해 / 요즘

밑줄 친 부분에 유의하여 다음 문장을 해석하시오.

정답 및 해설 p.15

164 I was bitten / by mosquitoes / today.
나는 물렸다 / 모기한테 / 오늘

165 The window is not locked.

166 Paris is visited by lots of tourists.

167 The children were not injured in the accident.

168 Every year, many houses are destroyed by tornadoes.

169 I drink milk every day. It is delivered to my house every morning.

구문 해석 기법

☐ 수동태는 '주어가 (행위자에 의해) ~되다/당하다/해지다'로 해석한다.

다음 문장의 네모 안에서 어법상 알맞은 것을 고르고, 문장을 해석하시오.

170 The hotel has a nice swimming pool. It is [locating / located] on the top floor.

171 These computers are made [by / to] a big company. And they [supply / are supplied] to public schools.

---

bite 물다(-bit-bitten) injure 다치게 하다 accident 사고 destroy 파괴하다 tornado 토네이도 deliver 배달하다 locate 위치하게 하다 top floor 맨 위층 supply (특히 대량으로) 공급하다, 제공하다 public 대중의; *공공의

Point 04

수동태의 시제 표현

be동사의 시제로 수동태의 현재시제 및 과거시제를 나타내며, 조동사 **will**을 사용하여 **미래시제**를 나타낸다.

수동태의 시제	현재	am/are/is+v-ed
	과거	was/were+v-ed
	미래	will be+v-ed

172 Most people **are influenced** / by their friends.
S V by+행위자
대부분의 사람들은 영향을 받는다 / 그들의 친구들에 의해

173 Blue jeans **were** first **made** / in America.
S M_1 V M_2
청바지는 처음으로 만들어졌다 / 미국에서

174 This product **will be sent** / by Friday.
S V M
이 제품은 보내질 것이다 / 금요일까지

밑줄 친 부분에 유의하여 다음 문장을 해석하시오.

정답 및 해설 p.16

175 The book was published / in 1987.
그 책은 출판되었다 / 1987년에

176 Your questions will be answered soon.

177 The bread was baked this morning.

178 Many rumors are spread on the internet.

179 New laws on smoking will be introduced next week.

180 I lost my dog yesterday. But he was found by a police officer today.

구문 해석 기법
- □ 과거시제 수동태는 '~되었다/해졌다'로 해석한다.
- □ 미래시제 수동태는 '~될/해질 것이다'로 해석한다.

다음 문장의 네모 안에서 어법상 알맞은 것을 고르고, 문장을 해석하시오.

181 The meals [are / were] prepared by the chef, and they were served to the guests.

182 English [is / be] used by many people all over the world. So it is [speaking / spoken] with many different accents.

---

influence 영향을 주다 publish 출판하다 rumor 소문, 유언비어 spread 펼치다; *퍼뜨리다, 유포하다 law 법 introduce 소개하다; *도입하다 serve 제공하다 all over the world 전 세계에서 accent 말씨, 억양

Unit Practice

STEP 1 직독직해에 맞게 ( ) 안의 단어를 사용하여 문장을 쓰시오. (필요시 형태를 바꿔 쓸 것)

1 그 동네는 위치해 있다 / 강 건너편에 (across the river / the town / locate)

_____ _____ _____ _____ / _____ _____ _____.

2 그 소포는 배달될 것이다 / 우체부에 의해 / 이틀 후 (the postman / in two days / the package / deliver)

_____ _____ _____ _____ _____ / _____

_____ _____ / _____ _____ _____.

3 그 공원에 있는 나무들은 / 심어지지 않았다 / 누구에 의해서도 (the trees / anyone / plant / in the park)

_____ _____ _____ _____ _____ / _____

_____ _____ / _____ _____.

STEP 2 다음 문장에서 수동태인 동사구를 찾아 밑줄 긋고, 문장을 해석하시오.

1 The animated movie will be released next month.

2 The photo was taken by the photographer in the studio.

3 I saw many fish were caught by the fisherman in the lake.

4 The meeting will be held in the conference room on the second floor.

5 At the museum, it is not allowed to bring outside food or beverages.

6 The windows of that building are cleaned by the workers every week.

postman 우체부 package 소포 plant (나무·씨앗 등을) 심다 animated 활기찬; *만화 영화로 된 release 풀어 주다; *개봉하다 photographer 사진작가 fisherman 어부, 낚시꾼 hold 잡고 있다; *열다, 개최하다(-held-held) conference room 회의실 outside 외부의 beverage 음료

STEP 3

1 (A), (B), (C)의 각 네모 안에서 어법에 맞는 표현을 고르시오.

Very special eucalyptus trees (A) [was / were] found by scientists from Australia. These trees have tiny bits of gold in their cells. The greatest amount of gold (B) [finds / is found] in the leaves. The scientists have a good explanation for this. The gold **is** probably **absorbed** by the roots. Then it is (C) [transporting / transported] through the trees to the leaves.

*eucalyptus tree 유칼립투스 나무

Reading Q 윗글의 제목으로 가장 적절한 것은?

① How Trees Absorb Water
② Scientists Discovered Gold in Trees
③ Why Eucalyptus Grows Well in Australia

NEW 내신기출

2 밑줄 친 우리말 (A), (B)를 조건에 맞게 써서 요약문을 완성하시오.

Do you know about National Mustard Day? In the US, it **is celebrated** on the first Saturday of August each year. It **was created by** the National Mustard Museum. On that day, delicious foods **are offered** for free. People enjoy pretzels, sausages, and sandwiches with mustard. Of course, ketchup **is** strictly **banned**!

*pretzel 프레첼 (매듭 모양의 짭짤한 비스킷)

Mustard Day is an annual event in the US. It (A) ~에 의해 만들어졌다 the National Mustard Museum. During this celebration, delicious foods (B) 제공된다 for free with mustard.

조건
· 수동태로 쓸 것
· 제시된 단어를 사용할 것 (필요시 형태를 바꿔 쓸 것)
· serve / make

(A) ____________ ____________ ____________ (B) ____________ ____________

1 bit 조각 cell 세포 amount 양 good 좋은; *타당한 explanation 설명 absorb 흡수하다 root 뿌리 transport 이동시키다 discover 발견하다
2 celebrate 기념하다, 축하하다 offer 제공하다 for free 무료로 strictly 엄격하게 ban 금지하다 annual 연례의 event 사건; *행사 celebration 기념 행사

Wrap Up

정답 및 해설 p.17

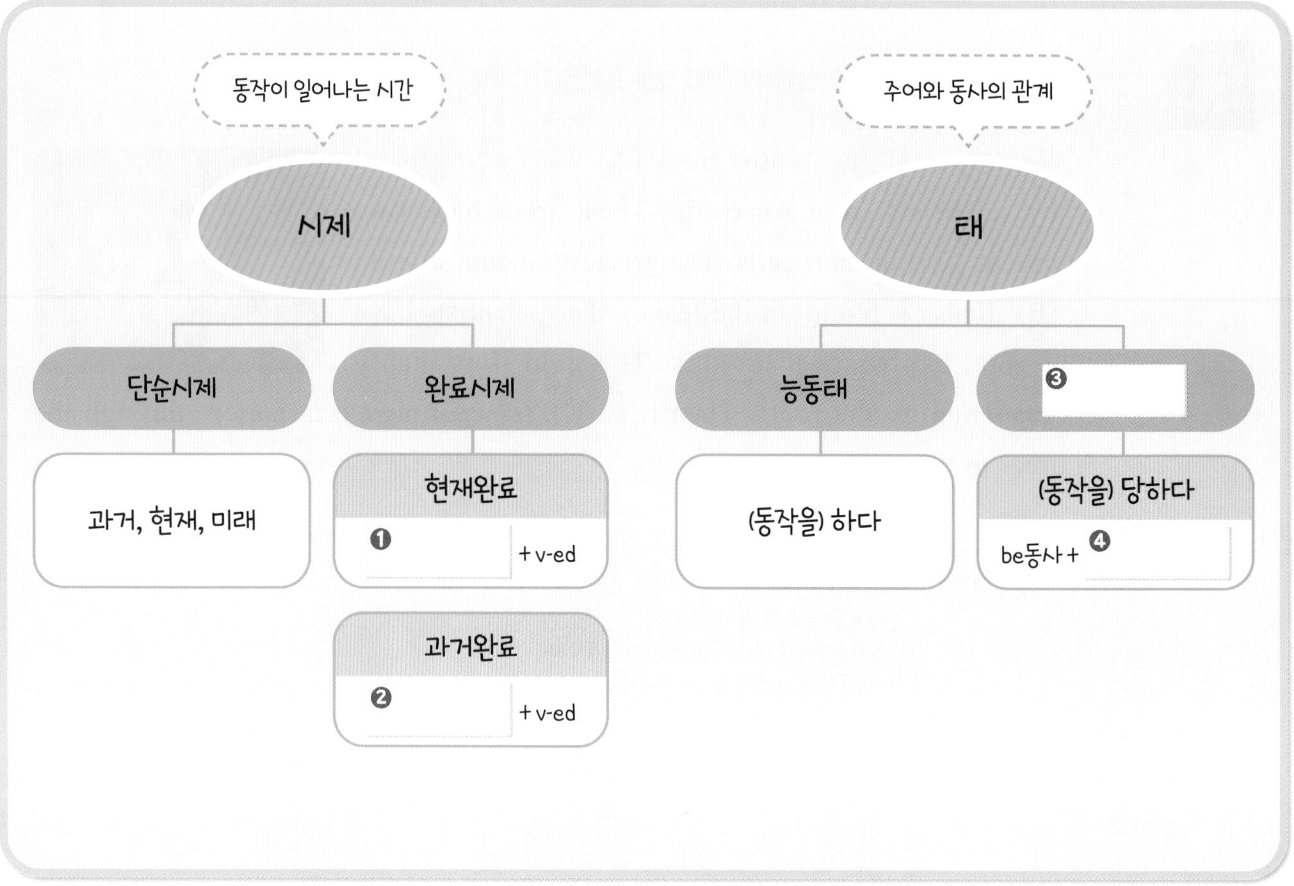

주요 예문을 다시 한번 확인하고, 우리말에 맞게 ( ) 안의 단어를 사용하여 문장을 쓰시오.

1 대부분의 사람들은 그들의 친구들에 의해 영향을 받는다. (influenced / friends) Point 04

2 이 노래는 유명한 기타 연주자에 의해 연주된다. (played / song / a famous guitarist) Point 03

3 많은 사람들이 전쟁 동안 죽임을 당했다. (during the war / people / killed / many) Point 03

4 그것의 가격은 오랫동안 변하지 않았었다. (changed / price / for a long time) Point 02

5 청바지는 미국에서 처음으로 만들어졌다. (first / made / blue jeans / in America) Point 04

6 우리는 베트남을 한 번 방문한 적이 있다. (Vietnam / once / visited) Point 01

UNIT 05

조동사의 이해

Point 01 can, may

Point 02 must/have to/should, had better

Point 03 must, may/might, can/could, cannot

Point 04 used to, would

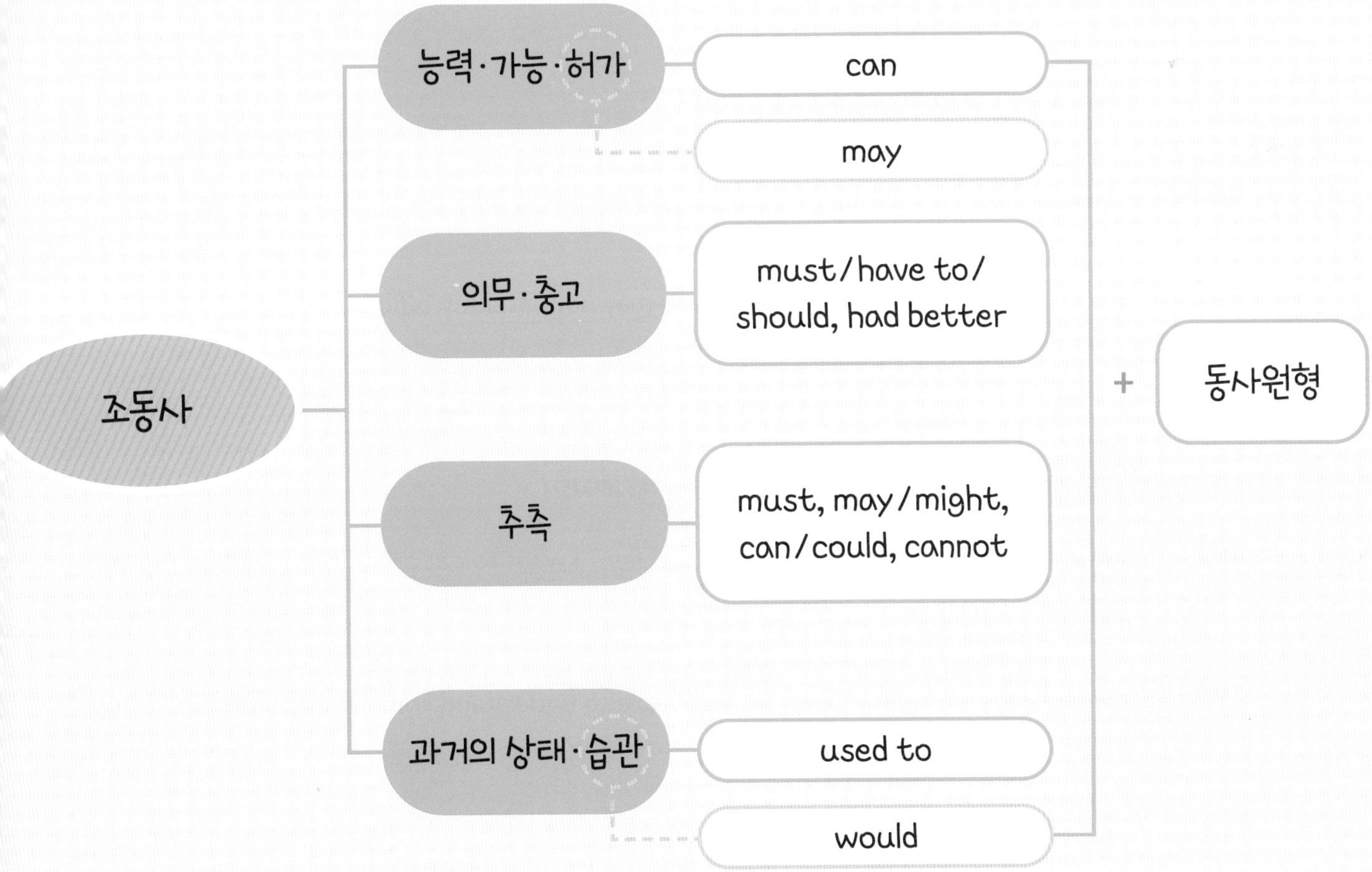

Point 01 can, may

can은 **능력·가능**(~할 수 있다), **허가**(~해도 된다)를 나타내는 조동사로 뒤에 동사원형을 쓴다.
• 능력·가능: be able to로 바꿔 쓸 수 있으며 be동사는 주어와 시제에 맞게 쓴다.
• 허가: 조동사 **may**로 바꿔 쓸 수 있으며 **can보다 격식 있는 표현**이 된다.

과거시제	could, was/were able to	미래시제	will be able to
부정형	cannot[can't]/could not[couldn't]		

183 Austin **can** play / the violin.
S V O
Austin은 연주할 수 있다 / 바이올린을

184 You **may** take / my umbrella.
S V O
너는 가져가도 된다 / 내 우산을

밑줄 친 부분에 유의하여 다음 문장을 해석하시오.

정답 및 해설 p.18

185 You can tell me / your concerns.
너는 나에게 말해도 된다 / 네 걱정을

186 May I wear your jacket today?

187 The cat can climb up the tree effortlessly.

188 Frank couldn't open the jar of pickles.

189 My little sister will be able to have her own room in our new house.

190 You may wait for me in the hall. But you may not enter my office.

> **구문 해석 기법**
> ☐ cannot[can't]은 '~할 수 없다'(불가능) 또는 '~하면 안 된다'(금지)로 해석한다.

다음 문장의 네모 안에서 어법상 알맞은 것을 고르고, 문장을 해석하시오.

191 Can you [bake / baked] muffins for breakfast? I want to eat them, but I [cannot make / can make not] them.

192 Chimpanzees are smart. They [be / are] able to understand some words and [use / using] tools.

take 가지고 가다 concern 우려, 걱정 effortlessly 노력하지 않고, 쉽게 jar 병, 단지 own 자기 자신의 hall 복도 enter 들어오다 tool 도구

Point 02 must/have to/should, had better

must/have to/should는 **의무**(~해야 한다), **had better**는 **강한 충고 · 경고**(~하는 것이 낫다)를 나타내는 조동사로 뒤에 동사원형을 쓴다.

• **should**는 **must보다 강제성이 약한 의무**를 나타내며 **충고**(~하는 것이 낫다)의 의미로도 쓰인다.

과거시제	had to	미래시제	will have to
부정형	must not (강한 금지, ~해서는 안 된다)		should not (금지, ~해서는 안 된다)
	don't[doesn't] have to (불필요, ~할 필요가 없다)		had better not (강한 충고, ~을 안 하는 게 낫다)

193 You **must** wear your seat belt / in the car.
S V O M
너는 네 안전벨트를 매야 한다 / 차 안에서

194 He **had better** listen / to his parents' advice.
S V O
그는 듣는 것이 낫다 / 그의 부모님의 충고를

밑줄 친 부분에 유의하여 문장을 해석하시오.

정답 및 해설 p.18

195 You had better not eat / spicy food / at night.
너는 안 먹는 게 낫다 / 매운 음식을 / 밤에

196 You should not call your teacher late at night.

197 We must not throw trash on the street.

198 Lisa has to go to the hospital with her mother.

199 We will have to wait in line at the restaurant for an hour.

200 The test is not difficult. So you don't have to worry about it.

구문 해석 기법

□ must not과 should not은 '~해서는 안 된다(금지)'로, don't[doesn't] have to는 '~할 필요가 없다(불필요)'로 해석한다.

다음 문장의 네모 안에서 어법상 알맞은 것을 고르고, 문장을 해석하시오.

201 Many guests cannot [come / came] to the party. We had better [delay / to delay] it.

202 You [have / had] better make your report simpler. And you should [give / given] it to me by tomorrow.

advice 충고 throw 던지다; *내던지다 trash 쓰레기 wait in line 줄을 서서 기다리다 guest 손님 delay 미루다, 연기하다 report 보고서

Point 03 must, may/might, can/could, cannot

must, **may/might**, **can/could**, **cannot**은 모두 **추측**을 나타내지만, 강도가 조금씩 다르다. 과거형 조동사 **could**, **might**도 현재나 미래에 대한 추측을 나타낼 수 있으나 **can**, **may보다 불확실한 추측**을 나타낸다.

강한 확신 ↔ 약한 추측

must(~임이 틀림없다)	>	can	>	may	>	could > might(~일지도 모른다)
cannot(~일 리가 없다)	>	couldn't	>	may not	>	might not(~가 아닐지도 모른다)

203 She **must** be / at least forty years old.
S V SC
그녀는 틀림없다 / 적어도 마흔 살임이

204 Emily **may** know the recipe.
S V O
Emily는 요리법을 알지도 모른다.

205 That story **cannot** be true.
S V SC
그 이야기가 사실일 리가 없다.

밑줄 친 부분에 유의하여 다음 문장을 해석하시오. 정답 및 해설 p.18

206 Clara may know / the location <of this restaurant>.
Clara는 알지도 모른다 / 위치 <이 식당의>

207 His explanation couldn't be wrong.

208 Jim and Nick might go camping this summer.

209 The gym may not be open on Sundays.

210 Traveling around the world must be a great experience.

211 I know that Mia is in Busan now. So that woman can't be her.

다음 문장의 네모 안에서 어법상 알맞은 것을 고르고, 문장을 해석하시오.

212 I can't [find / to find] my book in the bag. It might [is / be] on my desk at home.

213 Brianna has many coins from different countries. She [must / have to] like collecting coins.

---

at least 적어도 location 위치, 장소 explanation 설명 go camping 캠핑을 가다 experience 경험 coin 동전 collect 모으다, 수집하다

Point 04

used to, would

used to + 동사원형	과거의 상태	~이었다
used to / would + 동사원형	과거의 습관, 반복된 행동	~하곤 했다

214 A big maple tree / **used to** stand / there.
S V M
큰 단풍나무 한 그루가 / 서 있었다 / 저기에

215 I **used to** walk / to school / every morning.
S V M_1 M_2
나는 걸어가곤 했다 / 학교에 / 매일 아침

216 He **would** give flowers / to me / once a month.
S V O M_1 M_2
그는 꽃을 주곤 했다 / 내게 / 한 달에 한 번

밑줄 친 부분에 유의하여 다음 문장을 해석하시오.

정답 및 해설 p.19

217 In the past, / Avril used to own a boat.
과거에, / Avril은 배 한 척을 소유했었다.

218 I would often go to the park in my childhood.

219 Kate used to read comic books before she went to bed.

220 I used to make Christmas cards for my friends.

221 I would visit Jimmy's house and play games with him.

222 When I was young, my family would go climbing on weekends.

구문 해석 기법

□ 조동사 used to는 '(과거에) ~했으나 지금은 그렇지 않다'는 의미를 담고 있다.

다음 문장의 네모 안에서 어법상 알맞은 것을 고르고, 문장을 해석하시오.

223 Timmy used to [be / being] lazy, but now he is the most diligent student in his class.

224 There [used to / would] be a café on this street. Bruno would [spend / spends] time with his friends there.

maple tree 단풍나무 once 한 번 own 소유하다 childhood 어린 시절 comic book 만화책 go climbing 등산을 가다 diligent 부지런한

Unit Practice

STEP 1

직독직해에 맞게 ( ) 안의 단어를 사용하여 문장을 쓰시오. (필요시 형태를 바꿔 쓸 것)

1 우리는 내려야 한다 / 여기서 (here / get off)

_______ _______ _______ _______ _______ / _______.

2 그녀는 걸었기 때문에 / 하루 종일, / Tiffany는 무척 피곤한 것임이 틀림없다 (walk / tired / because / all day / very)

_______ _______ _______ / _______ _______, / _______

_______ _______ _______ _______.

3 그는 1마일을 뛸 수 있었다 / 6분 안에 / 그가 고등학교에 다녔을 때 (when / in high school / a mile / be / in six minutes / run)

_______ _______ _______ _______ _______ / _______ _______

_______ / _______ _______ _______ _______ _______ _______.

STEP 2

다음 문장에서 조동사를 찾아 밑줄 긋고, 문장을 해석하시오.

1 May I have your attention, please?

2 The flowers should not be picked without permission.

3 You don't have to apologize for not knowing something.

4 That animal can't be a bird, since it doesn't have any wings.

5 You had better not look at your phone when you cross the street.

6 Our school used to have a uniform policy, but now we can wear our own clothes.

get off 내리다 all day 하루 종일 attention 주목 pick 고르다; *(꽃을) 꺾다 permission 허락, 허가 apologize for ~에 대해 사과하다 wing 날개 cross (가로질러) 건너다 policy 정책, 방침

STEP 3

1 (A), (B), (C)의 각 네모 안에서 문맥상 적절한 것을 고르시오.

Do you love baking? Then come to the third Seoul Bakery Festival on May 5. You (A) can / used to make your own special cake and take it home. All adults **may** join this special event, but children (B) can / must be over five. You only (C) cannot / have to pay 15,000 won for a ticket. Don't miss this great opportunity!

Reading Q 윗글의 목적으로 가장 적절한 것은?

① 베이커리 축제를 홍보하려고
② 입장표 가격 변동을 안내하려고
③ 신입 제빵사 채용을 공고하려고

NEW 내신기출

2 밑줄 친 우리말 (A), (B)를 조건 에 맞게 써서 각 문장을 완성하시오.

(A) 연구에 따르면 아기들은 부모의 감정을 감지할 수 있다. What's more, angry parents **can** damage their babies' mental development. When babies hear loud arguments, they experience stress. This stress **can** make them more anxious later in life. Therefore, parents **should** keep their voices calm. (B) 정말 말다툼이 필요할 때, 그들은 밖으로 나가는 것이 낫다.

*mental development 정신적[심리적] 발달

조건
· 조동사를 쓸 것
· 제시된 단어를 사용할 것 (필요시 형태를 바꿔 쓸 것)
· baby / step outside / sense

(A) According to research, ________ ________ ________ ________ ________ their parents' emotions.

(B) When they really need to argue, ________ ________ ________ ________ ________.

1 adult 성인, 어른 event 사건[일]; *행사 over ~ 위에; *~ 이상의 pay 지불하다 miss 놓치다 opportunity 기회
2 argument 말다툼(*v.* argue 언쟁을 하다) anxious 불안해하는 step outside 밖으로 나가다 sense 감지하다, 느끼다 research 연구

정답 및 해설 p.20

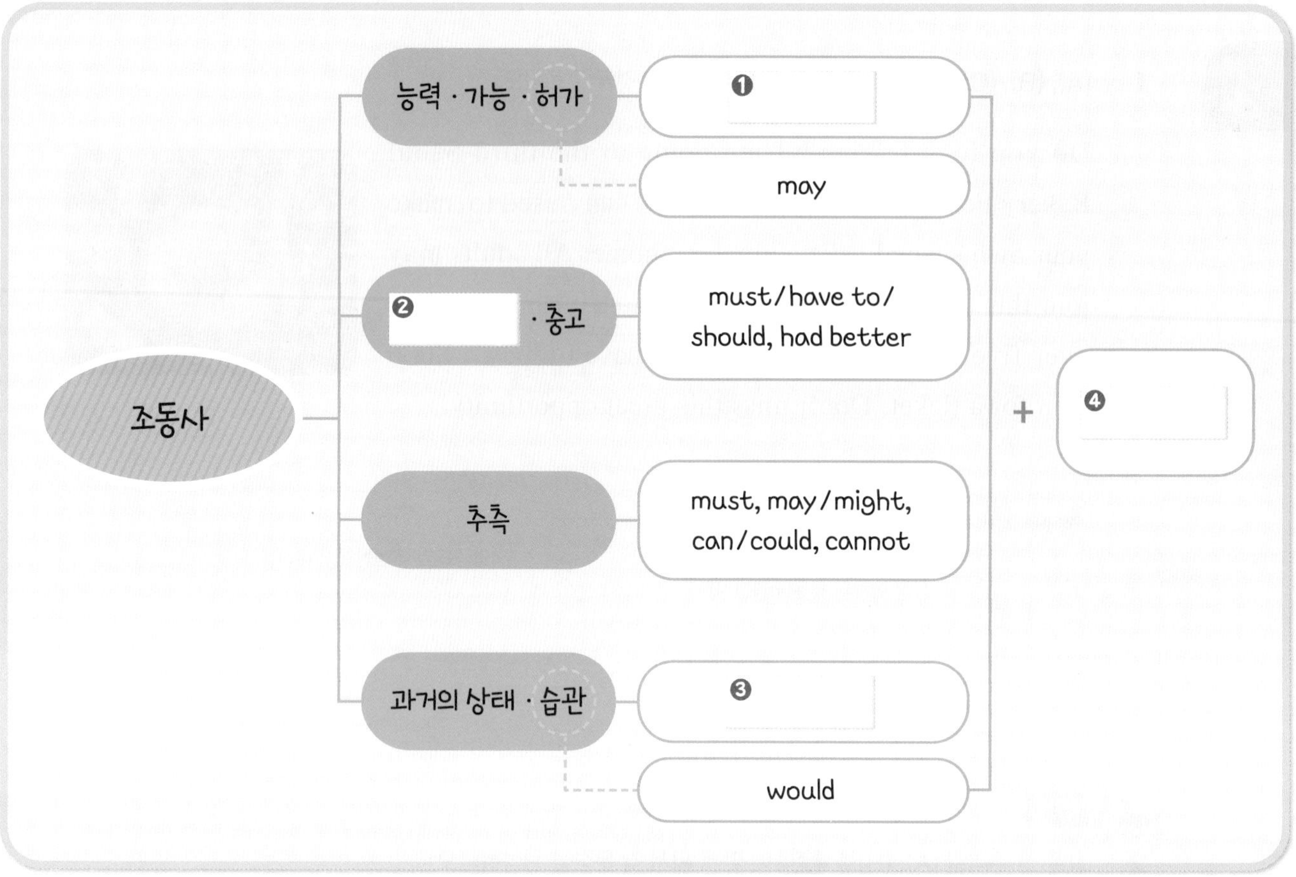

주요 예문을 다시 한번 확인하고, 우리말에 맞게 (　) 안의 단어를 사용하여 문장을 쓰시오.

1 그녀는 적어도 마흔 살임이 틀림없다. (forty years / at least / old) Point 03

2 너는 내 우산을 가져가도 된다. (umbrella / take) Point 01

3 그는 그의 부모님의 충고를 듣는 것이 낫다. (parents' advice / listen to) Point 02

4 큰 단풍나무 한 그루가 저기에 서 있었다. (stand / a big maple tree / there) Point 04

5 그는 한 달에 한 번 내게 꽃을 주곤 했다. (flowers / a month / once / give / to me) Point 04

6 너는 차 안에서 네 안전벨트를 매야 한다. (seat belt / in the car / wear) Point 02

UNIT 06

수식어구의 쓰임

Point 01 형용사와 부사
Point 02 분사와 전치사구
Point 03 형용사 역할의 to부정사
Point 04 부사 역할의 to부정사

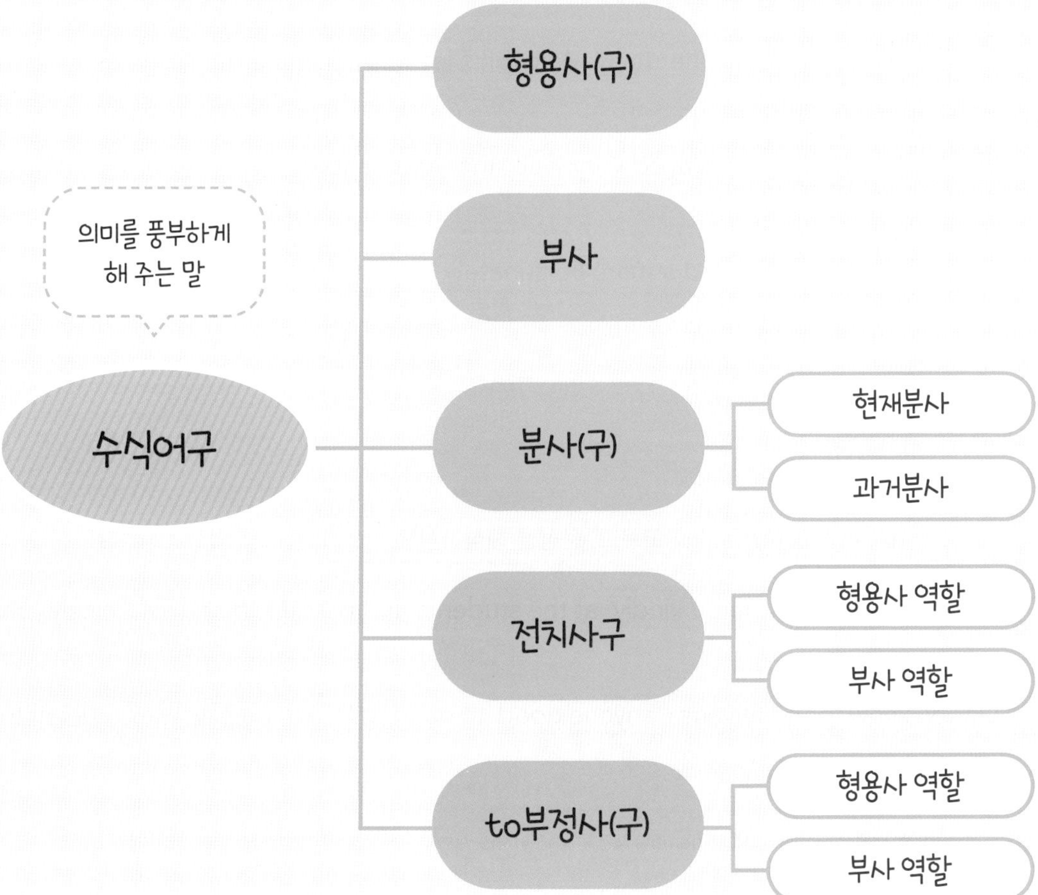

Point 01 형용사와 부사

형용사는 **명사**를 수식하며 한 단어일 때는 명사 앞에서, 두 단어 이상일 때는 명사 뒤에서 주로 수식한다. 부사는 **동사**, **형용사**, **부사**, **문장 전체**를 수식하며, **대부분 「형용사+-ly」 형태**로 쓴다.

• -thing, -body, -one으로 끝나는 대명사는 형용사가 뒤에서 수식한다.

-ly로 끝나지만 형용사인 단어	friendly, lovely, daily, ugly, silly, lonely 등

225 Henry bought me / a **nice** dress.
S V IO DO
Henry가 나에게 사 주었다 / 멋진 드레스를

226 The weather is **quite** good.
S V SC
날씨가 꽤 좋다.

다음 문장에서 밑줄 친 부분을 수식하는 수식어를 찾아 동그라미 하고, 문장을 해석하시오.

정답 및 해설 p.21

227 Stella had a (wonderful) time / with David.
Stella는 멋진 시간을 보냈다 / David와

228 We want to drink something cold.

229 I'm pretty sure that Jessica will forgive you.

230 I'm terribly sorry about the delay. We won't let this happen again.

231 The baseball team has played very well since last season.

232 A tiger suddenly attacked a man. Fortunately, he wasn't seriously hurt.

다음 문장의 네모 안에서 어법상 알맞은 것을 고르고, 문장을 해석하시오.

233 The teacher smiled [kind / kindly] at the students and praised their [nice / nicely] drawings.

234 Do you know [good anyone / anyone good] at dancing? I [real / really] want to learn to dance.

quite 꽤, 상당히 pretty 꽤, 매우 forgive 용서하다 terribly 대단히 delay 지연, 지체 attack 공격하다 fortunately 다행히도 seriously 심하게 praise 칭찬하다 drawing 그림 good at ~을 잘하는

Point 02 분사와 전치사구

분사는 **명사를 수식**하는 형용사 역할을 한다. 현재분사(v-ing)는 **능동 및 진행**의 의미를, 과거분사(v-ed)는 **수동 및 완료**의 의미를 지닌다. 전치사구는 **명사를 수식**하는 형용사 역할을 하거나 **동사를 수식**하는 부사 역할을 한다.

235 A **growing** child needs / plenty of sleep.
S V O
성장하는 아이는 필요로 한다 / 많은 잠을

236 I want to live / in a house <**made of brick**>.
S V O M
나는 살고 싶다 / 집에서 <벽돌로 지은>

237 Dinner <**under the night sky**> / was fantastic.
S V SC
저녁 식사는 <밤하늘 아래에서의> / 환상적이었다

다음 문장에서 밑줄 친 부분을 수식하는 수식어구를 찾아 동그라미 하고, 문장을 해석하시오. 정답 및 해설 p.21

238 We studied / for the exam.
우리는 공부했다 / 시험을 위해

239 Do you know the boy swimming in the pool?

240 Can I take a seat next to you?

241 They ran towards each other and hugged tightly.

242 We gave the police officer the wallet found on the bus.

243 The dishes served in this restaurant are expensive, but they taste great.

구문 해석 기법

□ 명사를 수식하는 현재분사(구)는 **'~하는/하고 있는'**, 과거분사(구)는 **'~해진/된'**으로 해석한다.

다음 문장의 네모 안에서 어법상 알맞은 것을 고르고, 문장을 해석하시오.

244 The [shocking / shocked] news about the war spread throughout the world.

245 The trees outside my window [block / blocks] the light. But the birds [singing / sung] in the trees make me feel good.

grow 커지다; *자라다 plenty of 많은 brick 벽돌 fantastic 환상적인 take a seat 자리에 앉다 hug 껴안다 tightly 단단히, 꽉 shock 충격을 주다 throughout 도처에 block 막다, 차단하다

Unit Practice

STEP 1

직독직해에 맞게 ( ) 안의 단어를 사용하여 문장을 쓰시오. (필요시 형태를 바꿔 쓸 것)

1 우리는 경찰관에게 주었다 / 지갑을 / 버스에서 발견된 (on the bus / find / give / the wallet)

________ ________ ________ ________ ________ / ________

________ / ________ ________ ________ ________.

2 유감스럽게도, / Ella는 약간의 커피를 쏟았다 / 그녀의 새 치마에 (some / on her new skirt / spill / unfortunately)

________, / ________ ________ ________ ________ / ________

________ ________ ________.

3 그 배낭은 / 파란색 지퍼가 있는 / 그의 것이다 (belong to / with the blue zipper / the backpack)

________ ________ / ________ ________ ________ ________ /

________ ________ ________.

STEP 2

다음 문장에서 밑줄 친 부분을 수식하는 수식어구를 찾아 동그라미 하고, 문장을 해석하시오.

1 I bought a novel written by a famous author.

2 We saw a beautiful rainbow on our way to school.

3 The sleeping baby must be dreaming of something happy.

4 She has saved so much money over the years.

5 My friend told me a story scarier than any horror movie.

6 In the summer, the sun shines brightly for up to fifteen hours.

spill 흘리다, 쏟다(-spilled[spilt]-spilled[spilt]) unfortunately 불행하게도, 유감스럽게도 belong to ~의 것이다, ~에 속하다 author 작가
save 구하다; *저축하다 horror movie 공포 영화 shine 빛나다, (해·달이) 비치다 brightly 밝게 up to ~까지

STEP 3

1 (A), (B)의 각 네모 안에서 어법에 맞는 표현을 고르시오.

Do you like cooking but need help? Solve your problems **with a smart refrigerator**. It has programs **for all your needs**. For anyone (A) searches / searching for recipe ideas, this refrigerator recommends recipes (B) finding / found on the internet. And each week, your groceries are ordered **by the refrigerator** after it reviews the food **inside it**. How amazing!

Reading Q 스마트 냉장고에 관한 윗글의 내용과 일치하지 <u>않는</u> 것은?
① 조리법을 추천해 준다.
② 상한 음식이 있으면 알려 준다.
③ 식료품을 확인해 주문해 준다.

NEW 내신기출

2 밑줄 친 우리말 (A), (B)에 맞게 보기 의 단어를 배열하여 각 문장을 완성하시오.

(A) <u>당신은 기묘한 것들을 매우 좋아하는가?</u> Then visit the Hair Museum **in Turkey**. The strange attraction **created by Chez Galip** looks scary. There are 16,000 hair samples **in the museum**. It is located **under Galip's pottery shop**. (B) <u>여러 여성들로부터 온 머리카락이 그 박물관의 모든 벽을 뒤덮고 있다.</u>

보기 strange / of the museum / every / covers / love / wall / from different women / things

(A) Do you ______________________________?

(B) Hair ______________________________.

1 need 필요로 하다; *필요(성), 필요한 것 search for ~을 찾다 recommend 추천하다 grocery 식료품 review 확인하다, 검토하다 amazing 놀라운
2 strange 이상한, 기묘한 attraction (사람을 끄는) 명물, 명소 pottery 도자기 cover 가리다; *(뒤)덮다

Point **03**

형용사 역할의 to부정사

to부정사(to-v)는 **명사를 수식**하는 **형용사** 역할을 하며 「명사+to부정사」의 형태로 쓴다. -thing, -body, -one으로 끝나는 대명사를 뒤에서 수식하기도 한다.

246 You can bring / a book <**to read**>.
S V O
너는 가져와도 된다 / 책을 <읽을>

247 I have / many friends <**to talk with**>.
S V O
나는 가지고 있다 / 많은 친구들을 <이야기할>

Tip 수식을 받는 명사가 전치사의 목적어인 경우에는 「명사+to부정사+전치사」의 순서로 쓴다.

248 He is looking for / something <**to do** / **on the weekends**>.
S V O
그는 찾고 있는 중이다 / 어떤 것을 <할 / 주말에>

다음 문장에서 밑줄 친 부분을 수식하는 수식어(구)를 찾아 동그라미 하고, 문장을 해석하시오. 정답 및 해설 p.23

구문 해석 기법
□ 명사를 수식하는 to부정사(구)는 '~할[하는]'으로 해석한다.

249 Is there / anything <to eat> / in the refrigerator?
있나요 / 어떤 것이 <먹을> / 냉장고 안에

250 The child needs a toy to play with.

251 Matt is building a house to live in.

252 You can choose a movie to watch with me.

253 One way to lose weight is to exercise every day.

254 I spilled sauce on my hand. I need a napkin to clean it off.

다음 문장의 네모 안에서 어법상 알맞은 것을 고르고, 문장을 해석하시오.

255 Joining a club will give you a chance [making / to make] new friends.

256 Erica has a baby [of to take care / to take care of]. So she doesn't have much time [sleep / to sleep] these days.

---

look for ~을 찾다 lose weight 살을 빼다 spill 쏟다 clean off (깨끗이) 닦아내다 chance 기회 take care of ~을 돌보다

Point 04 부사 역할의 to부정사

to부정사는 **동사, 형용사, 부사, 문장 전체를 수식**하는 **부사** 역할뿐만 아니라 문맥에 따라 **목적, 감정의 원인, 결과, 판단의 근거** 등의 의미를 나타내기도 한다.

목적	~하기 위해, ~하려고	in order to-v 또는 so as to-v로 바꿔 쓸 수 있음
감정의 원인	~해서, ~하게 되어서	happy, glad, proud, surprised, sad, sorry, afraid 등의 감정 형용사와 자주 함께 쓰임
결과	(~해서 결국) …하다	live, grow up, awake 등의 동사와 자주 함께 쓰임
판단의 근거	~하다니, ~하는 것을 보면	nice, clever, foolish, rich 등의 형용사와 자주 함께 쓰임

257 I called my boyfriend / **to wake him up.**
S V O M(called의 목적)
나는 내 남자친구에게 전화했다 / 그를 깨우려고

258 The little girl grew up / **to become a firefighter.**
S V M(grew up의 결과)
그 어린 소녀는 커서 / 소방관이 되었다.

밑줄 친 부분에 유의하여 다음 문장을 해석하시오.

정답 및 해설 p.23

259 Victoria was glad / to be home / again.
Victoria는 기뻤다 / 집에 와서 / 다시

260 We decided to take a bus to save money.

261 Sam lived to have his 101st birthday party.

262 Kelly must be rich to buy such an expensive car.

263 I turned on the morning news to check the weather.

264 Kevin woke up late in the morning. He ran fast to catch the bus.

다음 문장의 네모 안에서 어법상 알맞은 것을 고르고, 문장을 해석하시오.

265 I am sorry [inform / to inform] you that the festival has been canceled.

266 That boy must be a diligent student [getting / to get] such good grades. He will grow up [to is / to be] successful.

save 절약하다 such 그런; *그 정도의 catch 잡다; *(버스·기차 등을 시간 맞춰) 타다 inform 알리다 diligent 성실한 grade 품질; *성적

Unit Practice

STEP 1 직독직해에 맞게 ( ) 안의 단어를 사용하여 문장을 쓰시오. (필요시 형태를 바꿔 쓸 것)

1 너희는 있니 / 물어볼 어떤 것이 / 그 과제에 대해 (have / ask / anything / about the assignment)

_______ _______ _______ / _______ _______ _______ /

_______ _______ _______?

2 그 운동선수는 행복했다 / 메달을 받게 되어 (be / receive / the athlete / a medal / happy)

_______ _______ _______ _______ / _______ _______

_______ _______.

3 그녀는 없었다 / 샤워할 시간이 / 오늘 아침에 (this / time / take a shower / have / morning)

_______ _______ _______ / _______ _______ _______

_______ _______ / _______ _______.

STEP 2 다음 문장에서 밑줄 친 부분을 수식하는 수식어(구)를 찾아 동그라미 하고, 문장을 해석하시오.

1 Can I have another <u>opportunity</u> to try again?

2 He must be <u>busy</u> not to reply to my text message.

3 Mason <u>quit</u> his job to start his own business.

4 I booked <u>a hotel</u> to stay in during our vacation.

5 I felt bored because I had <u>nothing</u> to watch on TV.

6 Jenny was <u>embarrassed</u> to call her teacher "Mom" by mistake.

assignment 과제 receive 받다 athlete (운동)선수 opportunity 기회 reply 답장을 보내다 text message 문자 메시지 quit 그만두다 job 일, 직장 business 사업 book 예약하다 bored 지루해하는 embarrassed 당황한

STEP 3

1 밑줄 친 ①~④ 중 역할이 다른 것을 고르시오.

Lots of people use perfume these days. But the first people ① to use it were the ancient Egyptians. They used ② scented oils for funerals. The oils were put onto dead bodies ③ to protect them from evil. However, perfume was only for socially important people. When the grave ④ of King Tutankhamun was discovered, several bottles of perfume were inside it.

Reading Q 고대 이집트인들의 향수 사용에 관한 윗글의 내용과 일치하면 T, 일치하지 않으면 F를 쓰시오.

(1) 향수는 장례식에 사용되었다. ______

(2) 모든 사람들이 향수를 사용하였다. ______

NEW 내신기출

2 밑줄 친 우리말을 조건 에 맞게 쓰시오.

A woman's son had some bad friends. **To teach him a lesson**, the woman made a plan. Together, they put ten delicious apples and a rotten one into a bag. Later, they opened the bag. 그녀의 아들은 썩은 사과들만 있는 것을 보고 놀랐다. He learned that one rotten apple can spoil the rest.

조건 · to부정사를 쓸 것	· 제시된 단어를 사용할 것
· see / only / surprised / rotten / son	· 총 9단어로 쓸 것

____

1 Egyptian 이집트 사람 scented 향기가 나는 funeral 장례식 evil 악 socially 사회적으로 grave 무덤 discover 발견하다 several 여러 (개의)
2 lesson 교훈 make a plan 계획을 세우다 rotten 썩은 spoil 망치다, 못쓰게 만들다 (the) rest 나머지

Wrap Up

정답 및 해설 p.25

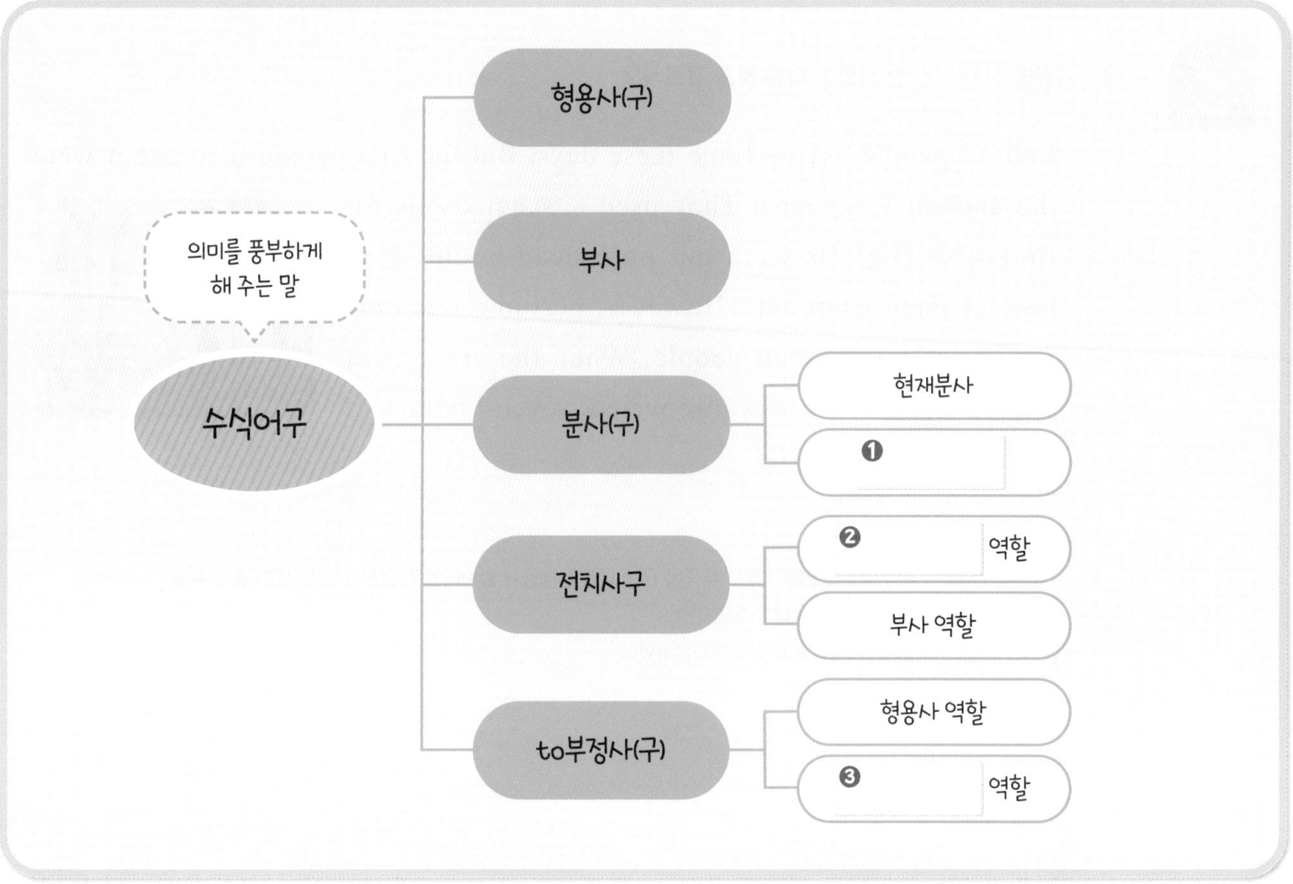

주요 예문을 다시 한번 확인하고, 우리말에 맞게 ( ) 안의 단어를 사용하여 문장을 쓰시오.

1 너는 읽을 책을 가져와도 된다. (a book / bring / read) Point 03

2 나는 벽돌로 지은 집에서 살고 싶다. (want / brick / live / in a house / made) Point 02

3 Henry가 나에게 멋진 드레스를 사 주었다. (nice / bought) Point 01

4 그 어린 소녀는 커서 소방관이 되었다. (a firefighter / grew up / become / the little girl) Point 04

5 성장하는 아이는 많은 잠을 필요로 한다. (plenty of / needs / sleep) Point 02

6 나는 내 남자친구를 깨우려고 그에게 전화했다. (called / wake up) Point 04

UNIT 07

비교 표현

Point 01 원급·비교급 구문
Point 02 원급·비교급 표현
Point 03 최상급 구문
Point 04 최상급 표현

비교 표현

- **원급 구문**
  - A as + 형용사/부사 + as B
- **원급 표현**
  - 배수사 + 원급 구문
  - as + 형용사/부사 + as possible
- **비교급 구문**
  - A 비교급 + than B
- **비교급 표현**
  - 배수사 + 비교급 than
  - the + 비교급 ~, the + 비교급 ...
  - 비교급 + and + 비교급
- **최상급 구문**
  - the + 최상급 + of/in/among ~
  - one of the + 최상급 + 복수명사
- **최상급 표현**
  - 원급 사용 표현
  - 비교급 사용 표현

Point 01 원급 · 비교급 구문

성격과 형태가 같은 두 대상이 상태, 정도 등에서 차이가 날 때, **형용사나 부사의 원급** 또는 **비교급 구문**을 써서 표현한다.

원급 구문	A as+형용사/부사+as B	A는 B만큼 ~한/하게
비교급 구문	A 비교급+than B	A는 B보다 더 ~한/하게 (비교 대상이 명확할 때 than B 생략 가능)
비교급 강조	much/even/a lot/far+비교급	훨씬 더 ~한/하게

267 The movie is **as popular** / **as** the book.
S V SC
그 영화는 인기 있다 / 그 책만큼

268 This desk is **cheaper** / **than** that one.
S V SC
이 책상은 더 저렴하다 / 저것보다

269 Horses run **much faster** / **than** camels.
S V M
말은 훨씬 더 빨리 달린다 / 낙타보다

밑줄 친 부분에 유의하여 다음 문장을 해석하시오.

정답 및 해설 p.25

270 Your hair is even longer / than mine.
네 머리카락이 훨씬 더 길다 / 내 머리카락보다

271 Today is as cold as yesterday.

272 Exercise is as important as a balanced diet.

273 Julie arrived at the airport earlier than her friends.

274 Elephants are more intelligent than most animals.

275 The baby sleeps as peacefully as an angel.

다음 문장의 네모 안에서 어법상 알맞은 것을 고르고, 문장을 해석하시오.

276 People say that vegetables are a lot [healthier than / than healthier] meat.

277 This couch is [more comfortable than / more than comfortable] that one. And its design is [prettier / more pretty].

camel 낙타 balanced 균형 잡힌 diet 식사, 식습관 peacefully 평화롭게, 평온하게 meat 고기 couch 긴 의자, 소파 comfortable 편안한

Point 02
원급 · 비교급 표현

형용사/부사의 원급, 비교급을 사용해 다양한 비교 표현을 나타낼 수 있다.

원급 표현	A 배수사+as+형용사/부사+as B	A는 B보다 ~ 배만큼 …한/하게
	as+형용사/부사+as possible[주어+can]	가능한 한[~가 할 수 있는 한] …한/하게
비교급 표현	A 배수사+비교급+than B	A는 B보다 ~ 배는 더 …한/하게
	the+비교급 ~, the+비교급 ...	~할수록 더 …하다
	비교급+and+비교급	점점 더 ~한/하게

278 This building is **twice as tall** / **as** that building.
S V SC
이 건물은 두 배만큼 높다 / 저 건물보다

Tip 배수사 (어떤 수의 '~배'가 되는 수) twice, three times, four times 등

279 **The higher** we go up, // **the colder** it gets.
SC_1 S_1 V_1 SC_2 S_2 V_2
우리가 높이 올라갈수록 // 더 추워진다.

280 The earth is getting / **hotter and hotter**.
S V SC
지구는 되고 있다 / 점점 더 더워지고

밑줄 친 부분에 유의하여 다음 문장을 해석하시오.

정답 및 해설 p.25

281 I became / more and more nervous.
나는 되었다 / 점점 더 긴장하게

282 Gia studied as hard as possible for the midterm exam.

283 That snake is three times as long as this snake.

284 The earlier you buy the ticket, the lower the price is.

285 Eating out costs two times more than eating at home.

286 Leo is growing taller and taller every day. Now he is as tall as his father.

다음 문장의 네모 안에서 어법상 알맞은 것을 고르고, 문장을 해석하시오.

287 The more popular a mall becomes, [more / the more] crowded it gets.

288 Since you have prepared for the exam as [more / much] as you can, you will pass it.

---

midterm exam 중간고사 low 낮은 price 가격 eat out 외식하다 cost 비용이 들다 mall 쇼핑센터 crowded 붐비는 prepare 준비하다

Unit Practice

STEP 1

직독직해에 맞게 ( ) 안의 단어를 사용하여 문장을 쓰시오. (필요시 형태를 바꿔 쓸 것)

1 네가 일찍 표를 구매할수록, / 가격이 더 낮다. (the ticket / be / the price / early / low / buy)

______ ______ ______ ______ ______ ______, /

______ ______ ______ ______ ______.

2 그 새 식당은 훨씬 더 분주하다 / 이전 식당보다 (far / be / the new restaurant / busy / the old one)

______ ______ ______ ______ ______ ______ /

______ ______ ______ ______.

3 저 골동품 시계는 / 열 배는 더 비싸다 / 내 것보다 (mine / expensive / be / that antique watch)

______ ______ ______ / ______ ______ ______

______ ______ / ______ ______.

STEP 2

밑줄 친 부분에 유의하여 다음 문장을 해석하시오.

1 This gold ring is a lot more expensive than the silver one.

2 The package needs to be delivered as soon as possible.

3 The fireworks exploded as loud as thunder in the night sky.

4 Sometimes taking the stairs is faster than taking the elevator.

5 The whale is more than five times heavier than the giraffe.

6 The rocket soared higher and higher into the air until it was almost out of sight.

antique (귀중한) 골동품인 package 소포 firework 폭죽 explode 터뜨리다, 폭발하다 take 가지고 가다; *이용하다 whale 고래 soar (허공으로) 솟구치다 air 공기; *하늘 almost 거의 out of sight 보이지 않는 곳에

STEP 3

1 밑줄 친 ①~④ 중 어법상 틀린 것을 모두 고르시오.

Many people think energy bars are ① healthier than candy bars. But in reality, they are as ② worse as candy bars. They often have a lot of fat and sugar in them. Therefore, they are high in calories. In addition, they're usually twice ③ so expensive as candy bars. So to get **more** energy, try fresh fruit instead. It is a ④ much better choice.

*candy bar 초코바

Reading Q 윗글의 요지로 가장 적절한 것은?

① 다이어트를 위해서는 과일을 먹는 것이 좋다.
② 에너지바는 건강에 해로울 수 있다.
③ 초코바가 에너지를 얻는 데 도움이 되기도 한다.

NEW 내신기출

2 밑줄 친 우리말을 조건에 맞게 쓰시오.

Can ice cream glow in the dark? Thanks to British inventor Charlie Francis, it sure can! He adds proteins from jellyfish to ice cream. These proteins start to work when they touch the tongue. So when you lick the ice cream, it glows. 당신이 그것을 많이 핥을수록 그것은 더 밝아진다. It's **much more expensive than** most ice cream, but many people want to try it.

*protein 단백질

조건
· 「the+비교급 ~, the+비교급 ...」을 쓸 것
· 제시된 단어를 사용할 것 (필요시 형태를 바꿔 쓸 것)
· lick / bright / much / become / it
· 총 9단어로 쓸 것

____

1 in reality 실제로는, 사실은 fat 뚱뚱한; *지방 sugar 설탕, 당분 high in ~의 함유량이 높은 in addition 게다가 instead 대신에 choice 선택
2 glow 빛나다 British 영국의, 영국인의 inventor 발명가 sure 물론; *정말 jellyfish 해파리 work 일하다; *작용하다 tongue 혀 lick 핥다

Point 03 최상급 구문

셋 이상의 대상 중 **상태·정도 등이 가장 큰 것**을 나타낼 때 **형용사나 부사의 최상급**으로 표현하며, 최상급 앞에는 the를 쓴다.

최상급 형태	A the+최상급(+명사)+of/in/among ~	A가 ~ 안에서[중에서] 가장 …한/하게
	one of the+최상급+복수 명사	가장 ~한 것들 중 하나
최상급 강조	by far/the very+최상급	단연코 가장 ~한

289 Monday is / **the busiest** day <of the week>.
S V SC
월요일은 ~이다 / 가장 바쁜 날 <일주일 중에서>

290 Ms. Han explains grammar / **the most clearly**.
S V O M
한 선생님은 문법을 설명해 주신다 / 가장 명확하게

291 Dolphins are / **one of the smartest animals**.
S V SC
돌고래는 ~이다 / 가장 똑똑한 동물들 중 하나

비교 범위를 나타낼 필요가 없을 경우, 「of/in/among ~」은 생략할 수 있다.

밑줄 친 부분에 유의하여 다음 문장을 해석하시오. 정답 및 해설 p.27

292 Today is / the very happiest day <of my life>.
오늘은 ~이다 / 단연코 가장 행복한 날 <내 인생에서>

293 Kevin gets up the earliest in his family.

294 The roller coaster is the scariest ride in this amusement park.

295 Melissa is by far the most talented among us.

296 Rome is one of the most wonderful cities in the world.

297 The tornado was one of the worst disasters in history.

다음 문장의 네모 안에서 어법상 알맞은 것을 고르고, 문장을 해석하시오.

298 This cooking video is one of the most popular [video / videos] on the website.

299 That black horse is the [faster / fastest] horse on this farm. She is also the [beautifulest / most beautiful] one.

clearly 틀림없이; *명확히 ride (자전거 등을) 타다; *(놀이) 기구 amusement park 놀이공원 talented 재능[재주]이 있는 in history 역사상

Point 04

최상급 표현

원급이나 비교급을 사용하여 최상급의 의미를 표현할 수 있다.

최상급 표현	no (other)+명사+as+형용사/부사+as A	어떤 ~도 A만큼 …하지 않은/않게
	no (other)+명사+비교급+than A	어떤 ~도 A보다 더 …하지 않은/않게
	비교급+than any other+단수 명사	다른 어떤 ~보다도 더 …한/하게

300 **No student** <in my school> / is **as kind** / **as** Jim.
S / V SC
어떤 학생도 <우리 학교의> / 친절하지 않다 / Jim만큼

301 = **No student** <in my school> / is **kinder** / **than** Jim.
S / V SC
어떤 학생도 <우리 학교의> / 더 친절하지 않다 / Jim보다

302 = Jim is **kinder** / **than any other student** <in my school>.
S V SC
Jim은 더 친절하다 / 다른 어떤 학생보다도 <우리 학교의>

밑줄 친 부분에 유의하여 다음 문장을 해석하시오.

정답 및 해설 p.27

303 No other desert is as wide / as the Sahara Desert.
어떤 사막도 넓지 않다 / 사하라 사막만큼

304 This test is harder than any other test.

305 No player plays tennis better than Cathy.

306 My brother is taller than any other student in his class.

307 No one in the room finished the puzzle as fast as Howard.

308 This is not a famous horror movie, but it's scarier than any other one.

다음 문장의 네모 안에서 어법상 알맞은 것을 고르고, 문장을 해석하시오.

309 Everyone loves Amanda's cookies. [No / Not] one can make cookies [well / better] than her.

310 My family is [more precious / preciouser] than any other [thing / things] to me. They always give me a lot of support.

desert 사막 wide 넓은 finish 끝내다 horror movie 공포 영화 scary 무서운 precious 귀중한, 소중한 support 지원, 지지

Unit Practice

STEP 1 직독직해에 맞게 (   ) 안의 단어를 사용하여 문장을 쓰시오. (필요시 형태를 바꿔 쓸 것)

1 Kevin은 가장 일찍 일어난다 / 그의 가족 중에서 (in his family / early / get up)

_______ _______ _______ _______ _______ / _______

_______ _______.

2 치타는 더 빨리 달린다 / 다른 어떤 동물보다도 (run / animal / fast / the cheetah)

_______ _______ _______ _______ / _______ _______

_______ _______.

3 독감은 ~이다 / 가장 흔한 병들 중 하나 / 요즘 (these days / common / be / the flu / diseases)

_______ _______ _______ / _______ _______ _______

_______ _______ _______ / _______ _______.

STEP 2 밑줄 친 부분에 유의하여 다음 문장을 해석하시오.

1 This was <u>one of the most difficult questions</u> on the exam.

2 From my experience, <u>no other thing</u> is <u>better than</u> being loved.

3 Chloe said this book is <u>by far the most interesting</u> one of the series.

4 When I heard her sing, I thought that <u>no singer</u> could sing a song <u>as well as</u> Bella.

5 <u>The most delicious dessert</u> among all the ones in the bakery is the chocolate cake.

6 It was reported that New York is <u>more crowded than any other city</u> in America.

common 흔한 flu 독감 disease (질)병 experience 경험 by far 단연코 series 연속; *시리즈 among ~의 가운데에; *~ 중에 report 알리다; *보고하다 crowded 붐비는

STEP 3

1 **(A), (B), (C)의 각 네모 안에서 어법에 맞는 표현을 고르시오.**

Reading webtoons is one of the (A) [most popular / popularest] online (B) [activity / activities] among young people today. Why are webtoons so popular? For one, most of them are free. Also, webtoons have interesting characters. Finally, people can easily access them with the (C) [most late / latest] smart devices. For these reasons, many young people love reading them.

*webtoon 웹툰(인터넷 만화) **smart device 스마트 기기

Reading Q 윗글의 주제로 가장 적절한 것은?

① problems with reading webtoons
② reasons why webtoons are popular
③ the difference between webtoons and comic books

NEW 내신기출

2 **밑줄 친 우리말을 조건 에 맞게 써서 요약문을 완성하시오.**

Which animal lives **the longest of all the animals**? It's not the elephant. It's not the tortoise either. It's the glass sponge! **No animal** lives **longer than** this sponge. It is **one of the simplest animals** on Earth. It doesn't have arms, organs, or even a head. But it's an animal, and it can live for 15,000 years.

*glass sponge 육방해면

조건
· 최상급 표현을 쓸 것
· live / animal / long
· 제시된 단어를 사용할 것 (필요시 형태를 바꿔 쓸 것)
· 총 7단어로 쓸 것

The glass sponge is one of the simplest animals on Earth, and <u>그것은 다른 어떤 동물보다도 더 오래 산다</u>.

____

1 character 등장인물 access 접근[접속]하다 late 늦은; *요즘의, 최근의 difference 차이(점) comic book 만화책
2 tortoise 거북 on Earth 지구상에서 organ (인체 내의) 장기 simple 간단한; *단순한

Wrap Up

정답 및 해설 p.29

비교 표현

원급 구문
A as + 형용사/부사 + ❶ ________ B

원급 표현
배수사 + 원급 구문
as + 형용사 / 부사 + as possible

비교급 구문
A 비교급 + ❷ ________ B

비교급 표현
배수사 + 비교급 than
the + 비교급 ~, ❸ ________ ...
비교급 + and + 비교급

최상급 구문
the + 최상급 + of / in / among ~
one of the + 최상급 + ❹ ________ 명사

최상급 표현
원급 사용 표현
비교급 사용 표현

주요 예문을 다시 한번 확인하고, 우리말에 맞게 (   ) 안의 단어를 사용하여 문장을 쓰시오.

1 돌고래는 가장 똑똑한 동물들 중 하나이다. (animals / dolphins) Point 03

2 이 건물은 저 건물보다 두 배만큼 높다. (that / twice / building / tall) Point 02

3 한 선생님은 가장 명확하게 문법을 설명해 주신다. (clearly / explains / grammar / Ms. Han) Point 03

4 우리가 높이 올라갈수록 더 추워진다. (it / go up / gets) Point 02

5 이 책상은 저것보다 더 저렴하다. (one / that / desk) Point 01

6 Jim은 우리 학교의 다른 어떤 학생보다도 더 친절하다. (in my school / student) Point 04

UNIT 08

관계사

Point 01 주격 관계대명사
Point 02 목적격 관계대명사
Point 03 소유격 관계대명사
Point 04 관계부사

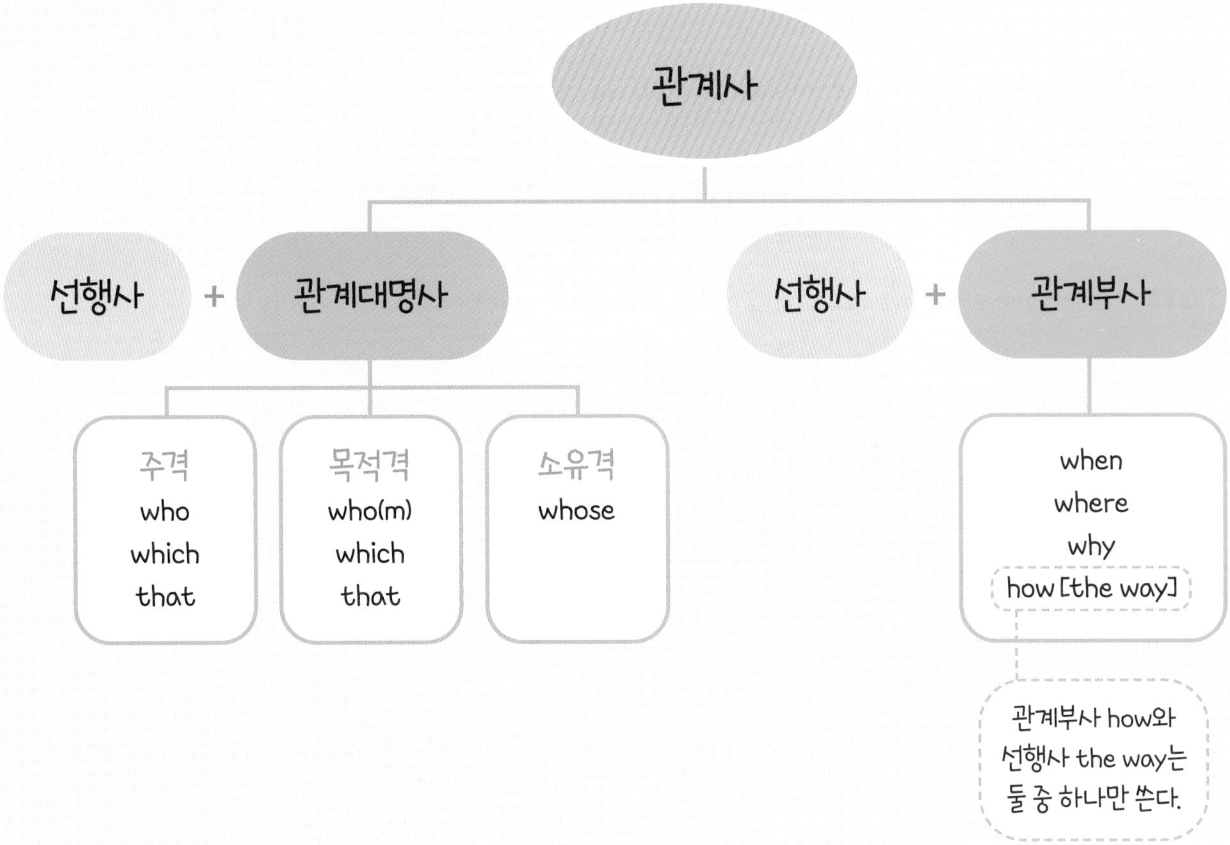

Point 01 주격 관계대명사

관계대명사는 두 개의 절을 연결하는 **관계사**와 바로 앞 명사를 대신하는 **대명사** 역할을 동시에 한다.

- 관계대명사 바로 앞에 있는 명사를 **선행사**라고 하고, 관계대명사가 이끄는 절은 선행사를 수식한다.
- 관계대명사가 **절 안에서 주어 역할**을 할 때 **주격 관계대명사**라고 하고, 선행사에 따라 관계대명사는 달라진다.

선행사가 사람	who, that	선행사가 사물, 동물	which, that

311 I like / *people* <**who** keep their promises>.
(S: I, V: like, O: people / S′: who, V′: keep, O′: their promises)
나는 좋아한다 / 사람들을 <자기 약속을 지키는>

312 Daisy prefers / eating *food* <(**which** is) spicy>.
(S: Daisy, V: prefers, O: eating food / S′: which, V′: is, SC′: spicy)
Daisy는 선호한다 / 음식을 먹는 것을 <매운>

「주격 관계대명사+be동사」는 생략 가능

313 *The cat* <**that** has white fur> / is my pet.
(S: The cat, V: is, SC: my pet / S′: that, V′: has, O′: white fur)
그 고양이가 <흰색 털을 가진> / 나의 반려동물이다

다음 문장에서 관계대명사절을 찾아 밑줄 긋고 선행사에 동그라미 한 후, 문장을 해석하시오. 정답 및 해설 p.29

314 This is / (the dog) <which can guide the blind>.
이것은 ~이다 / 개 <시각 장애인들을 안내할 수 있는>

315 I saw a man that looked like my father.

316 People who always complain don't have many friends.

317 Do you know a coffee shop that is open for 24 hours?

318 Anyone who loves climbing mountains can join our club.

319 I will buy a house that has a nice garden, and grow flowers which smell nice.

구문 해석 기법

☐ 관계대명사절은 선행사를 수식하는 형용사절이므로, '~하는'으로 해석한다.

다음 문장의 네모 안에서 어법상 알맞은 것을 고르고, 문장을 해석하시오.

320 The thief [who / which] stole my bag was arrested.

321 Emma read an article about a bear and a man [who / that] live together in a house.

the blind 시각 장애인들 complain 불평하다 join 연결하다; *가입하다 steal 훔치다(-stole-stolen) arrest 체포하다 article (신문·잡지의) 글, 기사

Point 02

목적격 관계대명사

관계대명사가 **절 안에서 목적어 역할**을 할 때 **목적격 관계대명사**라고 하고, 선행사에 따라 관계대명사는 달라진다. **목적격 관계대명사는 생략**할 수 있다.

선행사가 사람	who(m), that	선행사가 사물, 동물	which, that

322 I have / *a friend* <**who(m)** I trust / completely>.
(S: I, V: have, O: a friend / O′: who(m), S′: I, V′: trust, M′: completely)
나는 가지고 있다 / 한 친구를 <내가 믿는 / 완전히>

323 *The piano* <**which** Sam is playing> / is very old.
(S: The piano / O′: which, S′: Sam, V′: is playing / V: is, SC: very old)
피아노는 <Sam이 치고 있는> / 매우 오래되었다

324 *The dream* <**that** I had / last night> / was strange.
(S: The dream / O′: that, S′: I, V′: had, M′: last night / V: was, SC: strange)
그 꿈은 <내가 꿨던 / 어젯밤에> / 이상했다

다음 문장에서 관계대명사절을 찾아 밑줄 긋고 선행사에 동그라미 한 후, 문장을 해석하시오. 정답 및 해설 p.29

325 Jenny gave me / (cookies) <that she baked by herself>.
Jenny는 내게 주었다 / 쿠키를 <그녀가 직접 구운>

326 Do you have an adult who you can consult?

327 Is this the key which you need for the door?

328 The fish which we caught yesterday is still alive.

329 The cook whom we will meet was introduced on a TV show.

330 I read the book that you recommended, and I found it enjoyable.

> **구문 해석 기법**
> □ 관계대명사 바로 뒤에 동사가 나오면 주격 관계대명사, 「주어+동사」가 나오면 목적격 관계대명사이다.

다음 문장의 네모 안에서 어법상 알맞은 것을 고르고, 문장을 해석하시오.

331 Since I know the man [who / which] the detectives are chasing, I was shocked to hear the news.

332 The farmer has a son and a sheepdog [that / which] help him on the farm.

by oneself 혼자; *스스로 consult 상담하다 enjoyable 재미있는 detective 형사, 수사관 chase 뒤쫓다, 추적하다 sheepdog 양치기 개

Unit Practice

STEP 1 직독직해에 맞게 (　) 안의 단어를 사용하여 문장을 쓰시오. (필요시 형태를 바꿔 쓸 것)

1 누구나 / 등산하는 것을 매우 좋아하는 / 우리 동아리에 가입할 수 있다 (club / love / mountains / anyone / join / climbing / can)

_______ / _______ _______ _______ _______ / _______

_______ _______ _______.

2 그 책은 / 내가 도서관에서 빌린 / 매우 재미있었다 (very / from the library / interesting / borrow)

_______ _______ / _______ _______ _______ _______

_______ _______ / _______ _______ _______.

3 판매원은 / 네가 도움을 요청했던 / 친절했다 (help / friendly / ask for / the salesperson / be)

_______ _______ / _______ _______ _______ _______ /

_______ _______.

STEP 2 다음 문장에서 관계대명사절을 찾아 밑줄 긋고, 문장을 해석하시오.

1 Have you seen the backpack which has my laptop in it?

2 The flight we booked was delayed due to bad weather.

3 The concert ticket she bought for me for my birthday was expensive.

4 I saw a man and a dog that were wearing the same kind of shirt in the park.

5 Phillip met an old friend whom he had not seen in years at the grocery store.

6 Daisy heard that the teacher who taught her English would retire this year.

friendly 친절한　salesperson 판매원　laptop 노트북 컴퓨터　flight 여행; *항공편　book 예약하다　delay 연기하다　due to ~ 때문에　kind 종류　grocery store 식료품점　retire 은퇴하다

STEP 3

1 **빈칸 (A), (B)에 들어갈 관계대명사로 가장 적절한 것을 고르시오.**

Have you heard of fish ____(A)____ live in the desert? They're lungfish, and they are found in Africa. Sometimes, rivers flood dry regions, and small ponds form. Lungfish move with the flood and live in the ponds. When the water dries, the lungfish hide in the mud. Then they live there for months on nutrients ____(B)____ they have saved inside their body.

*lungfish 폐어(폐로 호흡하는 어류)

	(A)		(B)
①	that	……	who
②	which	……	that
③	who	……	which

Reading Q 폐어에 관한 윗글의 내용과 일치하면 T를, 그렇지 않으면 F를 쓰시오.
(1) 물 없이도 몇 달을 살 수 있다. ______
(2) 사막에서 태어난다. ______

NEW 내신기출

2 **밑줄 친 우리말을 조건에 맞게 쓰시오.**

The holiday story *A Christmas Carol* is about a stingy man named Scrooge. In fact, there was a real Scrooge in the eighteenth century. His name was John Elwes. <u>그는 엄청난 재산을 가진 정치인이었다.</u> However, he refused to spend it. He lived in an old, dirty house **which** didn't have owners. He also ate rotten food to save money.

*stingy 인색한, 아끼는

조건
· 관계대명사를 쓸 것
· a politician / great / had / wealth
· 제시된 단어를 사용할 것
· 총 8단어로 쓸 것

____

1 desert 사막 flood 홍수; *(물이) 범람하다[시키다] region 지역 pond 연못 form 형성되다 mud 진흙 live on ~을 먹고 살다 nutrient 영양분
2 century 세기(100년) refuse 거절하다 rotten 썩은 save 저장하다; *절약하다 politician 정치인 wealth 부(富), 재산

Point 03 소유격 관계대명사

관계대명사가 **절 안에서 소유격 대명사의 역할**을 하면 소유격 관계대명사를 쓴다. 소유격 관계대명사는 선행사에 관계없이 whose를 쓰며, **뒤에는 항상 명사**가 온다.

333 I have / *a friend* <**whose** father is a lawyer>.
S V O (S′ V′ SC′)
나는 가지고 있다 / 친구를 <그의 아버지가 변호사인>

334 They live / in *a house* <**whose** door is painted red>.
S V M (S′ V′ SC′)
그들은 산다 / 집에 <그것의 문이 빨간색으로 페인트칠 된>

335 *The bird* <**whose** feathers are beautiful> / sings / every morning.
S (S′ V′ SC′) V M
그 새는 <그것의 깃털이 아름다운> / 노래한다 / 매일 아침

다음 문장에서 관계대명사절을 찾아 밑줄 긋고 선행사에 동그라미 한 후, 문장을 해석하시오. 정답 및 해설 p.31

336 Robert bought / a necklace <whose price is high> / for his wife.
Robert는 샀다 / 목걸이를 <그것의 가격이 비싼> / 그의 아내를 위해

337 Christina gave me a skirt whose size was big for her.

338 The pen whose cap is missing is Andy's.

339 A man whose hair was blond asked my name.

340 She is a writer whose book has sold millions of copies.

341 I saw a movie whose reviews were good, but to me it was boring.

다음 문장의 네모 안에서 어법상 알맞은 것을 고르고, 문장을 해석하시오.

342 There is a friend [who / whose] name is the same as mine in my class.

343 This is a café [whose / whose owner] is a famous actor. So people [who / whose] want to see him often come here.

lawyer 변호사 paint 페인트를 칠하다 necklace 목걸이 cap 뚜껑 missing (원래 있던 것이) 없는, 빠진 blond 금발의 sell 팔리다(-sold-sold) copy 복사; *(책의) 한 부 review 논평, 평가 owner 주인

Point 04 관계부사

관계부사는 **절 안에서 부사의 역할**을 하며, 관계부사가 이끄는 절은 **장소**, **시간**, **이유**, **방법**을 나타내는 선행사를 수식한다. 선행사에 따라 다른 관계부사를 쓴다.

선행사	장소	시간	이유	방법
관계부사	where	when	why	how

344 We visited / the place <**where** we first met>.
(S: We, V: visited, O: the place / S′: we, M′: first, V′: met)
우리는 방문했다 / 장소를 <우리가 처음 만난>

345 This is / <**how[the way]** the machine works>.
(S: This, V: is, SC: how[the way] the machine works / S′: the machine, V′: works)
이것이 ~이다 / <그 기계가 작동하는 방법>

Tip 관계부사 how는 선행사 the way와 함께 쓰지 않고, 둘 중 하나만 쓴다.

다음 문장에서 관계부사절을 찾아 밑줄 긋고, 문장을 해석하시오.

정답 및 해설 p.32

346 Let me know / the place <where you will be>.
나에게 알려 줘 / 장소를 <네가 있을>

347 The doctors explained how they cured the patient.

348 Peter wondered the reason why Helen didn't call him.

349 I live in a town where I can see many stars at night.

350 The date when the movie was released was March 24.

351 Spring is a time when many people like to go hiking in the mountains.

다음 문장의 네모 안에서 어법상 알맞은 것을 고르고, 문장을 해석하시오.

352 Do you know the reason [why / how] he was absent from school yesterday?

353 She showed me [the way / the way how] she solved the math problem step by step.

---

machine 기계 work 일하다; *작동하다 explain 설명하다 cure 치료하다 patient 환자 wonder 궁금하다 release 풀어 주다; *공개[발표]하다 time 시간; *시기 go hiking 하이킹을 가다 absent 결석한, 결근한 step by step 차근차근

Unit Practice

STEP 1

직독직해에 맞게 (　) 안의 단어를 사용하여 문장을 쓰시오. (필요시 형태를 바꿔 쓸 것)

1 표지가 찢어진 그 책은 / Sarah의 것이다. (belong to / be / the book / torn / cover)

______ ______ ______ ______ ______ ______ /

______ ______ ______.

2 너는 역을 기억하니 / 우리가 내려야 하는 (get off / the station / remember / have to)

______ ______ ______ ______ ______ / ______

______ ______ ______ ______ ______?

3 내가 이유를 알게 해줘 / 네가 스트레스를 느끼고 있는 / 최근에 (know / stressed / lately / the reason / feeling / be / let)

______ ______ ______ ______ ______ / ______

______ ______ ______ ______ / ______.

STEP 2

다음 문장에서 관계사절을 찾아 밑줄 긋고, 문장을 해석하시오.

1 I will refund a jacket whose sleeves are too long for me.

2 The chef never tells us the way he makes his secret sauce.

3 Isabella has a son whose birthday is the same as mine.

4 There must be a reason why he isn't answering his phone.

5 I was there at the time when Ethan performed in the school play.

6 The teacher explained to the students how plants adapt to their environment.

tear 찢어지다(-tore-torn) cover 덮개; *표지 get off 내리다 lately 최근에 refund 환불하다 sleeve 소매 perform 행하다; *공연[연기]하다 play 놀이; *연극 explain 설명하다 adapt 조정하다; *적응하다 environment 환경

정답 및 해설 p.32

STEP 3

1 빈칸 (A), (B)에 들어갈 적절한 관계사를 쓰시오.

One cold night, a woman ___(A)___ clothes were worn out was brought to court. She had stolen bread for her children. She looked pitiful, but the judge said, "The law doesn't make exceptions. I fine you $10." Then he took out $10 from his wallet and paid her fine. He said, "I also fine everyone here $1 for living in a town ___(B)___ people have to steal bread to live."

(A) ______________ (B) ______________

Reading Q 윗글의 내용으로 보아 판사를 묘사하는 말로 가장 적절한 것은?
① greedy ② honest
③ thoughtful

NEW 내신기출

2 밑줄 친 ①~④ 중 어법상 틀린 2개를 찾아 해당 번호를 쓰고 바르게 고쳐 쓰시오.

In South America, there is a bird ① <u>which</u> bill is longer than its body. It is the sword-billed hummingbird. There is a reason ② <u>when</u> its bill is so long. It enjoys ③ <u>eating</u> from deep flowers, like fuchsia. ④ <u>To do</u> so, the sword-billed hummingbird developed a long bill over time.

*sword-billed hummingbird 칼부리벌새 **fuchsia 후크시아 (바늘꽃과 식물)

번호	적절하지 않은 단어	고쳐 쓴 단어

1 worn out 닳고 닳은 court 법정 pitiful 측은한, 불쌍한 judge 판사 exception 예외 fine 벌금을 물리다; 벌금 take out ~을 꺼내다 greedy 탐욕스러운 thoughtful 생각에 잠긴; *사려 깊은 **2** bill 청구서; *(새의) 부리 develop 발달시키다, 성장시키다 over time 시간이 흐르면서

Wrap Up

정답 및 해설 p.33

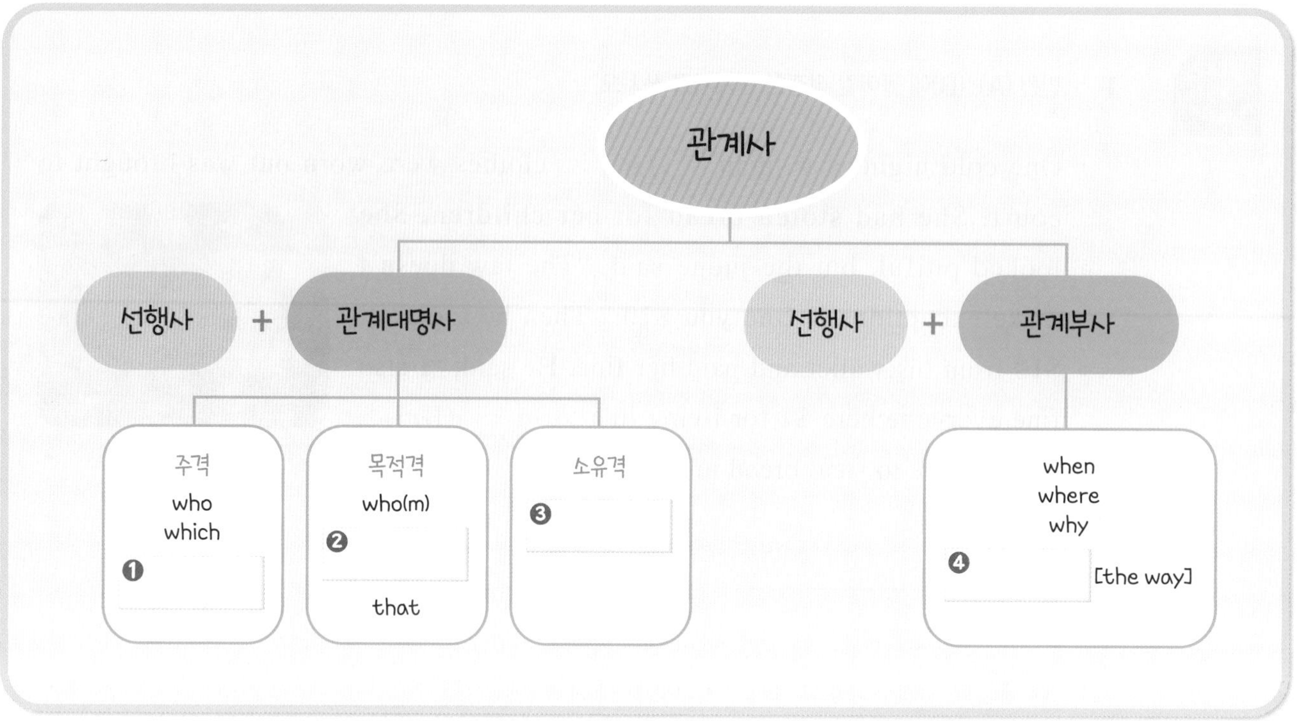

주요 예문을 다시 한번 확인하고, 우리말에 맞게 (   ) 안의 단어를 사용하여 문장을 쓰시오.

1 우리는 우리가 처음 만난 장소를 방문했다. (met / the place / first / visited) Point 04

2 나는 자기 약속을 지키는 사람들을 좋아한다. (promises / people / keep / like) Point 01

3 흰색 털을 가진 그 고양이가 나의 반려동물이다. (pet / fur / the cat / has) Point 01

4 그들은 문이 빨간색으로 페인트칠 된 집에 산다. (in a house / red / live / painted / door) Point 03

5 내가 어젯밤에 꿨던 그 꿈은 이상했다. (had / last / the dream / strange / night) Point 02

6 이것이 그 기계가 작동하는 방법이다. (works / the machine) Point 04

UNIT 09

접속사와 분사구문

Point 01 시간 접속사
Point 02 이유·조건 접속사
Point 03 분사구문 _ 동시상황
Point 04 분사구문 _ 시간, 이유

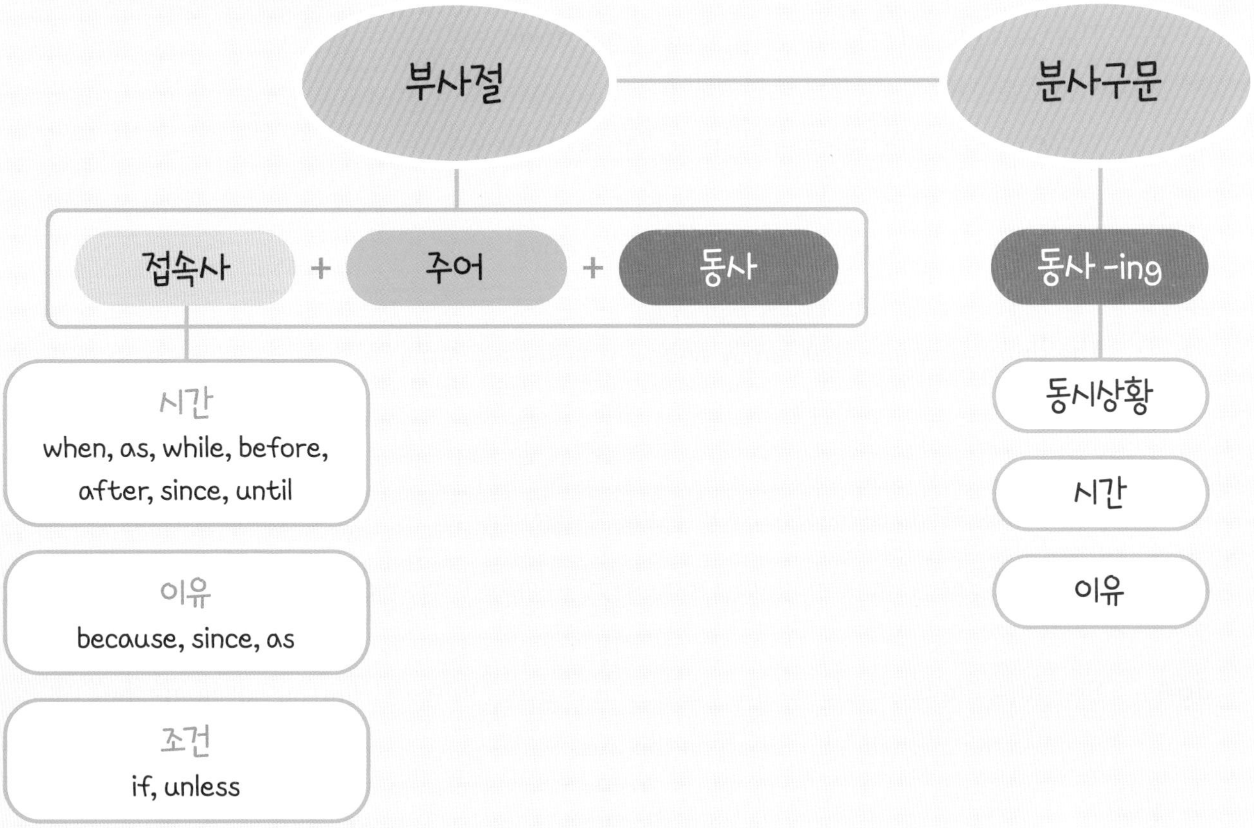

Point 01 시간 접속사

접속사 **when, as, while, before, after, since, until**은 시간을 나타내는 접속사로 **시간 부사절**을 이끈다.

when, as	~할 때, ~하면서	before	~하기 전에	since	~한 이후로
while	~하는 동안	after	~한 뒤에	until	~(할 때)까지

354 <**When** I hear / the sound of rain>, / I feel relaxed.
(I: S′, hear: V′, the sound of rain: O′ / I: S, feel: V, relaxed: SC)
<내가 들을 때 / 빗소리를> / 나는 편안함을 느낀다

355 Clara watched TV / <**while** I cooked>.
(Clara: S, watched: V, TV: O / I: S′, cooked: V′)
Clara는 TV를 시청했다 / <내가 요리하는 동안>

356 Eric will wait / <**until** I return>.
(Eric: S, will wait: V / I: S′, return: V′)
Eric은 기다릴 것이다 / <내가 돌아올 때까지>

Tip 시간 부사절에서는 현재시제로 미래를 나타낸다.

다음 문장에서 시간 부사절을 찾아 밑줄 긋고, 문장을 해석하시오.

정답 및 해설 p.34

357 <When I had a terrible cold>, / I couldn't eat anything.
<지독한 감기에 걸렸을 때>, / 나는 아무것도 먹을 수 없었다.

358 As I got off the bus, I saw my father at the stop.

359 The boys played soccer until the sun went down.

360 While I was in the hospital, I kept a diary every day.

361 You must fasten your seat belt before you drive.

362 The dog has been in her family since it was just a puppy.

구문 해석 기법

☐ 콤마(,)나 접속사를 기준으로 부사절을 찾는다.

다음 문장의 네모 안에서 문맥상 알맞은 것을 고르고, 문장을 해석하시오.

363 [While / Since] I was hiking up a mountain, I twisted my ankle.

364 Paul took the bus [before / after] school was over. [When / Until] he got home, he realized that he had left his bag on the bus.

relaxed 느긋한; *편안한 terrible 끔찍한; *지독한 get off (차 등에서) 내리다 fasten 매다 twist (발목·손목 등을) 삐다 ankle 발목

Point 02 이유·조건 접속사

접속사 **because, since, as**는 **이유 부사절**을, 접속사 **if, unless**는 **조건 부사절**을 이끈다.

because / since / as	~하기 때문에		
if	(만약) ~한다면	unless	(만약) ~하지 않으면 (= if ~ not)

365 I went / to the market / <**because** I needed eggs>.
(S V M / S′ V′ O′)
나는 갔다 / 시장에 / <나는 달걀이 필요했기 때문에>

366 <**If** Steve trusts you>, / he'll tell you / everything.
(S′ V′ O′ / S V IO DO)
<Steve가 너를 믿는다면>, / 그는 너에게 말할 것이다 / 전부

조건 부사절에서는 현재시제로 미래를 나타낸다.

367 <**Unless** you hurry>, / we'll leave / without you.
(S′ V′ / S V M)
<네가 서두르지 않으면>, / 우리는 떠날 것이다 / 너 없이

다음 문장에서 이유 또는 조건 부사절을 찾아 밑줄 긋고, 문장을 해석하시오. 정답 및 해설 p.34

368 Your mom will be upset / <if you get home / late>.
네 엄마가 속상해하실 것이다 / <네가 집에 도착하면 / 늦게>

369 She wore a coat since it was quite cold that evening.

370 You can't enter the museum unless you buy a ticket.

371 As I didn't have breakfast this morning, I feel really hungry now.

372 Ricky was happy because his parents threw him a surprise party.

373 Since Becky and I don't like crowded places, we won't go to the beach.

다음 문장의 네모 안에서 문맥상 알맞은 것을 고르고, 문장을 해석하시오.

374 He couldn't get on the plane [because / before] he left his passport at home.

375 [If / Unless] you are missing the receipt, you can return the item to us. But you can't get a refund [if / before] you removed the price tag.

---

throw a party 파티를 열다 miss 빗나가다; *빠뜨리다 receipt 영수증 item 항목; *물품 get a refund 환불받다 remove 제거하다 price tag 가격표

Unit Practice

STEP 1. 직독직해에 맞게 (   ) 안의 단어를 사용하여 문장을 쓰시오. (필요시 형태를 바꿔 쓸 것)

1 Kate는 있었다 / 집에 / 그녀의 어머니가 오실 때까지 (at home / come / mother / stay)

_____ _____ / _____ _____ / _____ _____

_____ _____.

2 그들은 잠을 잘 수 없었다 / 지난밤에 / 너무 더웠기 때문에 (hot / sleep / too / last night / be)

_____ _____ _____ / _____ _____ / _____

_____ _____ _____ _____.

3 네가 네 식물들을 돌보지 않으면, / 그것들은 죽을 것이다. (plants / take care of / die)

_____ _____ _____ _____ _____ _____

_____ _____, / _____ _____ _____.

STEP 2. 다음 문장에서 부사절을 찾아 밑줄 긋고, 문장을 해석하시오.

1 Please turn off your cell phone before the performance begins.

2 David hasn't eaten ice cream since he started his diet.

3 When I catch a cold, my mom makes hot tea with honey.

4 I couldn't focus on the exam because I stayed up all night.

5 You can't go into the swimming pool unless you wear a swimming cap.

6 Harper enjoys chatting with her friends while she is having lunch at school.

take care of ~을 돌보다   turn off (전기·가스·수도 등을) 끄다   performance 공연   diet 식사; *다이어트   catch a cold 감기에 걸리다   focus on ~에 집중하다
stay up 깨어 있다   swimming cap 수영 모자   chat 수다를 떨다

정답 및 해설 p.34

STEP 3

1 (A), (B)의 각 네모 안에서 문맥상 알맞은 것을 고르고, 밑줄 친 부분을 해석하시오.

Like other animals, cats can ____________. For example, (A) [if / while] your cat sneezes a lot, it will probably rain soon. And **when** your cat snores or lies on its back for a long time, it's bad news. Get your snow boots ready, (B) [when / because] the weather will probably get worse!

(A) ____

(B) ____

Reading Q 빈칸에 들어갈 말로 가장 적절한 것은?
① sleep all day ② catch a cold easily ③ sense changes in weather

NEW 내신기출

2 밑줄 친 우리말을 조건 에 맞게 써서 요약문을 완성하시오.

If you plan to live in the Netherlands with your dog, remember this: most cities in the Netherlands charge a dog tax. **When** you arrive, you must register your dogs with the local city hall. The amount of tax depends on the number of dogs that you have. **As** prices vary from city to city, you should check **before** you decide to bring your pet.

In the Netherlands, most cities charge a dog tax. So 만약 당신이 당신의 개와 함께 그곳에 살 계획이라면, you should check the specific tax amount for the city you want to live in.

조건
· 접속사를 쓸 것
· live / with your dog / there / plan
· 제시된 단어를 사용할 것
· 총 9단어로 쓸 것

____

1 sneeze 재채기를 하다 probably 아마(도) snore 코를 골다 get ~ ready ~을 준비하다 all day 하루 종일 sense 감지하다, 느끼다
2 charge (요금 등을) 청구하다 register 등록하다 local 현지의 depend on ~에 의해 결정되다 vary (~에 따라) 다르다 specific 구체적인

Point 03 분사구문 _ 동시상황

분사구문이란 접속사가 있는 부사절을 간단하게 줄인 형태로, 부사절의 접속사를 생략하고 부사절의 주어와 주절의 주어가 같으면 **부사절의 주어를 생략한 뒤, 동사를 v-ing로 바꾼다.** 분사구문은 문맥에 맞게 해석하면 되는데, **동시에 일어나는 상황**으로 가장 많이 쓰이며, **'~하면서, ~한 채'**로 해석한다.

- 부사절 [접속사 + 주어 + 동사], 주어+동사 ~
- ↓
- 분사구문 [생략 동사-ing], 주어+동사 ~

376 <Watching(V′) a movie(O′)>, / Ava(S) ate(V) popcorn(O). (← **While** she watched a movie, ~.)
<영화를 보면서>, / Ava는 팝콘을 먹었다.

377 <Waving(V′) his hand(O′)>, / he(S) said(V) hello(O). (← **As** he waved his hand, ~.)
<손을 흔들며>, / 그는 인사를 했다.

다음 문장에서 분사구문을 찾아 밑줄 긋고, 문장을 해석하시오. 정답 및 해설 p.36

378 <Sitting quietly>, / all of the students studied / hard.
<조용히 앉아서>, / 모든 학생이 공부했다 / 열심히

379 He lay on the beach, watching the sunset.

380 Holding some flowers, Dorothy knocked on the door.

381 Cleaning his room, he talked with his mother on the phone.

382 Listening to the radio, I heard the weather forecast for today.

383 Jimmy drove down the road, singing his favorite song.

다음 문장의 네모 안에서 어법상 알맞은 것을 고르고, 문장을 해석하시오.

384 [Sit / Sitting] by the lake, Rachel enjoyed the fresh air and sunshine.

385 [Handing / Handed] Joanna a letter of apology, Dana said that she was sorry.

wave 흔들다 quietly 조용히 lie 누워 있다, 눕다(-lay-lain) sunset 일몰 hold 잡고[들고] 있다 weather forecast 일기 예보 hand 건네주다

Point **04**

분사구문 _ 시간, 이유

분사구문은 **시간**이나 **이유**의 의미를 표현하기도 하며, **'~할 때, ~한 뒤'**, **'~하기 때문에'**로 해석한다.

V' O'

386 <**Opening the window**>, / he saw a blue bird. (← **When** he opened the window, ~.)

S V O

<창문을 열었을 때>, / 그는 파란 새를 보았다.

V' O'

387 <**Turning on the oven**>, / she started to cook. (← **After** she turned on the oven, ~.)

S V O

<오븐을 켠 뒤>, / 그녀는 요리하기 시작했다.

V' SC'

388 <**Being tired**>, / I drank a cup of coffee. (← **Because[Since/As]** I was tired, ~.)

S V O

<피곤했기 때문에>, / 나는 커피 한 잔을 마셨다.

밑줄 친 분사구문과 부사절의 의미가 같도록 ( ) 안에서 알맞은 접속사를 고르고, 문장을 해석하시오. 정답 및 해설 p.36

389 <Standing up>, / he stretched his legs.
= <(After / Because) he stood up>
<일어선 뒤에>, / 그는 다리를 뻗었다.

390 Living by the sea, I always enjoy fresh seafood.
= (Before / Because) I live by the sea

391 Being afraid of snakes, he didn't even look at my pet snake.
= (Because / When) he was afraid of snakes

392 Walking to the store, Sarah found some money on the ground.
= (Because / When) she was walking to the store

393 Waking up in the morning, I smelled something delicious.
= (When / Since) I woke up in the morning

394 Being ill, he was absent from work for a few days.
= (Before / Since) he was ill

다음 문장의 네모 안에서 어법상 알맞은 것을 고르고, 문장을 해석하시오.

395 [Knowing / Know] Hazel always keeps a secret, I talk about my worries with her.

396 [Leaving / Left] the house, she took her jacket and surveyed herself in the mirror.

---

even ~도[조차] ill 아픈, 몸[기분]이 안 좋은 absent 결석한, 결근한 keep a secret 비밀을 지키다 worry 걱정; *걱정거리 survey 살피다, 점검하다

Unit Practice

STEP 1 직독직해에 맞게 ( ) 안의 단어를 사용하여 문장을 쓰시오. (필요시 형태를 바꿔 쓸 것)

1 가게로 걸어갈 때, / Sarah는 약간의 돈을 발견했다 / 땅바닥에서 (money / to the store / find / walk / on the ground / some)

________ ________ ________ ________, / ________ ________

________ ________ / ________ ________ ________.

2 내 침대에 누워서, / 나는 내가 가장 좋아하는 만화책을 읽었다. (on my bed / comic books / lie)

________ ________ ________ ________, / ________ ________

________ ________ ________ ________.

3 그 정답을 알기 때문에, / 그녀는 그녀의 손을 들었다 / 자신 있게 (raise / know / confidently)

________ ________ ________, / ________ ________ ________

________ / ________.

STEP 2 다음 문장에서 분사구문을 찾아 밑줄 긋고, 문장을 해석하시오.

1 I nodded, saying that I agreed with David's opinion.

2 Hearing the news, he immediately called his best friend.

3 Brushing his daughter's hair, Hudson hummed a lullaby.

4 Being so busy these days, he must work on weekends.

5 Entering her room, she was surprised to find a small bug.

6 Feeling like challenging ourselves, we planned to go skydiving together.

confidently 자신 있게 nod (고개를) 끄덕이다 agree with ~에 동의하다 immediately 즉시 brush 솔질[빗질/칫솔질]을 하다 hum (노래를) 흥얼거리다 lullaby 자장가 bug 벌레 challenge 도전하다

STEP 3

1 **밑줄 친 (A), (B), (C)의 문맥상 의미로 바르게 짝지어진 것을 고르시오.**

(A) Arriving at the restaurant, Mike saw that many people were waiting. He asked the hostess, "Will it be long?" She kept writing in her notebook. (B) Receiving no response, Mike asked, "How long is the wait?" (C) Looking up, she responded, "It will be fifteen minutes." Several minutes later, the hostess came over and announced, "Willette B. Long, your table is ready."

	(A)		(B)		(C)
①	식당에 도착했기 때문에	……	답변을 받지 못했을 때	……	올려다보며
②	식당에 도착했을 때	……	답변을 받지 못해서	……	올려다보며
③	식당에 도착했을 때	……	답변을 받지 못해서	……	올려다볼 때
④	식당에 도착했기 때문에	……	답변을 받지 못한 뒤	……	올려다보았기 때문에

Reading Q 여자 종업원이 Mike의 첫 물음에 대답하지 않은 이유는?

① 주변이 시끄러워 물음을 듣지 못해서 ② 다른 대기 손님을 응대하느라 바빠서
③ 물음을 남자의 이름으로 착각해서

NEW 내신기출

2 **(A), (B)의 ( ) 안의 단어를 문맥상 의미가 통하도록 조건에 맞게 배열하시오.**

Sitting in my seat on the airplane, I started to look around. (A) (do / nothing else / have / to), I took the airline magazine out of the seat pocket. (B) (the pages / over / turn), I tried to find something interesting. However, it was mostly full of advertisements. I put down the magazine and stared out the window.

조건 · 분사구문을 쓸 것 · 필요시 형태를 바꿔 쓸 것

(A) ______________________________

(B) ______________________________

1 hostess 여자 종업원 receive 받다 response 대답(*v.* respond 대답하다) several 몇몇의 come over (다가)오다 announce 알리다, 발표하다
2 airline 항공사 turn over (페이지 등을) 넘기다 mostly 대부분 full of ~으로 가득한 advertisement 광고 stare 응시하다

Wrap Up

정답 및 해설 p.38

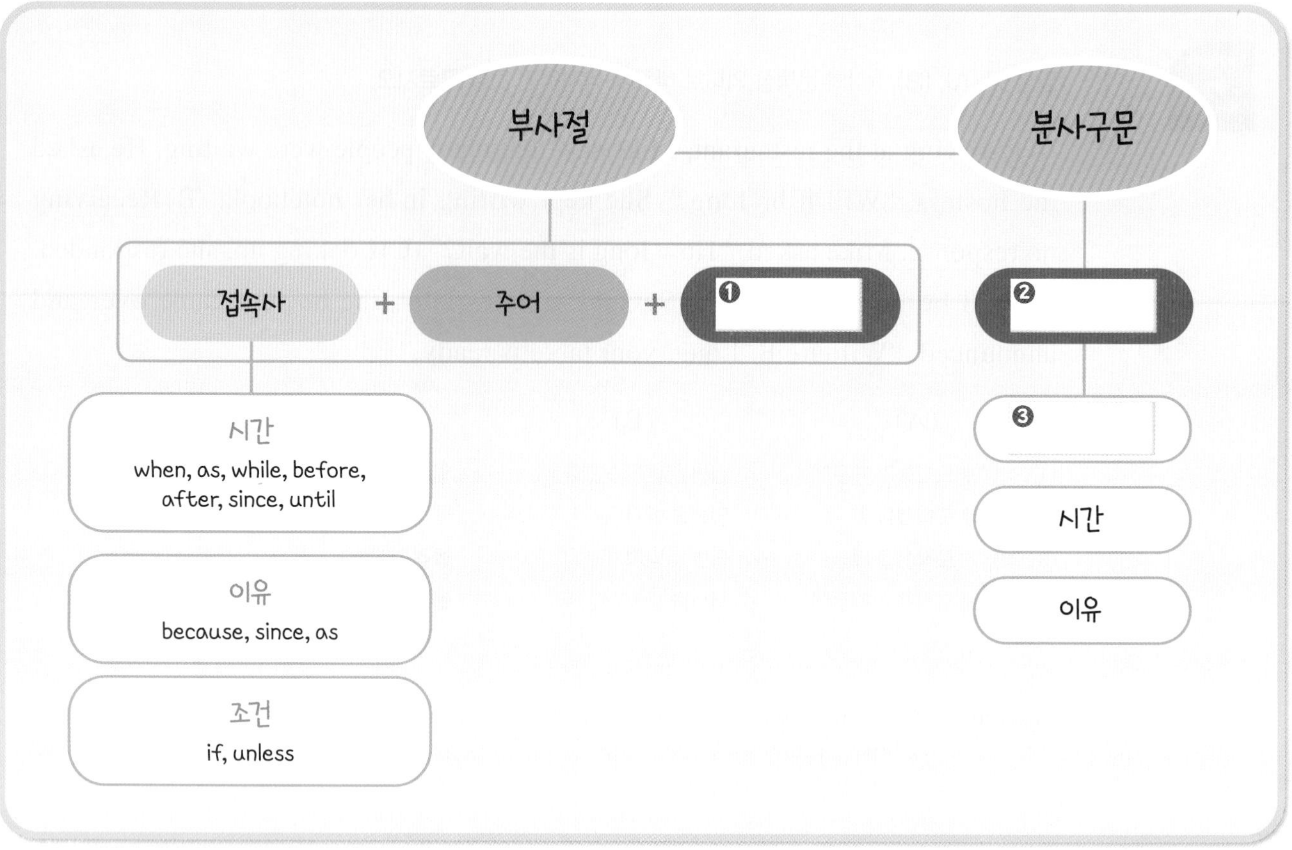

주요 예문을 다시 한번 확인하고, 우리말에 맞게 (　) 안의 단어를 사용하여 문장을 쓰시오.

1 Steve가 너를 믿는다면 그는 너에게 전부 말할 것이다. (trusts / everything / tell) Point 02

2 피곤했기 때문에 나는 커피 한 잔을 마셨다. (a cup of / tired / coffee / drank) Point 04

3 Eric은 내가 돌아올 때까지 기다릴 것이다. (wait / return) Point 01

4 나는 빗소리를 들을 때 편안함을 느낀다. (relaxed / the sound / feel / hear / of rain) Point 01

5 그의 손을 흔들며 그는 인사를 했다. (said / hand / hello) Point 03

UNIT 10

가정법

Point 01 가정법 과거
Point 02 가정법 과거완료

- 현재 사실과 반대되는 일을 가정
- 일어날 가능성이 거의 없는 일을 가정

↓

가정법

가정법 과거

If + 주어 + 동사의 과거형 / were ~, 주어 + 조동사 과거형 + 동사원형 ...

가정법 과거완료

If + 주어 + had + 과거분사 ~, 주어 + 조동사 과거형 + have + 과거분사 ...

↑

과거 사실과 반대되는 일을 가정

Point **01**

가정법 과거

가정법 과거는 **현재 사실과 반대되는 일**, 또는 **일어날 가능성이 거의 없는 일을 가정**하거나 상상할 때 쓴다.

형태	**If + 주어 + 동사의 과거형 / were ~, 주어 + 조동사 과거형(would / could / might) + 동사원형 ...**
	가정법 과거의 if절에서 be동사는 주어의 인칭과 상관없이 항상 were를 사용
의미	만약 ~라면[하다면] …할 텐데[할 수 있을 텐데 / 할지도 모를 텐데]

397 <**If** Mary **loved** me>, / I **would be** happy.
(Mary: S′, loved: V′, me: O′ / I: S, would be: V, happy: SC)
<만약 Mary가 나를 사랑한다면>, / 난 행복할 텐데.

398 <**If** I **were** a child>, / I **could play** / all day.
(I: S′, were: V′, a child: SC′ / I: S, could play: V, all day: M)
<만약 내가 아이라면>, / 놀 수 있을 텐데 / 하루 종일

399 <**If** I **left** / tomorrow>, / I **might be able to see** the show.
(I: S′, left: V′, tomorrow: M′ / I: S, might be able to see: V, the show: O)
<만약 내가 떠난다면 / 내일>, / 그 쇼를 볼 수 있을지도 모를 텐데

밑줄 친 부분에 유의하여 다음 문장을 해석하시오.

정답 및 해설 p.38

400 <If there were no air>, / we couldn't live.
<만약 공기가 없다면>, / 우리는 살 수 없을 텐데.

401 If I had a sister, I could go shopping with her.

402 If you studied harder, you might get better grades.

403 We could play baseball if it were not raining.

404 If I met God, I would ask him to give me a nice voice.

405 If Charles won the lottery, he would travel around the world with his family.

다음 문장의 네모 안에서 어법상 알맞은 것을 고르고, 문장을 해석하시오.

406 It would be so cool if it [were / is] snowing right now.

407 If they worked together, they might [solve / have solved] the problem more effectively.

grade (상품의) 품질; *성적 win the lottery 복권에 당첨되다 around the world 전 세계로 solve 해결하다 effectively 효과적으로

Point 02 가정법 과거완료

가정법 과거완료는 **과거 사실과 반대되는 일을 가정**할 때 쓴다.

형태	If+주어+had+과거분사 ~, 주어+**조동사 과거형(would/could/might)+have+과거분사** ...
의미	만약 ~했더라면[였다면] …했을 텐데[할 수 있었을 텐데 / 했을지도 모를 텐데]

S′ V′ O′
408 <**If** I **had saved** my money>, / I **could have bought** the house.
S V O
<만약 내가 돈을 저축했더라면>, / 그 집을 살 수 있었을 텐데.

S′ V′ M′
409 You **might have become** a violinist / <**if** you **had practiced** / harder>.
S V SC
너는 바이올리니스트가 되었을지도 모를 텐데 / <만약 네가 연습했더라면 / 더 열심히>

S′ V′ O′
410 [**If** I **had known** / <you were coming>], / I **would have prepared** dinner.
S V O
[만약 내가 알았더라면 / <네가 오는 중이었다는 것을>], / 나는 저녁을 준비했을 텐데

밑줄 친 부분에 유의하여 다음 문장을 해석하시오. 정답 및 해설 p.39

411 <If Nate had not lied>, / Blaire would have forgiven him.
<만약 Nate가 거짓말하지 않았더라면>, / Blaire는 그를 용서했을 텐데.

412 If I had listened to you, I might not have lost my friends.

413 You could have exchanged your jacket if you had had your receipt.

414 Ken wouldn't have been stuck in traffic if he had gotten up early.

415 If she had been at home at that time, she could have helped her mother.

416 If I had known it was his birthday, I would have given a birthday gift to him.

다음 문장의 네모 안에서 어법상 알맞은 것을 고르고, 문장을 해석하시오.

417 If my father [allowed / had allowed] me to go out, I could have played with my friends.

418 If Peter had not [be / been] tired, he might not [have / had] dozed off during the class.

forgive 용서하다(-forgave-forgiven) exchange 교환하다 receipt 영수증 stuck in traffic 교통이 막힌[정체된] doze off 깜빡 잠이 들다, 졸다

Unit Practice

STEP 1 **직독직해에 맞게 (   ) 안의 단어를 사용하여 문장을 쓰시오. (필요시 형태를 바꿔 쓸 것)**

1 내 소원들이 이루어질 텐데 / 만약 내게 마법 지팡이가 있다면 (a magic wand / come true / have / wishes)

______ ______ ______ ______ ______ / ______

______ ______ ______ ______ ______.

2 만약 Gavin이 높은 곳을 무서워하지 않는다면, / 그는 번지 점프를 하러 갈 수 있을 텐데. (heights / go / afraid of / bungee jumping)

______ ______ ______ ______ ______ ______

______, / ______ ______ ______ ______ ______.

3 만약 네가 그 책을 읽었더라면, / 너는 그 영화를 이해할 수 있었을 텐데 / 더 잘 (the movie / read / understand / the book / better)

______ ______ ______ ______ ______ ______, / ______

______ ______ ______ ______ ______ / ______.

STEP 2 **다음 문장에서 if절을 찾아 밑줄 긋고, 문장을 해석하시오.**

1 If they had taken the highway, they could have avoided the traffic jam.

2 If you gave up this opportunity, you might regret it for the rest of your life.

3 We would have brought umbrellas if we had checked the weather forecast.

4 If I were a time traveler, I would witness some of the greatest moments in history.

5 If Heidi weren't busy, she could come with us to the party tonight.

6 If we had booked the tickets earlier, we might have gotten better seats.

wand (마술사의) 지팡이 height 높이; *높은 곳 highway 고속도로 opportunity 기회 regret 후회하다 rest 나머지 weather forecast 일기 예보
time traveler 시간 여행자 witness 목격하다 moment 순간 book 예약하다 seat 자리

정답 및 해설 p.39

STEP 3

1 가정법에 유의하여 밑줄 친 문장을 해석하시오.

Last weekend, I went to a store. On my way back home, I realized that the clerk had given me too much change. I thought about keeping it, but I soon decided to return it. **If** I **had kept** the money, I **could have bought** some snacks. However, I don't regret giving it back. I feel good about being honest.

____

Reading Q 윗글에 드러난 'I'의 심경 변화로 가장 적절한 것은?

① nervous → bored
② proud → disappointed
③ confused → pleased

NEW 내신기출

2 밑줄 친 ①~④ 중 어법상 틀린 2개를 찾아 해당 번호를 쓰고 바르게 고쳐 쓰시오.

If gravity ① disappeared, what would happen? Everything ② would have floated away if there were no force holding us to the earth. But if gravity suddenly ③ has doubled, that would be bad as well. Everything might suddenly ④ become much heavier, and many buildings might collapse.

번호	적절하지 않은 단어	고쳐 쓴 단어

1 on one's way (~으로) 가는 길에 realize 깨닫다 clerk 점원 change 변화; *거스름돈 proud 자랑스러운 confused 혼란스러워하는
2 gravity 중력 disappear 사라지다 float away 떠다니다 force 힘 double 두 배가 되다 as well 또한, 역시 collapse 붕괴되다, 무너지다

Wrap Up

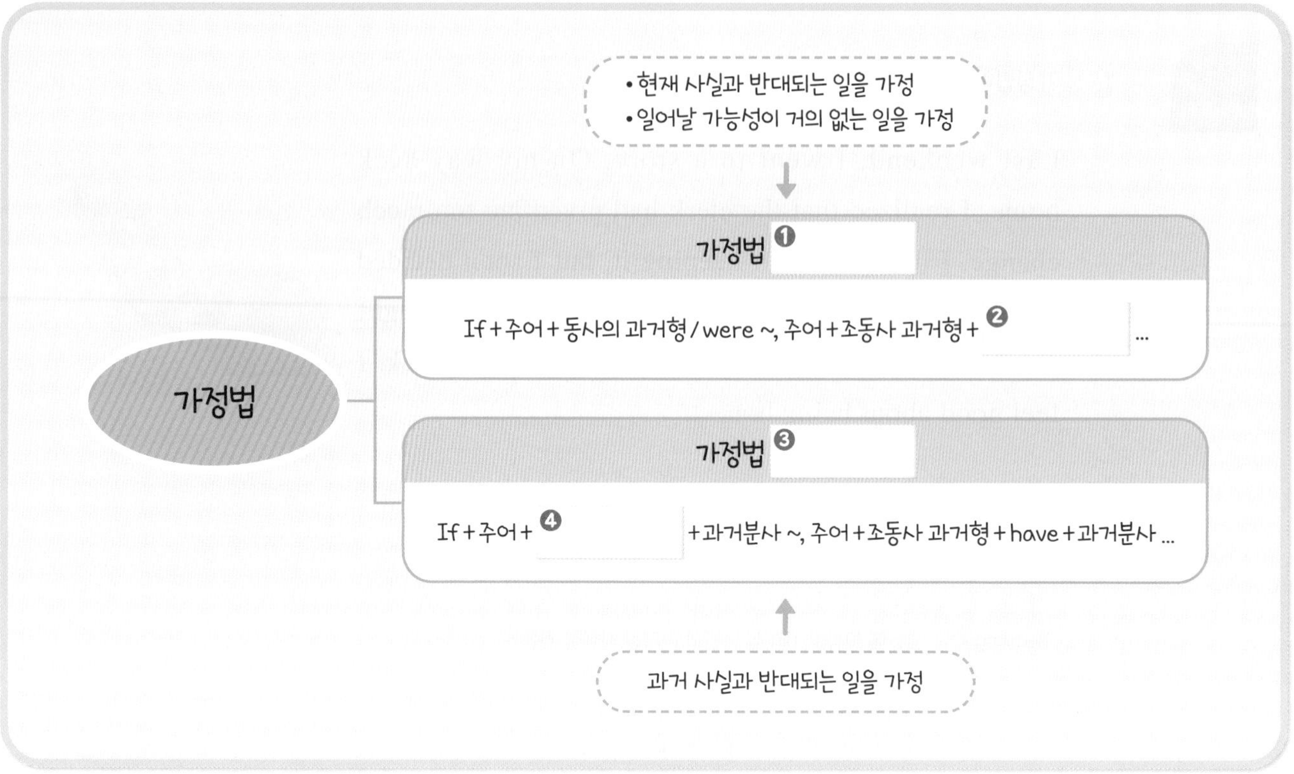

주요 예문을 다시 한번 확인하고, 우리말에 맞게 (   ) 안의 단어를 사용하여 문장을 쓰시오.

1 만약 내가 돈을 저축했더라면 그 집을 살 수 있었을 텐데. (the house / bought / saved) Point 02

2 만약 네가 오는 중이었다는 것을 알았더라면 나는 저녁을 준비했을 텐데. (prepared / known / dinner) Point 02

3 만약 네가 더 열심히 연습했더라면 너는 바이올리니스트가 되었을지도 모를 텐데. (become / harder) Point 02

4 만약 Mary가 나를 사랑한다면 난 행복할 텐데. (happy / loved) Point 01

5 만약 내가 아이라면 하루 종일 놀 수 있을 텐데. (all day / play / a child) Point 01

MEMO

MEMO

MEMO

지은이

NE능률 영어교육연구소

NE능률 영어교육연구소는 혁신적이며 효율적인 영어 교재를 개발하고
영어 학습의 질을 한 단계 높이고자 노력하는 NE능률의 연구조직입니다.

중학 천문장 〈LEVEL 2〉

펴 낸 이 주민홍
펴 낸 곳 서울특별시 마포구 월드컵북로 396(상암동) 누리꿈스퀘어 비즈니스타워 10층
(주)NE능률 (우편번호 03925)
펴 낸 날 2024년 1월 5일 개정판 제1쇄 발행
2024년 2월 15일 제2쇄
전 화 02 2014 7114
팩 스 02 3142 0356
홈페이지 www.neungyule.com
등록번호 제 1-68호
I S B N 979-11-253-4294-6
정 가 13,000원

NE 능률

고객센터

교재 내용 문의 : contact.nebooks.co.kr (별도의 가입 절차 없이 작성 가능)
제품 구매, 교환, 불량, 반품 문의 : 02-2014-7114
☎ 전화문의는 본사 업무시간 중에만 가능합니다.

NE능률 교재 MAP

문법 구문

아래 교재 MAP을 참고하여 본인의 현재 혹은 목표 수준에 따라 교재를 선택하세요.
NE능률 교재들과 함께 영어실력을 쑥쑥~ 올려보세요!
MP3 등 교재 부가 학습 서비스 및 자세한 교재 정보는 www.nebooks.co.kr 에서 확인하세요.

초1-2

초3
- 그래머버디 1
- 초등영어 문법이 된다 Starter 1

초3-4
- 그래머버디 2
- 초등영어 문법이 된다 Starter 2
- 초등 Grammar Inside 1
- 초등 Grammar Inside 2

초4-5
- 그래머버디 3
- Grammar Bean 1
- Grammar Bean 2
- 초등영어 문법이 된다 1
- 초등 Grammar Inside 3
- 초등 Grammar Inside 4

초5-6
- Grammar Bean 3
- Grammar Bean 4
- 초등영어 문법이 된다 2
- 초등 Grammar Inside 5
- 초등 Grammar Inside 6

초6-예비중
- 능률중학영어 예비중
- Grammar Inside Starter
- 원리를 더한 영문법 STARTER

중1
- 능률중학영어 중1
- Grammar Zone 입문편
- Grammar Zone 워크북 입문편
- 1316 Grammar 1
- 문제로 마스터하는 중학영문법 1
- Grammar Inside 1
- 열중 16강 문법 1
- 쓰기로 마스터하는 중학서술형 1학년
- 중학 천문장 1

중1-2
- 능률중학영어 중2
- 1316 Grammar 2
- 문제로 마스터하는 중학영문법 2
- Grammar Inside 2
- 열중 16강 문법 2
- 원리를 더한 영문법 1
- 중학영문법 총정리 모의고사 1
- 중학 천문장 2

중2-3
- Grammar Zone 기초편
- Grammar Zone 워크북 기초편
- 1316 Grammar 3
- 원리를 더한 영문법 2
- 중학영문법 총정리 모의고사 2
- 쓰기로 마스터하는 중학서술형 2학년
- 중학 천문장 3

중3
- 능률중학영어 중3
- 문제로 마스터하는 중학영문법 3
- Grammar Inside 3
- 열중 16강 문법 3
- 중학영문법 총정리 모의고사 3
- 쓰기로 마스터하는 중학서술형 3학년

예비고–고1
- 문제로 마스터하는 고등영문법
- 올클 수능 어법 start
- 천문장 입문

고1
- Grammar Zone 기본편 1
- Grammar Zone 워크북 기본편 1
- Grammar Zone 기본편 2
- Grammar Zone 워크북 기본편 2
- 필히 통하는 고등 영문법 기본편
- 필히 통하는 고등 서술형 기본편
- 천문장 기본

고1-2
- 필히 통하는 고등 영문법 실력편
- 필히 통하는 고등 서술형 실전편
- TEPS BY STEP G+R Basic

고2-3
- Grammar Zone 종합편
- Grammar Zone 워크북 종합편
- 올클 수능 어법 완성
- 천문장 완성

고3

수능 이상/ 토플 80-89 · 텝스 600-699점
- TEPS BY STEP G+R 1

수능 이상/ 토플 90-99 · 텝스 700-799점
- TEPS BY STEP G+R 2

수능 이상/ 토플 100 · 텝스 800점 이상
- TEPS BY STEP G+R 3

중학

천문장

LEVEL 2

「구문이 독해로 연결되는 해석 공식」

정답 및 해설

NE 능률

UNIT 01

주어의 형태

Point 01 명사와 대명사 p.8

005 Sweet desserts have / lots of sugar.
달콤한 디저트는 가지고 있다 / 많은 설탕을
달콤한 디저트는 많은 설탕을 가지고 있다.

006 He writes a letter / to me / every week.
그는 편지를 쓴다 / 나에게 / 매주
그는 매주 나에게 편지를 쓴다.

007 The airplane <from London> / just landed / at the airport.
비행기가 <런던에서 온> / 방금 착륙했다 / 공항에
런던에서 온 비행기가 방금 공항에 착륙했다.

008 Some famous painters visited / this art museum / yesterday.
몇몇 유명한 화가들이 방문했다 / 이 미술관을 / 어제
몇몇 유명한 화가들이 어제 이 미술관을 방문했다.

009 Olivia invited her friends / to her house. She will have a party / tomorrow.
Olivia는 그녀의 친구들을 초대했다 / 그녀의 집으로. 그녀는 파티를 할 것이다 / 내일
Olivia는 그녀의 친구들을 집으로 초대했다. 그녀는 내일 파티를 할 것이다.

010 The causes <of the accident> / are not clear. The police are looking for clues.
원인은 <그 사고의> / 분명하지 않다. 경찰은 단서를 찾고 있다.
그 사고의 원인은 분명하지 않다. 경찰은 단서를 찾고 있다.

011 Jake and his mother went / to the restaurant. He ordered pasta // and she ordered a steak.
Jake와 그의 어머니는 갔다 / 식당에. 그는 파스타를 주문했다 // 그리고 그녀는 스테이크를 주문했다
Jake와 그의 어머니는 식당에 갔다. 그는 파스타를 주문했고 그녀는 스테이크를 주문했다.

Point 02 동명사와 to부정사 p.9

016 Lying <on this sofa> / relaxes me.
누워 있는 것은 <이 소파에> / 나를 편안하게 한다
이 소파에 누워 있는 것은 나를 편안하게 한다.

017 To break a promise / destroys trust.
약속을 어기는 것은 / 신뢰를 무너뜨린다.

018 Becoming an astronaut / was my dream / long ago.
우주 비행사가 되는 것은 / 나의 꿈이었다 / 오래전
우주 비행사가 되는 것은 오래전 나의 꿈이었다.

019 Never forgetting / to say "thank you" / shows respect <for others>.
절대 잊지 않는 것은 / '감사합니다'라고 말하는 것을 / 존중을 보여 준다 <다른 사람들에 대한>
'감사합니다'라고 말하는 것을 절대 잊지 않는 것은 다른 사람들에 대한 존중을 보여 준다.

020 Cooking delicious meals / gives her great pleasure.
맛있는 식사를 요리하는 것은 / 그녀에게 큰 즐거움을 준다.

021 Not to accept the invitation / would be rude.
그 초대를 받아들이지 않는 것은 / 무례할 것이다.

022 Listening to music / relieves stress. To take a walk <for a few minutes> / also helps.
음악을 듣는 것은 / 스트레스를 덜어 준다. 산책을 하는 것은 <잠시 동안> / 또한 도움이 된다
음악을 듣는 것은 스트레스를 덜어 준다. 잠시 동안 산책을 하는 것도 도움이 된다.

Unit Practice pp.10~11

STEP 1

1 Chloe was talking on the phone / at that time.
풀이 명사 Chloe가 문장의 주어이고, 동사는 과거진행형인 점에 유의하여 단어를 배열한다.
구문 ▶ was/were+v-ing: ~하고 있었다 (과거진행)
▶ at that time: 그때

2 To exercise regularly / is good for your health.
풀이 주어의 빈칸 개수로 보아, to부정사구 To exercise regularly가 문장의 주어로 오도록 단어를 배열한다.
구문 good for: ~에 좋은

3 Learning a new language / is challenging but exciting.
풀이 동명사구 Learning a new language가 문장의 주어이고 be동사 is 다음에 주격보어 challenging but exciting이 오도록 단어를 배열한다.

STEP 2

1 To talk loudly during a movie is annoying.
영화 상영 중에 큰 소리로 이야기하는 것은 짜증스럽다.

풀이 동사 is 앞까지가 주어이므로, to부정사구 To talk ~ movie가 문장의 주어이다. to부정사구 주어는 '~하는 것'으로 해석한다.

2 The sound of the bell surprised the students.
벨 소리가 학생들을 깜짝 놀라게 했다.
풀이 명사구 The sound of the bell이 문장의 주어이다.
구문 of the bell: 명사 the sound를 수식하는 전치사구

3 To become the president of a large company is my life goal.
대기업의 회장이 되는 것이 내 인생 목표이다.
풀이 동사 is 앞까지가 주어이므로, to부정사구 To become ~ company가 문장의 주어이다.
구문 of a large company: 명사 the president를 수식하는 전치사구

4 Spending time with family on weekends is important to him.
주말에 가족들과 시간을 보내는 것은 그에게 중요하다.
풀이 동사 is 앞까지가 주어이므로, 동명사구 Spending ~ weekends가 문장의 주어이다. 동명사구 주어는 '~하는 것'으로 해석한다.
구문 ▶ with family: 동명사구 Spending time을 수식하는 전치사구
▶ on weekends: 동명사구 Spending ~ family를 수식하는 전치사구

5 Doing volunteer work provides valuable experience for children.
자원봉사를 하는 것은 아이들에게 소중한 경험을 제공한다.
풀이 동사 provides 앞까지가 주어이므로, 동명사구 Doing volunteer work가 문장의 주어이다. 명사구 volunteer work는 동명사 doing의 목적어이다.

6 Teenagers love to take photos, and they also love sharing them on social media.
십 대들은 사진 찍는 것을 아주 좋아하고, 그들은 소셜 미디어에 그것들을 공유하는 것도 아주 좋아한다.
풀이 명사 Teenagers가 앞 절의 주어이고, 앞 절에서 언급된 Teenagers를 가리키는 대명사 they가 and 이하 절의 주어이다.
구문 love+to-v[v-ing]: ~하는 것을 대단히 좋아하다

STEP 3

1 (A) [Finding the doll inside your piece] makes you "king" for the day.
당신의 조각 안에서 그 인형을 찾는 것은
(B) [Becoming the king] allows you to make the rules all day.
왕이 되는 것은
Q ②

해석 킹 케이크는 재미있는 관습을 가진 프랑스의 전통 케이크이다. 작은 인형 하나가 그 케이크 안에 들어 있다. 누군가가 케이크를 자른 뒤에 모든 사람들은 한 조각씩 갖는다. (A) 당신의 조각 안에서 그 인형을 찾는 것은 당신을 그날의 '왕'으로 만든다. (B) 왕이 되는 것은 당신이 하루 종일 규칙을 만드는 것을 가능하게 한다. 그리고 당신의 친구들과 가족들은 당신의 규칙을 따라야 한다!

구문해설

1행 King cake is a traditional French cake **with an interesting custom**.
▶ 명사구 a traditional French cake를 수식하는 전치사구

3행 Finding the doll inside your piece **makes you "king"** for the day.
▶ make+목적어+목적격보어(명사): 목적어를 ~로 만들다

4행 Becoming the king **allows you to make** the rules all day.
▶ allow+목적어+목적격보어(to-v): 목적어가 ~하는 것을 가능하게 하다

문제해설

1 (A) 목적어 the doll과 수식어구 inside your piece가 있는 동명사구 Finding ~ piece가 문장의 주어이고 makes가 동사이다. 동명사구 주어는 '~하는 것'으로 해석한다.
(B) 보어 the king이 있는 동명사구 Becoming the king이 문장의 주어이고 allows가 동사이다.

Q 인형이 들어 있는 케이크 조각을 가진 사람이 그날의 왕이 되는 재미있는 관습을 가진 프랑스의 전통 케이크에 대한 글이므로, 글의 주제로 ② '킹 케이크의 관습'이 가장 적절하다.
① 킹 케이크의 기원
③ 킹 케이크를 만드는 방법

2 Walking on the salt lake is wonderful.

해석 Salar de Uyuni는 볼리비아에 있는 거대한 소금 사막이다. 그곳은 아름다운 경관으로 유명하다. 비가 온 뒤에 물은 넓지만 매우 얕은 소금 호수를 형성한다. 거대한 거울처럼, 그것은 하늘 전체를 비춘다. 그 소금 호수 위를 걷는 것은 멋지다. 당신은 당신의 발아래에 있는 하늘을 볼 수 있다. 그래서 사람들은 때때로 이 장소를 '지구상의 천국'이라고 부른다.

구문해설

1행 It is **famous for** its beautiful scenery.

▶ famous for: ~로 유명한

2행 After it rains, the water forms a large **but** very thin salt lake.

▶ but: '(하)지만'의 의미로, 형용사(구) large와 very thin을 연결

4행 So people sometimes **call this place "Heaven on Earth."**

▶ call+목적어+목적격보어(명사): 목적어를 ~라고 부르다

문제해설

2 동사 walk를 동명사 walking으로 바꾸고 그 뒤에 전치사구 on the salt lake가 오도록 배열하여 동명사구 주어를 만든다. 동명사구 주어는 단수 취급하므로, 뒤에 be동사의 3인칭 단수 is와 주격보어 wonderful을 배열한다.

Point 03 that절과 의문사절 p.12

027 <That so many people died / in the accident> / was shocking.

<그렇게 많은 사람이 죽었다는 것은 / 그 사고로> / 충격적이었다

그 사고로 그렇게 많은 사람들이 죽었다는 것은 충격적이었다.

028 <Where I hid my report card> / is a secret.

<내가 내 성적표를 어디에 숨겼는지는> / 비밀이다.

029 <What she asked me to do> / is unclear.

<그녀가 나에게 무엇을 해 달라고 부탁했는지는> / 불확실하다.

030 <That I passed the exam> / made my parents happy.

<내가 시험에 합격한 것은> / 나의 부모님을 행복하게 했다.

031 <That he escaped / from prison> / is big news. <Who helped him> / is a mystery.

<그가 탈출했다는 것은 / 감옥에서> / 심각한 소식이다. <누가 그를 도왔는지는> / 수수께끼이다.

그가 감옥에서 탈출했다는 것은 심각한 소식이다. 누가 그를 도왔는지는 수수께끼이다.

032 <That Bella was angry / at him> / is clear. But <why she was upset> / is uncertain.

<Bella가 화가 났다는 것은 / 그에게> / 분명하다. 하지만 <왜 그녀가 마음이 상했는지는> / 불확실하다.

Bella가 그에게 화가 났다는 것은 분명하다. 하지만 그녀가 왜 마음이 상했는지는 불확실하다.

033 It doesn't matter / <that the team won first prize>. <How it became the best> / is the important thing.

중요하지 않다 / <그 팀이 우승했다는 것은>. <그것이 어떻게 최고가 되었는지가> / 중요한 것이다.

그 팀이 우승했다는 것은 중요하지 않다. 그 팀이 어떻게 최고가 되었는지가 중요한 것이다.

Point 04 가주어와 비인칭 주어 p.13

038 It is impossible / to do everything well.

불가능하다 / 모든 것을 잘하는 것은

모든 것을 잘하는 것은 불가능하다.

039 It is hard / to imagine my life <without a smartphone>.

어렵다 / 내 삶을 상상하는 것은 <스마트폰이 없는>

스마트폰이 없는 내 삶을 상상하는 것은 어렵다.

040 It made me sad / <that he forgot my birthday>.

나를 슬프게 했다 / <그가 내 생일을 잊었다는 것은>

그가 내 생일을 잊었다는 것은 나를 슬프게 했다.

041 It is around 100 meters / from here to my house.

약 100미터이다 / 여기에서 우리 집까지는

여기에서 우리 집까지는 약 100미터이다.

042 It seems / <that my parents are sleeping deeply>.

~인 것 같다 / <우리 부모님께서 깊이 주무시고 계신 것>

우리 부모님께서 깊이 주무시고 계신 것 같다.

043 <When you feel sick>, / it is helpful / to take medicine / and rest at home.

<네가 아플 때는>, / 도움이 된다 / 약을 먹는 것이 / 그리고 집에서 쉬는 것이

네가 아플 때는 약을 먹고 집에서 쉬는 것이 도움이 된다.

044 It is getting hotter / every year. It is probably true / <that global warming is becoming / a serious problem>.

더 더워지고 있다 / 매년. 아마도 사실일 것이다 / <지구 온난화가 되고 있다는 것은 / 심각한 문제가>

매년 더 더워지고 있다. 지구 온난화가 심각한 문제가 되고 있다는 것은 아마도 사실일 것이다.

Unit Practice pp.14~15

STEP 1

1 It is interesting / that dogs can dream.

풀이 우리말 해석에서 주어가 뒤에 있으므로, 문장 맨 앞에 가주어 it을 쓰고, 진주어인 that절 that dogs can dream이 뒤에 오도록 단어를 배열한다.

2 It is Sunday today, and I will visit my grandparents.

풀이 요일을 나타내는 비인칭 주어 it이 앞 절의 주어이다. 등위접속사 and는 '~와[과]'의 뜻으로 두 개의 절 It ~ today와 I ~ grandparents를 연결한다.

3 When she will get back / from the trip / is not certain.

풀이 의문사절 When ~ trip이 문장의 주어가 된다. 또한 '확실하지 않다'라고 했으므로 동사 is 뒤에 not이 오도록 단어를 배열한다.

구문 from the trip: 동사구 will get back을 수식하는 전치사구

STEP 2

1 Why he committed the crime is still unknown.

그가 왜 그 범죄를 저질렀는지는 아직 알려지지 않았다.

풀이 의문사절 Why ~ crime이 문장의 주어이다. 의문사 why가 이끄는 명사절 주어는 '왜 ~하는지는'으로 해석한다.

2 It is fun to try new foods from different cultures.

다른 문화에서 온 새로운 음식을 시도해보는 것은 즐겁다.

풀이 가주어 it을 문장 맨 앞에 쓰고, 진주어인 to부정사구 to try ~ cultures를 뒤로 보낸 형태이다. 이러한 to부정사구는 '~하는 것은'으로 해석한다.

구문 from different cultures: 명사 foods를 수식하는 전치사구

3 It was dark in the cave, and I was scared of the bats.

동굴 안은 어두웠고 나는 박쥐가 무서웠다.

풀이 앞 절의 주어인 비인칭 주어 it은 명암을 나타내며, 이때 비인칭 주어는 해석하지 않는다. and 이하 절의 주어는 대명사 I이다.

구문 ▶ in the cave: 형용사 dark를 수식하는 전치사구
▶ and: 절 It ~ cave와 I was ~ bats를 연결
▶ scared of: ~이 무서운

4 That they canceled the concert was disappointing.

그들이 콘서트를 취소했다는 것은 실망스러웠다.

풀이 that절 That ~ concert가 문장의 주어이다. 접속사 that이 이끄는 명사절 주어는 '하는 것은'으로 해석한다.

구문 disappointing: 실망스러운 (현재분사)

5 What children watch on television affects their behavior.

아이들이 텔레비전에서 무엇을 보는지가 그들의 행동에 영향을 미친다.

풀이 의문사절 What ~ television이 문장의 주어이다. 의문사 what이 이끄는 명사절 주어는 '무엇을 ~하는지가'로 해석한다.

6 It seems that you are a big fan of superhero movies.

너는 슈퍼히어로 영화의 열혈 팬인 것 같다.

풀이 「It seems that ~」 구문에서 It은 가주어, that절 that you ~ movies는 진주어이며, '~인 것 같다'로 해석한다.

구문 of superhero movies: 명사구 a big fan을 수식하는 전치사구

STEP 3

1 (A) to make artificial eggs from beans
(B) that these eggs will make baking cookies and bread cheaper
문장 해석은 아래 해석 참조

Q ③

해석 (A)콩으로 인공 달걀을 만드는 것은 비현실적으로 들린다. 그러나 미국에 있는 한 회사는 이것을 할 수 있다! 진짜 달걀은 해로운 콜레스테롤을 가지고 있다. 그러나 인공 달걀은 전혀 가지고 있지 않다. 그래서 인공 달걀을 먹는 것이 건강에 더 좋다. 또한, 그것들을 만드는 것은 비용이 많이 들지 않는다. 그래서 (B)이 달걀들이 쿠키와 빵을 굽는 것에 돈이 더 적게 들도록 하는 것이 가능하다.

구문해설

1행 However, a company **in the US** can do *this*!
▶ in the US: 명사 a company를 수식하는 전치사구
▶ this: 앞 문장에 언급된 to make artificial eggs from beans를 가리키는 대명사

3행 So it is **healthier** to eat artificial *ones*.
▶ 형용사+-er: 더 ~한 (비교급)
▶ ones: eggs를 가리키는 대명사

문제해설

1 (A), (B) 가주어 it을 문장 맨 앞에 쓰고, 각각 진주어 to부정사구와 that절을 뒤로 보낸 형태이다. 진주어인 to부정사구와 that절은 '~하는 것은'으로 해석한다.

Q 인공 달걀을 먹는 것이 건강에 더 좋다고 했으므로, 글의 내용과 일치하지 않는 것은 ③이다.

2 (A) It is hard to hold short pencils
(B) How you use them is simple

해석 (A)짧은 연필들을 쥐는 것은 어렵다. 그래서 대부분의 사람들은 그것들을 그냥 버린다. 그러나 한 회사는 특별한 연필들을 만든다. (B)당신이 그것들을 어떻게 사용하는지는 간단하다. 그것들이 짧아지면 그것들을 흙에 심어라. 그 연필들은 안에 허브 씨앗을 가지고 있다. 그 씨앗은 싹이 나고 자란다. 당신이 지구를 도왔다는 것은 당신을 행복하게 할 것이다. 그리고 당신은 허브도 즐길 수 있다!

구문해설

1행 So most people just throw **them** away.
▶ short pencils를 가리키는 대명사

2행 When they **get short**, *plant* them in some soil.

▶ get+형용사: ~해지다

▶ plant: '~하라'라는 명령문의 경우, 주어를 생략하고 동사원형으로 시작

문제해설

2 (A) 가주어 it을 사용하되 빈칸이 총 7개이므로, 진주어는 to부정사구를 쓴다. 가주어 it을 문장 맨 앞에 쓰고, 진주어인 to부정사구 to hold short pencils를 뒤로 보낸다.
(B) '어떻게 ~하는지는'이라는 의미의 의문사절 「How+주어+동사 ~」가 문장의 주어로 오도록 단어를 배열한다.

Wrap Up p.16

❶ 주어 ❷ it ❸ that

1 Who found the answer doesn't matter.
2 Eating breakfast is good for teenagers.
3 It is necessary to keep your promise.
4 The ending of this novel is really interesting.
5 That everyone has worries is obvious.
[= It is obvious that everyone has worries.]
6 It was nice that you gave up your seat to the elderly woman.

UNIT 02 목적어의 형태

Point 01 명사와 대명사 p.18

050 You don't have to do it / now.
너는 그것을 할 필요가 없다 / 지금
너는 지금 그것을 할 필요가 없다.

051 My dad cooked us / pizza / at home.
아빠가 우리에게 요리해 주셨다 / 피자를 / 집에서
아빠가 집에서 우리에게 피자를 요리해 주셨다.

052 We made / him our team captain.
우리는 만들었다 / 그를 우리 팀 주장으로
우리는 그를 우리 팀 주장으로 만들었다.

053 We lost / our way <to the shopping mall>.
우리는 잃었다 / 길을 <쇼핑몰로 가는>
우리는 쇼핑몰로 가는 길을 잃었다.

054 <After Clara solved the math problem>, / she raised her hand.
<Clara는 그 수학 문제를 푼 뒤>, / 그녀는 손을 들었다.

055 Ava sent me / a text message / after school.
Ava는 내게 보냈다 / 문자 메시지를 / 방과 후에
Ava는 방과 후에 내게 문자 메시지를 보냈다.

056 I didn't drink coffee / <when I was young>. Now I drink it / every day.
나는 커피를 마시지 않았다 / <어렸을 때>. 이제 나는 그것을 마신다 / 매일
나는 어렸을 때 커피를 마시지 않았다. 이제 나는 그것을 매일 마신다.

Point 02 동명사와 to부정사 p.19

062 He began / looking for a new job.
그는 시작했다 / 새로운 직업을 찾기
그는 새로운 직업을 찾기 시작했다.

063 Leo always practices / dancing.
Leo는 항상 연습한다 / 춤추는 것을
Leo는 항상 춤추는 것을 연습한다.

064 My elder brother and I enjoy / watching soccer matches.
우리 형과 나는 즐긴다 / 축구 경기를 보는 것을
우리 형과 나는 축구 경기를 보는 것을 즐긴다.

065 She agreed / to accept my suggestion.
그녀는 동의했다 / 내 제안을 받아들이는 것에
그녀는 내 제안을 받아들이는 것에 동의했다.

066 I forgot / to bring my history textbook.
나는 잊었다 / 내 역사 교과서를 가져오는 것을
나는 내 역사 교과서를 가져오는 것을 잊었다.

067 Henry wants / to lose weight. He avoids / eating sweets / these days.
Henry는 원한다 / 살을 빼는 것을. 그는 피한다 / 단것을 먹는 것을 / 요즘
Henry는 살을 빼는 것을 원한다. 그는 요즘 단것을 먹는 것을 피한다.

068 I'm trying / to study <for my test>. Do you mind / turning down the volume?
나는 노력하고 있어 / 공부하려고 <시험을 위해서>. 너는 해 주겠니 / 소리를 낮추는 것을
나는 시험을 위해서 공부하려고 노력하고 있어. 소리를 낮춰 주겠니?

Unit Practice pp.20~21

STEP 1

1 My grandfather raises / cows and chickens / on his farm.

풀이 주어가 3인칭 단수이므로 동사 raise를 raises로 바꾸고, 목적어로 명사구 cows and chickens를 써서, 「주어(My grandfather)+동사(raises)+목적어(cows and chickens)+수식어구(on his farm)」의 순서로 배열한다.

2 Karen didn't recognize him / at first.

풀이 동사 recognize를 과거시제 부정형 didn't recognize로 바꾸고, 목적어로 대명사 him을 써서, 「주어(Karen)+동사(didn't recognize)+목적어(him)+수식어구(at first)」의 순서로 배열한다.

3 We gave up / waiting for the subway / and walked / home.

풀이 동사 give up을 과거시제 gave up으로 바꾸고, 목적어로 동명사구 waiting for the subwag를 써서, 「주어(We)+동사(gave up)+목적어(waiting for the subway) ~」의 순서로 배열한다.

구문 and: 동사 gave up과 walked 연결

STEP 2

1 Don will introduce her to his family next month.

Don은 다음 달에 그녀를 그의 가족에게 소개할 것이다.

풀이 동사 will introduce의 목적어로 대명사 her가 쓰였다.

구문 introduce A to B: A를 B에게 소개하다

2 She will try making a cake by herself for the first time.

그녀는 처음으로 혼자 케이크를 만들어 볼 것이다.

풀이 동사 will try의 목적어로 동명사구 making ~ herself가 쓰였다. a cake는 동명사 making의 목적어, by herself는 수식어구이다. 동사 try의 목적어로 동명사가 올 때는 '(시험 삼아) ~해 보다'로 해석한다.

구문 ▶ by oneself: 혼자
▶ for the first time: 처음으로

3 The dogs continued barking until late at night.

그 개들은 늦은 밤까지 짖는 것을 계속했다.
(= 그 개들은 늦은 밤까지 계속 짖었다.)

풀이 동사 continued의 목적어로 동명사 barking이 쓰였다. 동사 continue는 동명사와 to부정사 둘 다 목적어로 쓸 수 있으며 '~하는 것을 계속하다'로 해석한다.

구문 until: ~(때)까지

4 The athlete finished the marathon within three hours.

그 운동선수는 세 시간 이내에 마라톤을 완주했다.

풀이 동사 finished의 목적어로 명사 the marathon이 쓰였다.

구문 within: ~ 이내에[안에]

5 I learned to swim last year, but I still can't swim in the sea.

나는 작년에 수영을 배웠지만 여전히 바다에서 수영하지 못한다.

풀이 동사 learned의 목적어로 to부정사 to swim이 쓰였다. 동사 learn은 to부정사를 목적어로 쓰는 동사이며 '~하는 것을 배우다'로 해석한다.

6 Diana is expecting to get a good grade on the midterm exam.

Diana는 중간고사에서 좋은 점수를 받을 것을 기대하고 있다.

풀이 동사 is expecting의 목적어로 to부정사구 to get ~ exam이 쓰였다. a good grade는 to get의 목적어, on the midterm exam은 수식어구이다. 동사 expect는 to부정사를 목적어로 쓰는 동사이며 '~하기를 기대하다'로 해석한다.

STEP 3

1 everyone stops eating meat products

Q ②

해석 볼티모어에서 몇몇 학교들은 고기 없는 월요일을 즐긴다. 그 학교들에서는 월요일마다 모두가 고기 제품을 먹는 것을 멈춘다. 고기 대신에 식당 직원들은 채소, 과일, 그리고 곡물을 제공한다. 이것들은 건강에 좋은 저지방의 음식들이다. 또한, 그것들은 더 낮은 열량으로 사람들을 배부르게 만든다. 학교들은 고기 없는 월요일로 학생 건강 문제들을 줄이기를 기대한다.

구문해설

3행 Also, they **make people full** on *fewer* calories.
▶ make+목적어+목적격보어(형용사): 목적어를 ~하게 만들다
▶ fewer: 더 적은 (few의 비교급)

4행 The schools **expect to reduce** student health problems *with* Meatless Monday.
▶ expect+to-v: ~하기를 기대하다
▶ with: ~(으)로

문제해설

1 everyone은 단수 취급하므로, 3인칭 단수 동사 stops를 쓴다. 동사 stop은 목적어로 동명사를 쓰므로, 「stop+v-ing」로 나타낸다.

Q

고기 없는 월요일로 학교들은 그들의 (A) 학생들이 (B) 건강한 상태를 유지하는 데 도움을 줄 수 있다.

마지막 문장에서 고기 없는 월요일로 학생들의 건강 문제가 줄어들기를 기대한다고 했으므로, 빈칸에는 ② '(A) 학생들, (B) 건강한'이 가장 적절하다.

① (A) 노동자들 (B) 똑똑한
③ (A) 동물들 (B) 행복한

2 (1) Do you want to be a reporter?
(2) You should also practice writing about the things around you.

해석 당신은 기자가 되기를 원하는가? 그렇다면 당신은 학교에 있는 방송부에 가입하는 것이 좋다. 당신은 뉴스를 보도하고 특집 기사를 내보내는 것을 배울 수 있다. 당신은 또한 당신 주변의 일들에 관해서 쓰는 것을 연습하는 것이 좋다. 마지막으로 당신은 당신의 의사소통 기술에 노력을 기울여야 한다. 이것은 기자들이 잘 읽고, 쓰고, 말하고, 듣는 것이 필요하기 때문에 중요하다.

구문해설

1행 Then you **should** join the broadcasting club *at school*.
▶ should: ~해야 한다, ~하는 것이 좋다 (의무, 충고)
▶ at school: 명사 the broadcasting club을 수식하는 전치사구

4행 This is important because reporters **need to read**, **write**, **speak**, **and listen** well.
▶ need+to-v: ~하는 것이 필요하다

문제해설

2 (1) 동사 want는 to부정사를 목적어로 쓰므로, being을 to be로 고쳐야 한다.
(2) 동사 practice는 동명사를 목적어로 쓰므로, to write를 writing으로 고쳐야 한다.

Point 03 that절과 의문사절 p.22

074 You didn't say / <what the answer was>.
너는 말하지 않았다 / <정답이 무엇인지>
너는 정답이 무엇인지 말하지 않았다.

075 We all know / [(that) cheating <on exams> / is bad].
우리 모두는 안다 / [부정행위를 하는 것이 <시험에서> / 나쁘다는 것을]
우리 모두는 시험에서 부정행위를 하는 것이 나쁘다는 것을 안다.

076 I don't understand / <why you must leave>.
나는 이해할 수 없다 / <네가 왜 떠나야 하는지를>
나는 네가 왜 떠나야 하는지를 이해할 수 없다.

077 Hilary forgot / <how old the man was>.
Hilary는 잊어버렸다 / <그 남자가 몇 살인지>
Hilary는 그 남자가 몇 살인지 잊어버렸다.

078 Sometimes I imagine / <that I can communicate / with animals>.
가끔씩 나는 상상한다 / <내가 의사소통할 수 있다고 / 동물들과>
가끔씩 나는 내가 동물들과 의사소통할 수 있다고 상상한다.

079 Lisa doesn't believe / <that ghosts exist>. She thinks / <(that) the scary stories / are fake>.
Lisa는 믿지 않는다 / <귀신이 존재한다는 것을>. 그녀는 생각한다 / <무서운 이야기들이 / 가짜라고>
Lisa는 귀신이 존재한다는 것을 믿지 않는다. 그녀는 무서운 이야기들이 가짜라고 생각한다.

080 Kevin forgot / <when Amy's birthday was>. He thought / <(that) it was in May>.
Kevin은 잊었다 / <Amy의 생일이 언제인지를>. 그는 생각했다 / <그것이 5월에 있다고>
Kevin은 Amy의 생일이 언제인지를 잊었다. 그는 그것이 5월에 있다고 생각했다.

Point 04 가목적어, 전치사의 목적어 p.23

087 He finds it difficult / speaking <in public>.
그는 어렵다고 생각한다 / 말하는 것이 <대중 앞에서>
그는 대중 앞에서 말하는 것이 어렵다고 생각한다.

088 Please keep it a secret / <that Luhan is my boyfriend>.
비밀로 해 주세요 / <Luhan이 내 남자친구라는 것을>
Luhan이 내 남자친구라는 것을 비밀로 해 주세요.

089 The movie is / about surviving <on a desert island>.
그 영화는 ~이다 / 살아남는 것에 대한 것 <무인도에서>
그 영화는 무인도에서 살아남는 것에 대한 것이다.

090 The traffic jam made it impossible / to arrive <on time>.
교통 체증이 불가능하게 했다 / 도착하는 것을 <제시간에>
교통 체증이 제시간에 도착하는 것을 불가능하게 했다.

091 My parents consider it rude / to leave <without saying goodbye>.
나의 부모님은 무례하다고 여기신다 / 떠나는 것을 <작별 인사를 하지 않고>
나의 부모님은 작별 인사를 하지 않고 떠나는 것을 무례하다고 여기신다.

092 We think it essential / <that we maintain / a work-life balance>.
우리는 필수적이라고 생각한다 / <우리가 유지하는 것이 / 일과 생활의 균형을>

우리는 우리가 일과 생활의 균형을 유지하는 것이 필수적이라고 생각한다.

Unit Practice pp.24~25

STEP 1

1 You didn't say / what the answer was.

풀이 동사 didn't say의 목적어로 의문사절이 쓰였다. 의문사 what 다음에 「주어+동사 ~」가 오도록 단어를 배열한다.

2 Monica realized / that honesty is the best policy.

풀이 과거시제이므로 동사 realize를 realized로 쓰고, 목적어로 접속사 that이 이끄는 명사절을 써서 that 다음에 「주어+동사」가 오도록 단어를 배열한다. 명사절 목적어를 이끄는 접속사 that은 생략할 수 있다.

3 I'm tired / of wearing a school uniform.

풀이 전치사 of의 목적어로 동명사 wearing을 쓰고 그 뒤에 wearing의 목적어인 a school uniform이 오도록 배열한다.

구문 tired of: ~에 싫증이 난

STEP 2

1 They believe (that) you will pass the exam.

그들은 네가 시험에 합격할 것이라고 믿는다.

풀이 동사 believe의 목적어로 명사절이 쓰였고, 명사절을 이끄는 접속사 that이 생략되었다. that절 목적어는 '~라고'로 해석한다.

2 People thought it impossible to travel to space.

사람들은 우주로 여행을 가는 것이 불가능하다고 생각했다.

풀이 목적어 자리에 가목적어 it을 쓰고 진목적어인 to부정사구를 뒤로 보낸 형태이다. 가목적어 it 자리에 진목적어 to부정사구를 넣어 해석한다.

3 Colin considers it boring studying alone.

Colin은 혼자 공부하는 것이 지루하다고 생각한다.

풀이 목적어 자리에 가목적어 it을 쓰고 진목적어인 동명사구를 뒤로 보낸 형태이다. 가목적어 it 자리에 진목적어 동명사구를 넣어 해석한다.

구문 consider+목적어+목적격보어(형용사): 목적어를 ~라고 생각하다[여기다]

4 She agrees that saving money is important for the future.

그녀는 미래를 위해 돈을 저축하는 것이 중요하다는 것에 동의한다.

풀이 동사 agrees의 목적어로 that절이 쓰였다. 이때 명사절을 이끄는 접속사 that은 생략할 수 있다.

구문 saving money: that절의 동명사구 주어

5 He doesn't remember why he didn't pay the bills on time.

그는 그가 왜 제때 요금을 지불하지 않았는지 기억하지 못한다.

풀이 동사 doesn't remember의 목적어로 의문사절이 쓰였다. 의문사 why가 이끄는 명사절 목적어는 '왜 ~하는지(를)'로 해석한다.

6 We are thinking of attending a music festival.

우리는 음악 축제에 참석할 것을 생각하고 있다.

풀이 전치사 of의 목적어로 동명사구가 쓰였다. 동명사구 목적어는 '~하는 것을'로 해석한다.

구문 think of: ~을 생각하다

STEP 3

1 that

문장 해석은 아래 해석 참조

Q ②

해석 (a) 과거에 커피나무는 동아시아와 아라비아의 야생에서만 자랐다. 어느 이야기에 따르면 한 어린 양치기가 그의 양들이 커피 열매를 먹은 뒤에 이상하게 행동하는 것을 알아차렸다. 그는 몇 개를 먹어 보기로 했고 그것들이 (b) 형편없다(→ 맛있다)고 생각했다. 곧 커피는 아라비아 전역에서 인기를 얻었고 나중에 그것은 유럽으로 (c) 퍼졌다.

구문해설

3행 ~ his animals behaved **strangely** after *eating coffee berries*.

▶ strangely: 동사 behaved를 수식하는 부사

▶ eating coffee berries: 전치사 after의 동명사구 목적어

4행 He **decided to try** some and thought *that* ~.

▶ decide+to-v: ~하기로 결심하다

▶ that: 동사 thought의 명사절 목적어를 이끄는 접속사로 생략 가능

문제해설

1 동사 noticed의 목적어인 명사절을 이끄는 접속사가 필요한 자리이므로 빈칸에는 that이 알맞다. that절 목적어는 '~하다는 것을'로 해석한다.

Q 마지막 문장에서 곧 커피가 아라비아 전역에서 인기를 얻었다고 했으므로 커피 열매는 맛이 있었음을 알 수 있다. 따라서 ② (b) terrible(형편없는)을 delicious(맛있는)로 쓰는 것이 적절하다.

2 who they were, how rich they were

해석 신발은 고대 로마인들의 삶에서 중요한 역할을 했다. 로마인들은 신발이 중요한 메시지를 보낸다는 것을 알았다. 그들의 신발은 그들이 누구이며 그들이 얼마나 부유한지를 나타냈다. 또한, 로마의 아이들은 그들의 부모와 똑같은 종류의 신발을 신었다. 특정한 종류의 신발을 신는 것은 '나는 이 사회 계급의 구성원이다'라고 말하는 하나의 방식이었다.

구문해설

1행 The Romans knew **that** shoes sent an important message.

▶ that: 동사 knew의 명사절 목적어를 이끄는 접속사로 생략 가능

3행 Also, Roman kids wore **the same** kind of shoes **as** their parents.

▶ the same A as B: B와 똑같은 A

Wearing a certain kind of shoes was a way of *saying*, ~.

▶ Wearing ~ shoes: 동명사구 주어

▶ saying, ~: 전치사 of의 동명사구 목적어

문제해설

2 동사 expressed의 의문사절 목적어로 명사절을 이끄는 의문사 who 다음에 「주어+동사」가 오고, 의문사 how 다음에는 「형용사/부사+주어+동사」가 오도록 하여 문장을 완성한다.

Wrap Up p.26

❶ that ❷ it ❸ to부정사(구)

1 He thought (that) you were with Matt.
2 I made it a goal to improve my English.
3 I remember calling him yesterday.
4 Kate believes (that) James is innocent.
5 I forgot the name of the song.
6 She stays healthy by exercising every day.

UNIT 03 보어의 형태

Point 01 주격보어 _ 명사, 형용사, 분사 p.28

097 The weather suddenly got cold / this week.
날씨가 갑자기 추워졌다 / 이번 주에
날씨가 이번 주에 갑자기 추워졌다.

098 Over time, / the problem will grow worse.
시간이 흐르면서, / 그 문제는 더 나빠질 것이다.

099 Some seats remained empty / during the show.
몇몇 자리는 비어 있었다 / 공연을 하는 동안
몇몇 자리는 공연을 하는 동안 비어 있었다.

100 It was surprising / <that she became the winner>.
놀라웠다 / <그녀가 우승자가 된 것은>
그녀가 우승자가 된 것은 놀라웠다.

101 My favorite food is fried chicken. It tastes and smells delicious.
내가 가장 좋아하는 음식은 프라이드치킨이다. 그것은 맛있는 맛과 냄새가 난다.

102 The mission was successful. We felt satisfied / <after we finished it>.
그 임무는 성공적이었다. 우리는 만족했다 / <그것을 마친 뒤에>
그 임무는 성공적이었다. 우리는 그것을 마친 뒤에 만족했다.

103 Emma became disappointed / <when she saw her quiz grade>. She looks sad / now.
Emma는 실망했다 / <그녀가 그녀의 퀴즈 성적을 보았을 때>. 그녀는 속상해 보인다 / 지금
Emma는 그녀의 퀴즈 성적을 보았을 때 실망했다. 그녀는 지금 속상해 보인다.

Point 02 주격보어 _ 동명사와 to부정사 p.29

108 Our decision was / to cancel the party.
우리의 결정은 ~이었다 / 파티를 취소하는 것
우리의 결정은 파티를 취소하는 것이었다.

109 My father's job is / writing fairy tales <for children>.
우리 아버지의 직업은 ~이다 / 동화를 쓰는 것 <아이들을 위한>
우리 아버지의 직업은 아이들을 위한 동화를 쓰는 것이다.

110 Nana's dream is / to becoeme a famous guitarist.
Nana의 꿈은 ~이다 / 유명한 기타 연주자가 되는 것
Nana의 꿈은 유명한 기타 연주자가 되는 것이다.

111 The purpose <of the event> is / to raise money <for charity>.
목적은 <그 행사의> ~이다 / 돈을 모으는 것 <자선 단체를 위한>
그 행사의 목적은 자선 단체를 위한 돈을 모으는 것이다.

112 I did volunteer work / last weekend. My role was / taking care <of the elderly>.
나는 봉사 활동을 했다 / 지난 주말에. 나의 역할은 ~이었다 / 돌보는 것 <어르신들을>
지난 주말에 나는 봉사 활동을 했다. 나의 역할은 어르신들을 돌보는 것이었다.

113 I love to travel. My favorite thing <about traveling> is / meeting new people.

나는 여행하는 것을 매우 좋아한다. 내가 가장 좋아하는 것은 <여행에 관해> ~이다 / 새로운 사람들을 만나는 것
나는 여행하는 것을 매우 좋아한다. 내가 여행에 관해 가장 좋아하는 것은 새로운 사람들을 만나는 것이다.

114 The first step <to happiness> is / being kind <to yourself>. The next step is / to connect <with others>.
첫 번째 단계는 <행복을 향한> ~이다 / 친절한 것 <네 자신에게>. 그 다음 단계는 ~이다 / 관계를 가지는 것 <다른 사람들과>
행복을 향한 첫 번째 단계는 네 자신에게 친절한 것이다. 그 다음 단계는 다른 사람들과 관계를 가지는 것이다.

Unit Practice

pp.30~31

STEP 1

1 Their decision was / to divide the money / equally.
풀이 be동사의 과거시제를 쓰고 주격보어 자리의 빈칸 개수에 따라 to부정사구를 써서 「주어(Their decision)+동사(was)+주격보어(to divide the money) ~」의 순서로 배열한다. to부정사구 to divide the money는 주어를 보충 설명한다.

2 That novel is a bestseller / of this year.
풀이 현재시제이므로 be동사 is 다음에 주격보어로 명사 a bestseller를 써서 주어 That novel을 보충 설명한다.
구문 of this year: 명사 a bestseller를 수식하는 전치사구

3 Her hobby is / decorating her room / herself.
풀이 현재시제이므로 be동사 is 다음에 주격보어로 동명사구 decorating her room을 써서 주어 Her hobby를 보충 설명한다. 동명사구 대신 to부정사구로 쓸 수 있으나, 빈칸 개수에 맞게 단어를 배열한다.
구문 herself: 직접, 그녀[자기] 자신 (재귀대명사)

STEP 2

1 The song of the bird sounds beautiful.
그 새의 노래는 아름답게 들린다.
풀이 주어 The song of the bird를 보충 설명하는 주격보어로 형용사 beautiful이 쓰였다.
구문 ▶ of the bird: 명사 The song을 수식하는 전치사구
▶ sound+형용사: ~하게 들리다

2 The rules of the game are confusing.
그 게임의 규칙은 혼란스럽다.
풀이 주어 The rules of the game을 보충 설명하는 주격보어로 현재분사 confusing이 쓰였다. 현재분사는 주어가 느끼게 하는 감정을 나타낸다.
구문 of the game: 명사 The rules를 수식하는 전치사구

3 I felt worried about my parents' medical test results.
나는 부모님의 의료 검사 결과가 걱정되었다.
풀이 주어 I를 보충 설명하는 주격보어로 과거분사 worried가 쓰였다. 과거분사는 주어가 느끼게 된 감정을 나타낸다.

4 Her main means of transportation is biking and walking.
그녀의 주된 이동 수단은 자전거 타기와 걷기이다.
풀이 주어 Her ~ transportation을 보충 설명하는 주격보어로 동명사구 biking and walking이 쓰였다.
구문 ▶ of transportation: 명사 means를 수식하는 전치사구
▶ and: 동명사 biking과 walking을 연결

5 The snowman became the movie's most popular character.
그 눈사람은 그 영화의 가장 인기 있는 등장인물이 되었다.
풀이 주어 The snowman을 보충 설명하는 주격보어로 명사구 the movie's ~ character가 쓰였다.

6 My plan is to read one book per month.
내 계획은 매달 한 권의 책을 읽는 것이다.
풀이 주어 My plan을 보충 설명하는 주격보어로 to부정사구 to read ~ month가 쓰였다.
구문 per: ~당[마다]

STEP 3

1 (A) one tasty lion (B) scared
문장 해석은 아래 해석 참조

Q ②

해석 어느 날 아침, 배고픈 사자 한 마리가 개 뒤에 숨어 있었다. 그 영리한 개는 이것을 알아차리고 소리쳤다. "(A)그것은 맛있는 사자 한 마리였어! 더 많은 사자를 먹어야겠다." (B)그 사자는 겁이 나서 도망쳤다. 그때 다람쥐 한 마리가 그 사자에게 개의 속임수에 대해서 말해 주었다. 그 사자는 화가 났다. "나를 그 개에게 데려다줘!"라고 사자가 말했고, 그들은 달려서 돌아왔다. 그러나 그 개는 준비되어 있었고 소리쳤다. "그 다람쥐가 어디 있지? 내가 그에게 다른 사자 한 마리를 데려오라고 말했는데!"

구문해설

1행 One morning, a hungry lion **was hiding** behind a dog.
▶ was/were+v-ing: ~하고 있었다 (과거진행)

7행 I **told him to** ***bring*** *me another lion*!
▶ tell+목적어+목적격보어(to-v): 목적어에게 ~하라고 말하다[시키다]
▶ bring+간접목적어+직접목적어: ~에게 …을 가져오다

문제해설

1 (A) be동사 was 다음에 주격보어로 쓰인 명사구 one tasty lion

이 주어의 신분이나 자격 등을 보충 설명한다. '~는 보어였다'로 해석한다.

(B) 상태 변화를 나타내는 동사 get 다음에 주격보어로 쓰인 과거분사 scared가 주어의 상태를 보충 설명한다. '~한 감정을 느끼게) 된'으로 해석한다.

Q 자신을 잡아먹으려는 사자를 꾀를 내어 속인 것으로 보아 영리한 개이므로, 빈칸에 들어갈 말로 가장 적절한 것은 ② '영리한'이다.
① 게으른 ③ 탐욕스러운

2 ② be a cartoonist → to be[being] a cartoonist
③ truly → true

해석 Charles M. Schulz는 수줍음이 많은 소년이었고, 종종 나쁜 성적을 받았다. 그러나 그는 꿈을 가지고 있었다. 그의 목표는 만화가가 되는 것이었다. 그의 꿈은 그의 만화인 *Peanuts*로 실현되었다. 그것의 주인공인 Charlie Brown은 작고 연약하다. 그의 성격은 대부분의 영웅들과 다르다. Schulz는 자기 자신과 비슷한 인물을 그리고 싶었기 때문에 그를 선택했다.

구문해설

3행 His personality is **different from** most heroes.
▶ different from: ~와 다른

4행 Schulz chose him **because** he *wanted to draw* a character **like** *himself*.
▶ because: ~하기 때문에
▶ want+to-v: ~하기를 원하다
▶ like: ~와 비슷한
▶ himself: 그[자기] 자신 (재귀대명사)

문제해설

2 ② 주어 His goal을 보충 설명하는 주격보어이므로, to부정사구 to be a cartoonist 또는 동명사구 being a cartoonist로 고쳐야 한다.
③ 주어 His dream을 보충 설명하는 주격보어이므로, 부사 truly를 형용사 true로 고쳐야 한다.

Point 03 목적격보어_명사와 형용사 p.32

119 The drivers got / their cars ready / for the race.
운전자들은 ~되게 했다 / 그들의 차들이 준비되게 / 경주에
운전자들은 그들의 차들이 경주에 준비되게 했다.

120 Wendy thinks / him an incredibly handsome man.
Wendy는 생각한다 / 그를 대단히 잘생긴 남자라고
Wendy는 그를 대단히 잘생긴 남자라고 생각한다.

121 The chef named / the special dish Pacific Delight.
그 요리사는 이름지었다 / 그 특별 요리를 태평양의 기쁨이라고
그 요리사는 그 특별 요리를 태평양의 기쁨이라고 이름 지었다.

122 Last night, / my worries <about the exam> kept / me awake.
지난밤, / 걱정이 <시험에 대한> 유지시켰다 / 나를 깨어 있게
지난밤 시험에 대한 걱정이 나를 깨어 있게 했다.

123 A bad smell came / out of my room. So I left / the windows open.
나쁜 냄새가 났다 / 내 방에서. 그래서 나는 두었다 / 창문을 연 상태로
내 방에서 나쁜 냄새가 났다. 그래서 나는 창문을 열어 두었다.

124 The town elected / Nicole its leader. But the position made / her arrogant.
그 마을은 선출했다 / Nicole을 마을의 지도자로. 하지만 그 위치는 만들었다 / 그녀를 오만하게
그 마을은 Nicole을 마을의 지도자로 선출했다. 하지만 그 위치는 그녀를 오만하게 만들었다.

125 People find / making a speech difficult. But practice makes / it easy.
사람들은 여긴다 / 연설하는 것을 어렵게. 그러나 연습은 만든다 / 그것을 쉽게
사람들은 연설하는 것을 어렵게 여긴다. 그러나 연습은 그것을 쉽게 만든다.

Point 04 목적격보어_to부정사와 동사원형 p.33

130 This pill will help / you feel better.
이 알약은 도와줄 것이다 / 네가 나아지도록
이 알약은 네가 나아지도록 도와줄 것이다.

131 His boss doesn't let / him go home early.
그의 상사는 허락하지 않는다 / 그가 집에 일찍 가도록
그의 상사는 그가 집에 일찍 가도록 허락하지 않는다.

132 Amy noticed / some raindrops fall down / from the sky.
Amy는 알아차렸다 / 약간의 빗방울이 떨어지는 것을 / 하늘에서
Amy는 하늘에서 약간의 빗방울이 떨어지는 것을 알아차렸다.

133 Our teacher advised / us to study hard / for the final exam.
우리 선생님은 조언하셨다 / 우리가 열심히 공부하라고 / 기말고사를 위해
우리 선생님은 우리에게 기말고사를 위해 열심히 공부하라고 조언하셨다.

134 I heard / the phone ring. I asked / my friend to answer it.

나는 들었다 / 전화가 울리는 것을. 나는 부탁했다 / 내 친구에게 그것을 받을 것을

나는 전화가 울리는 것을 들었다. 나는 내 친구에게 그것을 받을 것을 부탁했다.

135 Mom doesn't allow / me to play computer games / before dinner. She wants / me to finish my homework first.

엄마는 허락하지 않는다 / 내가 컴퓨터 게임을 하는 것을 / 저녁 식사 전에. 그녀는 원한다 / 내가 우선 숙제를 끝내는 것을

엄마는 내가 저녁 식사 전에 컴퓨터 게임을 하는 것을 허락하지 않는다. 그녀는 내가 우선 숙제를 끝내길 원한다.

136 Edwin saw / a girl say something / to a dog. She ordered / the dog to sit.

Edwin은 보았다 / 한 여자아이가 무언가를 말하는 것을 / 개에게 / 그녀는 명령했다 / 그 개에게 앉으라고

Edwin은 한 여자아이가 개에게 무언가를 말하는 것을 보았다. 그녀는 그 개에게 앉으라고 명령했다.

Unit Practice pp.34~35

STEP 1

1 You can't order / me to give up my dream.

풀이 동사 order는 목적격보어로 동사가 올 경우 to부정사를 쓴다. 「주어(You)+동사(can't order)+목적어(me)+목적격보어(to give up my dream)」의 순서로 단어를 배열한다.

2 Most people consider / the movie's title quite unique.

풀이 동사 consider의 목적격보어로 형용사구 quite unique가 쓰였으므로, 「주어(Most people)+동사(consider)+목적어(the movie's title)+목적격보어(quite unique)」의 순서로 단어를 배열한다.

3 The new program helped / us save time.

풀이 동사 helped는 목적격보어로 동사가 올 경우 to부정사와 동사원형 둘 다 쓸 수 있으나, 빈칸이 총 7개이므로 동사원형을 쓴다. 「주어(The new program)+동사(helped)+목적어(us)+목적격보어((to) save time)」의 순서로 단어를 배열한다.

STEP 2

1 Henry named his son Austin.

Henry는 그의 아들을 Austin이라고 이름 지었다.

풀이 동사 named의 목적격보어로 명사 Austin을 썼다. 「name+목적어+목적격보어(명사)」는 '목적어를 ~라고 이름 짓다'로 해석한다.

2 We found the dress on display beautiful.

우리는 진열된 그 드레스가 아름답다고 생각했다.

풀이 동사 found의 목적격보어로 형용사 beautiful을 썼다. 「find+목적어+목적격보어(형용사)」는 '목적어가 ~하다고 여기다[생각하다]'로 해석한다.

구문 on display: 명사 the dress를 수식하는 전치사구

3 I heard my father snore in the living room.

나는 아버지가 거실에서 코를 고는 소리를 들었다.

풀이 지각동사 heard의 목적격보어로 동사원형 snore를 썼다. 「hear+목적어+목적격보어(동사원형)」는 '목적어가 ~하는 것을 듣다'로 해석한다.

구문 in the living room: 목적격보어로 쓰인 동사 snore를 수식하는 전치사구

4 The hot soup caused me to burn my tongue.

그 뜨거운 수프는 내 혀를 데게 했다.

풀이 동사 caused의 목적격보어로 to부정사구 to burn my tongue을 썼다. to부정사구 to burn my tongue에서 my tongue은 burn의 목적어이다. 「cause+목적어+목적격보어(to-v)」는 '목적어가 ~하도록 하다'로 해석한다.

5 My teacher expects us to learn from our mistakes.

선생님은 우리가 실수에서 배우기를 기대하신다.

풀이 동사 expects의 목적격보어로 to부정사구 to learn ~ mistakes를 썼다. 「expect+목적어+목적격보어(to-v)」는 '목적어가 ~하기를 기대하다'로 해석한다.

6 Mom sometimes had me do the dishes after dinner.

엄마는 가끔 나에게 저녁 식사 후 설거지를 하게 하셨다.

풀이 사역동사 had의 목적격보어로 동사원형 do를 썼다. 「have+목적어+목적격보어(동사원형)」는 '목적어가 ~하게 하다'로 해석한다.

구문 ▶ sometimes: 가끔, 때때로 (빈도부사)

▶ after dinner: 동사구 do the dishes를 수식하는 전치사구

STEP 3

1 ②, ③

Q ②

해석 몇몇 학교들은 나무 의자를 고무공 의자로 교체하고 있다. 이 고무공 의자들은 아이들이 더 잘 배우도록 돕는다. 그 공 위에서 학생들은 균형을 위해 집중해야 한다. 이것은 수업 동안 그들의 뇌를 활동적이게 만든다. 또한, 공 의자는 학생들이 더 좋은 자세를 갖게 한다. 무엇보다도 학생들은 공 의자가 재미있고 편안하다고 여긴다.

구문해설

1행 Some schools **are *replacing*** wooden chairs *with* rubber ball chairs.

▶ am/are/is+v-ing: ~하고 있다 (현재진행)

▶ replace A with B: A를 B로 바꾸다

4행 Best of all, students **find the ball chairs fun and comfortable**.

▶ find+목적어+목적격보어(형용사): 목적어가 ~하다고 여기다[생각하다]

문제해설

1 ② 부사 actively는 목적격보어로 쓰일 수 없으며, '목적어를 ~하게 만들다'는 「make+목적어+목적격보어(형용사)」로 표현한다. 따라서 형용사 active가 되어야 한다.

③ let은 목적격보어로 동사가 올 때 동사원형을 써서 「let+목적어+목적격보어(동사원형)」로 표현한다. 따라서 to have는 동사원형 have가 되어야 한다.

Q 고무공 의자가 학생들의 학습과 자세에 도움이 될 뿐만 아니라 재미와 편안함을 주는 등 긍정적인 효과가 있음을 말해 주는 글이므로, ②가 글의 주제로 가장 적절하다.

2 because people considered them signs of God's anger

해석 때때로 달이 낮 동안에 태양을 가린다. 낮이 밤처럼 어두워진다. 당신은 잠시 동안 태양을 볼 수 없다. 사람들은 이러한 현상을 일식이라고 부른다. 수년 전에, 사람들은 태양을 신이라고 여겼다. 그들은 일식이 신의 분노의 징후라고 생각했다. 그들은 일식을 두려워했고 그것들을 불길하다고 생각했다.

구문해설

1행 The day **becomes dark** *as* night.

▶ become+형용사: ~해지다

▶ as: ~처럼

2행 You cannot see the sun **for a while**.

▶ for a while: 잠시 동안, 잠깐

3행 They thought **(that)** eclipses were signs of God's anger.

▶ 동사 thought의 명사절 목적어를 이끄는 접속사 that이 생략됨

문제해설

2

Q. 사람들은 왜 일식을 두려워했나? **A.** 사람들은 그것들이 신의 분노의 징후라고 생각했기 때문이다.

동사 considered의 목적격보어로 명사구 signs of God's anger를 써서 「이유의 접속사(because)+주어(people)+동사(considered)+ 목적어(them)+목적격보어(signs of God's anger)」의 순서로 단어를 배열한다. 과거시제이므로 과거형 동사 considered를 쓴다.

Wrap Up p.36

❶ 형용사(구) ❷ 과거분사 ❸ 목적격보어 ❹ 동사원형

1 A kind man helped me (to) find the way.
2 Liam felt exhausted after the long trip.
3 His dream is to explore[exploring] the whole world.
4 The teacher told them to be quiet.
5 People call her a genius.
6 Smartphones make our lives more convenient.

UNIT 04 시제와 수동태

Point 01 현재완료 p.38

142 Jessica has already left / the country.
Jessica는 이미 떠났다 / 그 나라를
Jessica는 이미 그 나라를 떠났다. <완료>

143 Sarah has had heart surgery / before.
Sarah는 심장 수술을 받은 적이 있다 / 전에
Sarah는 전에 심장 수술을 받은 적이 있다. <경험>

144 My uncle has just arrived / at the train station.
나의 삼촌이 방금 도착하셨다 / 기차역에
나의 삼촌이 기차역에 방금 도착하셨다. <완료>

145 We have not decided / on a topic <for the presentation> / yet.
우리는 결정하지 못했다 / 주제를 <발표를 위한> / 아직
우리는 발표 주제를 아직 결정하지 못했다. <완료>

146 Have you met Clare / recently? I have not seen her / for several weeks.
너는 Clare를 만난 적 있니 / 최근에? 나는 그녀를 못 봤어 / 몇 주 동안
너는 최근에 Clare를 만난 적 있니? 나는 몇 주 동안 그녀를 못 봤어. <경험, 계속>

147 Irene has been ill / since last month. I hope / <she gets better soon>.
Irene은 아팠다 / 지난달부터. 나는 바란다 / <그녀가 곧 낫기를>
Irene은 지난달부터 아팠다. 나는 그녀가 곧 낫기를 바란다. <계속>

148 My neighbor's dog has been barking / for two hours. I can't stand it / anymore.
나의 이웃집 개가 짖고 있다 / 두 시간 동안. 나는 참을 수가 없

다 / 더 이상
이웃집 개가 두 시간 동안 짖고 있다. 나는 더 이상 참을 수가 없다. <계속>

Point 02 과거완료 p.39

154 Martin had not been / on an airplane / before.
Martin은 타본 적이 없었다 / 비행기를 / 전에
Martin은 전에 비행기를 타본 적이 없었다.

155 He had been waiting / for thirty minutes / <when I arrived>.
그는 기다리고 있었다 / 30분 동안 / <내가 도착했을 때>
내가 도착했을 때 그는 30분 동안 기다리고 있었다.

156 David couldn't take notes / <because he had hurt / his hands>.
David는 필기를 할 수 없었다 / <그가 다쳤기 때문에 / 그의 손을>
David는 그의 손을 다쳤기 때문에 필기를 할 수 없었다.

157 I had just finished / taking a shower / <when my mother called me>.
나는 막 끝냈었다 / 샤워하는 것을 / <어머니가 나에게 전화하셨을 때>
어머니가 나에게 전화하셨을 때 나는 샤워하는 것을 막 끝냈었다.

158 Sammy had been studying Chinese / for a year / <before he went to China>.
Sammy는 중국어를 공부해 왔다 / 일 년 동안 / <그가 중국에 가기 전에>
Sammy는 중국에 가기 전에 일 년 동안 중국어를 공부해 오고 있었다.

159 I thought / <Matt had already had dinner>. So I ate / all the food <on the table>.
나는 생각했다 / <Matt가 이미 저녁 식사를 했다고>. 그래서 나는 먹었다 / 모든 음식을 <식탁 위에 있는>
나는 Matt가 이미 저녁 식사를 했다고 생각했다. 그래서 나는 식탁 위에 있는 모든 음식을 먹었다.

160 Alex and Jay had just returned / home. They had traveled around Europe / for three months.
Alex와 Jay는 막 돌아왔었다 / 집에. 그들은 유럽을 여행했었다 / 세 달 동안
Alex와 Jay는 집에 막 돌아왔었다. 그들은 세 달 동안 유럽을 여행했었다.

Unit Practice pp.40~41

STEP 1

1 Dante said / he had taken a nap / for three hours.
풀이 Dante가 3시간 동안 낮잠을 잔 것은 그가 그것에 대해 말하기 이전에 일어난 일이므로, 과거완료로 표현한다. 과거완료는 「had+과거분사」이므로, take를 taken으로 바꿔 쓴다.
구문 ▶ Dante said (that) he had taken ~.: 동사 said의 명사절 목적어를 이끄는 접속사 that 생략
▶ for+기간: ~ 동안

2 Erica and I have been best friends / since childhood / for over ten years.
풀이 Erica와 내가 가장 친한 친구인 것은 어린 시절부터 10년 넘게 현재까지 계속된 일이므로, 현재완료 have been으로 표현한다.
구문 ▶ since+시점: '~부터[이후로]'의 뜻으로 '계속'을 의미하는 현재완료와 사용됨
▶ for+기간: ~ 동안
▶ over: ~이 넘는, ~ 이상의

3 I had just finished / taking a shower / when my mother called me.
풀이 내가 샤워하는 것을 막 끝낸 것이 어머니가 나에게 전화하신 것보다 먼저 일어난 일이므로, 과거완료 had finished로 써야 한다. 또한 finish는 동명사(구)를 목적어로 쓰므로, take를 taking으로 바꿔 쓴다.
구문 finish+v-ing: ~하는 것을 끝내다

STEP 2

1 She has moved to Seattle with her family.
그녀는 그녀의 가족과 함께 시애틀로 이사를 갔다.
풀이 현재완료 중 '완료'의 의미로 쓰인 문장으로, '(막) ~했다'로 해석한다.

2 Frankie had not driven his new car until yesterday.
Frankie는 어제까지 그의 새 차를 운전한 적이 없었다.
풀이 과거완료 중 '경험'의 의미로 쓰인 부정문으로, '~한 적이 없었다'로 해석한다.

3 I didn't know that he had been sick with the flu.
나는 그가 독감으로 아팠었는지 몰랐다.
풀이 과거완료 중 '계속'의 의미로 쓰인 문장으로, '(과거의 어느 시점까지 계속) ~해 왔다'로 해석한다.
구문 that: 동사 didn't know의 명사절 목적어를 이끄는 접속사로 생략 가능

4 Grace has worn eyeglasses for reading since last year.
Grace는 작년부터 독서를 위해 안경을 써 왔다.

풀이 현재완료 중 '계속'의 의미로 쓰인 문장으로, '(지금까지 계속) ~해 왔다'로 해석한다.

구문 reading: 전치사 for의 목적어로 쓰인 동명사

5 They have sold all the tickets for the concert.
그들은 콘서트 표를 모두 다 팔았다.

풀이 현재완료 중 '결과'의 의미로 쓰인 문장으로, '표를 다 팔아서 그 결과 현재 남은 표가 없다'는 의미를 나타낸다.

6 He had been cleaning his room before his cousins came to his house.
그는 그의 사촌들이 집에 오기 전에 자신의 방을 청소하고 있었다.

풀이 과거완료 진행형으로, '~해 오고 있었다'로 해석한다.

구문 before: '~하기 전에'의 의미로 시간 부사절을 이끄는 접속사

STEP 3

1 ②, ④
Q ①

해석 1945년에 한 기술자가 레이더 시스템으로 일을 하고 있었다. 갑자기 그는 자기 주머니에 있던 초코바가 녹아 버렸다는 것을 알아차렸다. 그 순간 그는 자신이 특별한 무언가를 발견했다는 것을 깨달았다. 그는 레이더 앞에 마른 옥수수 몇 알을 놓았고, 그것들은 빠르게 펑 하고 터졌다. 이것이 전자레인지의 시작이었다.

구문해설

2행 Suddenly, he noticed **that** the candy bar *in his pocket* had melted.
▶ that: 동사 noticed의 명사절 목적어를 이끄는 접속사로 생략 가능
▶ in his pocket: 명사구 the candy bar를 수식하는 전치사구

3행 At that moment, he realized (**that**) he *had discovered* something special.
▶ (that): 동사 realized의 명사절 목적어를 이끄는 접속사 that 생략
▶ had+v-ed: 과거시제 realized보다 앞서 일어난 일을 나타내는 과거완료

문제해설

1 주머니 안에 있던 초코바가 녹은 것이 그가 그 일을 알아차린 것보다 먼저 일어난 일이므로, ② has melted를 과거완료 had melted로 고쳐야 한다. 또한 그가 레이더 앞에 마른 옥수수 몇 알을 놓은 것과 그것이 빠르게 터진 것은 연이어 일어난 일이므로 시제를 일치시켜서 ④ had popped를 과거시제 popped로 고쳐야 한다.

Q 레이더 시스템으로 일을 하던 한 기술자가 우연히 깨닫게 된 원리로 전자레인지가 발명되었다는 내용이므로, ①이 글의 주제로 가장 적절하다.

2 (A) has had a strange job
(B) had dreamed of becoming an actor

해석 (A) Chuck Lamb은 2005년 이후로 색다른 직업을 가져왔다. 그의 직업은 영화에서 죽은 사람처럼 연기하는 것이다. (B) Lamb은 어려서부터 배우가 되는 것을 꿈꿨었다. 그러나 그는 그가 배우가 될 재능을 갖고 있지 않다고 생각했다. 어느 날 그는 TV에 출연할 수 있는 가장 쉬운 방법은 시체 연기를 하는 것임을 깨달았다. 이제 그는 전문적인 시체로서 유명해졌다.

구문해설

1행 His job is **to act *like* a dead person in movies**.
▶ to act ~ movies: to부정사구 주격보어
▶ like+명사: ~처럼

2행 However, he thought (**that**) he didn't have the talent *to be* ***one***.
▶ (that): 동사 thought의 명사절 목적어를 이끄는 접속사 that 생략
▶ to be one: 명사 the talent를 수식하는 형용사 역할의 to부정사구
▶ one: an actor를 가리키는 대명사

4행 Now he **has become** famous *as* a professional corpse.
▶ have/has+v-ed: ~해 버렸다[해졌다] (현재완료, 결과)
▶ as: ~로서

문제해설

2 (A) since가 있는 것으로 보아 과거에 시작된 일이 현재까지 이어진다는 것을 알 수 있다. 따라서 현재완료를 써서 「동사(has had)+목적어(a strange job)」의 순서로 단어를 배열한다.
(B) 어려서부터 배우가 되는 것을 꿈꿨었다고 했으므로, 배우가 된 과거의 시점 이전부터 꿈꿔 왔다는 것을 나타내는 과거완료를 써야 한다. 따라서 「동사(had dreamed of)+목적어(becoming an actor)」의 순서로 단어를 배열한다.

Point 03 수동태의 개념 p.42

165 The window is not locked.
그 창문은 잠겨 있지 않다.

166 Paris is visited / by lots of tourists.
파리는 방문된다 / 많은 관광객에 의해
파리는 많은 관광객에 의해 방문된다.

167 The children were not injured / in the accident.
그 아이들은 다치지 않았다 / 그 사고로
그 아이들은 그 사고로 다치지 않았다.

168 Every year, / many houses are destroyed / by tornadoes.

매년, / 많은 집들이 파괴된다 / 토네이도에 의해
매년 많은 집들이 토네이도에 의해 파괴된다.

169 I drink milk / every day. It is delivered / to my house / every morning.
나는 우유를 마신다 / 매일. 그것은 배달된다 / 우리 집으로 / 매일 아침
나는 매일 우유를 마신다. 그것은 매일 아침 우리 집으로 배달된다.

170 The hotel has a nice swimming pool. It is located / on the top floor.
그 호텔은 멋진 수영장을 가지고 있다. 그것은 위치해 있다 / 맨 위층에
그 호텔은 멋진 수영장을 가지고 있다. 그것은 맨 위층에 위치해 있다.

171 These computers are made / by a big company. And they are supplied / to public schools.
이 컴퓨터들은 생산된다 / 대기업에 의해. 그리고 그것들은 공급된다 / 공립학교에
이 컴퓨터들은 대기업에 의해 생산된다. 그리고 그것들은 공립학교에 공급된다.

Point 04 수동태의 시제 표현 p.43

176 Your questions will be answered / soon.
너의 질문들은 답변받을 것이다 / 곧
너의 질문들은 곧 답변받을 것이다.

177 The bread was baked / this morning.
그 빵은 구워졌다 / 오늘 아침에
그 빵은 오늘 아침에 구워졌다.

178 Many rumors are spread / on the internet.
많은 유언비어가 유포된다 / 인터넷에서
많은 유언비어가 인터넷에서 유포된다.

179 New laws <on smoking> / will be introduced / next week.
새로운 법이 <흡연에 대한> / 도입될 것이다 / 다음 주에
흡연에 대한 새로운 법이 다음 주에 도입될 것이다.

180 I lost my dog / yesterday. But he was found / by a police officer / today.
나는 나의 개를 잃어버렸다 / 어제. 그러나 그는 발견되었다 / 한 경찰관에 의해 / 오늘
나는 어제 나의 개를 잃어버렸다. 그러나 그는 오늘 한 경찰관에 의해 발견되었다.

181 The meals were prepared / by the chef, // and they were served / to the guests.
음식들이 준비되었다 / 그 요리사에 의해 // 그리고 그것들은 제공되었다 / 손님들에게
음식들이 그 요리사에 의해 준비되었고, 그것들은 손님들에게 제공되었다.

182 English is used / by many people / all over the world. So it is spoken / with many different accents.
영어는 사용된다 / 많은 사람에 의해 / 전 세계에서. 그래서 그것은 말해진다 / 많은 다양한 억양으로
영어는 전 세계에서 많은 사람에 의해 사용된다. 그래서 그것은 많은 다양한 억양으로 말해진다.

Unit Practice pp.44~45

STEP 1

1 The town is located / across the river.
풀이 '~에 위치해 있다'는 현재시제 수동태 is located로 표현할 수 있으므로, 「주어(The town)+be동사(is)+과거분사(located)+수식어구(across the river)」의 순서로 배열한다.
구문 across: 건너편에, 맞은편에

2 The package will be delivered / by the postman / in two days.
풀이 '배달될 것이다'는 미래시제 수동태 will be delivered로 표현할 수 있으므로, 「주어(The package)+will be+과거분사(delivered)+by+행위자(the postman)+수식어구(in two days)」의 순서로 배열한다.

3 The trees in the park / were not planted / by anyone.
풀이 '심어지지 않았다'는 과거시제 수동태 부정형 were not planted로 표현할 수 있으므로, 「주어(The trees in the park)+be동사(were)+not+과거분사(planted)+by+행위자(anyone)」의 순서로 배열한다.
구문 in the park: 명사 The trees를 수식하는 전치사구

STEP 2

1 The animated movie will be released next month.
그 애니메이션 영화는 다음 달에 개봉될 것이다.
풀이 will be released는 미래시제 수동태로, '개봉될 것이다'로 해석한다.
구문 next month: 동사구 will be released를 수식하는 전치사구

2 The photo was taken by the photographer in the studio.
그 사진은 스튜디오에서 그 사진작가에 의해 찍혔다.
풀이 was taken은 과거시제 수동태로, '찍혔다'로 해석한다.

구문 in the studio: 동사구 was taken을 수식하는 전치사구

3 I saw many fish were caught by the fisherman in the lake.

나는 많은 물고기가 호수에서 그 낚시꾼에 의해 잡히는 것을 보았다.

풀이 were caught는 과거시제 수동태로, '잡혔다'로 해석한다. fish가 복수명사이므로 were가 쓰였다.

구문 I saw (that) many fish were caught ~: 동사 saw의 명사절 목적어를 이끄는 접속사 that 생략

4 The meeting will be held in the conference room on the second floor.

그 회의는 2층에 있는 회의실에서 열릴 것이다.

풀이 will be held는 미래시제 수동태로, '열릴 것이다'로 해석한다.

구문 on the second floor: 명사구 the conference room을 수식하는 전치사구

5 At the museum, it is not allowed to bring outside food or beverages.

박물관에는 외부 음식이나 음료를 가져오는 것이 허용되지 않는다.

풀이 is not allowed는 현재시제 수동태 부정형으로, '허용되지 않다'로 해석한다.

구문 ▶ it은 가주어, to bring 이하가 진주어
▶ allow+to-v: ~하는 것을 허락[허용]하다

6 The windows of that building are cleaned by the workers every week.

저 건물의 창문들은 매주 일꾼들에 의해 청소된다.

풀이 are cleaned는 현재시제 수동태로, '청소되다[닦이다]'로 해석한다. 주어가 복수 명사 windows이므로 동사도 복수형 are가 쓰였다.

구문 ▶ of that building: 명사 The windows를 수식하는 전치사구
▶ every+단수 명사: 모든[매] ~

STEP 3

1 (A) were (B) is found (C) transported
Q ②

해석 매우 특별한 유칼립투스 나무가 호주의 과학자들에 의해서 발견되었다. 이 나무들은 그것들의 세포 안에 아주 작은 금 조각들을 가지고 있다. 가장 많은 양의 금은 잎사귀에서 발견된다. 과학자들은 이에 대한 타당한 설명을 한다. 그 금은 아마도 뿌리에 의해 흡수되었을 것이다. 그러고 나서 그것은 나무를 통해 잎사귀로 이동된다.

구문해설

3행 **The greatest** amount of gold is found in the leaves.
▶ the+형용사-est: 가장 ~한 (최상급)

6행 Then **it** is transported *through* the trees *to* the leaves.
▶ it: the gold를 가리키는 대명사
▶ through A to B: A를 통하여 B로

문제해설

1 (A), (B), (C) 문장은 동작의 영향을 받는 대상을 주어로 쓰고 있으므로, 수동태로 써야 한다. 「be동사+과거분사(v-ed)」의 형태로 쓰되, 주어가 단수인지 복수인지를 확인해서 be동사를 선택한다.

Q 호주의 과학자들이 세포에 금 조각을 가진 매우 특별한 유칼립투스 나무를 발견했다는 내용의 글이므로, 글의 제목으로는 ② '과학자들이 나무에서 금을 발견했다'가 가장 적절하다.
① 나무들은 어떻게 물을 흡수하는가
③ 왜 유칼립투스 나무는 호주에서 잘 자라는가

2 (A) was made by
(B) are served

해석 당신은 전국 머스터드의 날에 대해서 알고 있는가? 미국에서는 그것이 매년 8월의 첫 번째 토요일에 기념된다. 그것은 국립 머스터드 박물관에 의해 만들어졌다. 그날에는 맛있는 음식들이 무료로 제공된다. 사람들은 프레첼, 소시지, 그리고 샌드위치를 머스터드와 함께 즐긴다. 물론 케첩은 엄격히 금지된다!

구문해설

1행 ~, it **is celebrated** *on* the first Saturday **of August** each year.
▶ am/are/is+v-ed: ~되다 (수동태)
▶ on+날짜: ~에
▶ of August: 명사구 the first Saturday를 수식하는 전치사구

문제해설

2

머스터드의 날은 미국의 연례 행사이다. 그것은 국립 머스터드 박물관에 (A) 의해 만들어졌다. 이 기념 행사 동안에는 맛있는 음식들이 머스터드와 함께 무료로 (B) 제공된다.

(A), (B) 모두 수동태로 표현해야 하므로, 「be동사+과거분사(+by+행위자)」의 순서로 배열한다.

Wrap Up

p.46

❶ have/has ❷ had ❸ 수동태 ❹ v-ed[과거분사]

1 Most people are influenced by their friends.
2 This song is played by a famous guitarist.
3 Many people were killed during the war.
4 Its price had not changed for a long time.
5 Blue jeans were first made in America.
6 We have visited Vietnam once.

UNIT 05 조동사의 이해

Point 01 can, may p.48

186 May I wear your jacket / today?
내가 네 재킷을 입어도 되니 / 오늘
내가 오늘 네 재킷을 입어도 되니?

187 The cat can climb up the tree / effortlessly.
그 고양이는 그 나무에 오를 수 있다 / 쉽게
그 고양이는 그 나무에 쉽게 오를 수 있다.

188 Frank couldn't open / the jar of pickles.
Frank는 열 수 없었다 / 그 피클 병을
Frank는 그 피클 병을 열 수 없었다.

189 My little sister will be able to have / her own room / in our new house.
내 여동생은 가질 수 있을 것이다 / 그녀 자신의 방을 / 우리의 새 집에
내 여동생은 우리의 새 집에 그녀 자신의 방을 가질 수 있을 것이다.

190 You may wait for me / in the hall. But you may not enter my office.
너는 나를 기다려도 된다 / 복도에서. 하지만 내 사무실에 들어오면 안 된다.
너는 복도에서 나를 기다려도 된다. 하지만 내 사무실에 들어오면 안 된다.

191 Can you bake muffins / for breakfast? I want to eat them, // but I cannot make them.
너는 머핀을 구워 줄 수 있니 / 아침으로? 나는 그것들을 먹고 싶다, // 하지만 나는 그것들을 만들 수 없어
너는 아침으로 머핀을 구워 줄 수 있니? 나는 그것들을 먹고 싶지만 만들 줄 몰라.

192 Chimpanzees are smart. They are able to understand / some words / and use tools.
침팬지들은 똑똑하다. 그들은 몇몇 단어들을 이해할 수 있다 / 그리고 도구를 사용할 수 있다
침팬지들은 똑똑하다. 그들은 몇몇 단어들을 이해할 수 있고 도구를 사용할 수 있다.

Point 02 must/have to/should, had better p.49

196 You should not call your teacher / late at night.
너는 선생님께 전화해서는 안 된다 / 밤늦게
너는 밤늦게 선생님께 전화해서는 안 된다.

197 We must not throw trash / on the street.
우리는 쓰레기를 내던지면 안 된다 / 길에
우리는 길에 쓰레기를 버리면 안 된다.

198 Lisa has to go to the hospital / with her mother.
Lisa는 병원에 가야 한다 / 그녀의 어머니와 함께
Lisa는 그녀의 어머니와 함께 병원에 가야 한다.

199 We will have to wait in line / at the restaurant / for an hour.
우리는 줄을 서서 기다려야 할 것이다 / 식당에서 / 한 시간 동안
우리는 식당에서 한 시간 동안 줄을 서서 기다려야 할 것이다.

200 The test is not difficult. So you don't have to worry / about it.
시험은 어렵지 않다. 그러니 너는 걱정할 필요가 없다 / 그것에 대해
시험은 어렵지 않다. 그러니 너는 그것에 대해 걱정할 필요가 없다.

201 Many guests cannot come / to the party. We had better delay it.
많은 손님들이 올 수 없다 / 그 파티에. 우리는 그것을 미루는 것이 좋겠다
많은 손님들이 그 파티에 올 수 없다. 우리는 그것을 미루는 것이 좋겠다.

202 You had better make / your report simpler. And you should give it to me / by tomorrow.
너는 만드는 것이 좋겠다 / 네 보고서를 더 간단하게. 그리고 그것을 나에게 주어야 한다 / 내일까지
너는 네 보고서를 더 간단하게 만드는 것이 좋겠다. 그리고 내일까지 그것을 나에게 주어야 한다.

Point 03 must, may/might, can/could, cannot p.50

207 His explanation / couldn't be wrong.
그의 설명이 / 틀릴 리가 없다.

208 Jim and Nick might go camping / this summer.
Jim과 Nick은 캠핑을 갈지도 모른다 / 이번 여름에
Jim과 Nick은 이번 여름에 캠핑을 갈지도 모른다.

209 The gym may not be open / on Sundays.
그 체육관은 열지 않을지도 모른다 / 일요일에
그 체육관은 일요일에 열지 않을지도 모른다.

210 Traveling <around the world> / must be a great experience.
여행하는 것은 <전 세계를> / 멋진 경험임이 틀림없다

전 세계를 여행하는 것은 멋진 경험임이 틀림없다.

211 I know / <that Mia is in Busan / now>. So that woman can't be her.
나는 안다 / <Mia가 부산에 있다는 것을 / 지금>. 그러니 저 여자는 그녀일 리가 없다.
나는 Mia가 지금 부산에 있다는 것을 안다. 그러니 저 여자는 그녀일 리가 없다.

212 I can't find my book / in the bag. It might be / on my desk <at home>.
나는 내 책을 찾을 수가 없다 / 가방 안에서. 그것은 있을지도 모른다 / 내 책상 위에 <집에 있는>
나는 가방 안에서 내 책을 찾을 수가 없다. 그것은 집에 있는 내 책상 위에 있을지도 모른다.

213 Brianna has many coins <from different countries>. She must like / collecting coins.
Brianna는 동전들을 많이 가지고 있다 <여러 나라에서 온>. 그녀는 좋아하는 것이 틀림없다 / 동전을 모으는 것을
Brianna는 여러 나라의 동전들을 많이 가지고 있다. 그녀는 동전을 모으는 것을 좋아하는 것이 틀림없다.

Point 04 used to, would p.51

218 I would often go to the park / in my childhood.
나는 종종 그 공원에 가곤 했다 / 어린 시절에
나는 어린 시절에 종종 그 공원에 가곤 했다.

219 Kate used to read comic books / <before she went to bed>.
Kate는 만화책을 읽곤 했다 / <그녀가 자기 전에>
Kate는 자기 전에 만화책을 읽곤 했다.

220 I used to make Christmas cards / for my friends.
나는 크리스마스카드를 만들곤 했다 / 친구들을 위해
나는 친구들을 위해 크리스마스카드를 만들곤 했다.

221 I would visit Jimmy's house / and play games / with him.
나는 Jimmy의 집을 방문하곤 했다 / 그리고 게임을 하곤 했다 / 그와
나는 Jimmy의 집을 방문해서 그와 게임을 하곤 했다.

222 <When I was young>, / my family would go climbing / on weekends.
<내가 어렸을 때>, / 나의 가족은 등산을 가곤 했다 / 주말에
내가 어렸을 때 나의 가족은 주말에 등산을 가곤 했다.

223 Timmy used to be lazy, // but now he is the most diligent student / in his class.
Timmy는 게을렀다, // 하지만 지금 그는 가장 부지런한 학생이다 / 그의 반에서
Timmy는 게을렀지만, 지금 그는 그의 반에서 가장 부지런한 학생이다.

224 There used to be a café / on this street. Bruno would spend time / with his friends / there.
카페가 있었다 / 이 거리에. Bruno는 시간을 보내곤 했다 / 그의 친구들과 / 그곳에서
이 거리에 카페가 있었다. Bruno는 그곳에서 그의 친구들과 시간을 보내곤 했다.

Unit Practice pp.52~53

STEP 1

1 We have to get off / here.
풀이 의무를 나타내는 조동사 have to를 쓰고, 「주어(We)+조동사(have to)+동사원형(get off)+수식어구(here)」의 순서로 배열한다.

2 Because she walked / all day, / Tiffany must be very tired.
풀이 강한 확신을 나타내는 조동사 must를 써서, 「주어(Tiffany)+조동사(must)+동사원형(be)+주격보어(very tired)」의 순서로 배열한다.
구문 because: ~하기 때문에(이유 부사절을 이끄는 접속사)

3 He could run a mile / in six minutes / when he was in high school.
풀이 능력을 나타내는 조동사 can의 과거형 could를 쓰고, 「주어(He)+조동사(could)+동사원형(run)+목적어(a mile)+수식어구(in six minutes) ~」의 순서로 배열한다.
구문 in+시간[기간]: ~ 안에, ~ 동안에

STEP 2

1 May I have your attention, please?
제가 여러분의 주목을 받아도 될까요? (=제게 주목해 주시겠어요?)
풀이 「May I ~?」는 부탁하는 표현으로 '~해도 될까요?'로 해석한다. may는 허가를 나타내는 조동사이다.

2 The flowers should not be picked without permission.
허락 없이 꽃을 꺾어서는 안 된다.
풀이 금지를 나타내는 조동사 should not은 '~해서는 안 된다'로 해석한다.
구문 ▶ be picked: 「am/are/is+v-ed」, ~되다 (수동태)
▶ without: ~ 없이

3 You don't have to apologize for not knowing something.
너는 무언가를 알지 못하는 것에 대해 사과할 필요가 없다.

풀이 불필요를 나타내는 조동사 don't have to는 '~할 필요가 없다'로 해석한다.

구문 not knowing something: 전치사 for의 동명사구 목적어

4 That animal can't be a bird, since it doesn't have any wings.

저 동물은 날개가 없기 때문에 새일 리가 없다.

풀이 강한 확신을 나타내는 조동사 can't[cannot]는 '~일 리가 없다'로 해석한다.

구문 ▶ since: ~하기 때문에(이유 부사절을 이끄는 접속사)

▶ it: That animal을 가리키는 대명사

5 You had better not look at your phone when you cross the street.

너는 길을 건널 때 너의 휴대 전화를 안 보는 게 낫다.

풀이 강한 충고를 나타내는 조동사 had better not은 '~을 안 하는 게 낫다'로 해석한다.

구문 when: ~할 때(시간 부사절을 이끄는 접속사)

6 Our school used to have a uniform policy, but now we can wear our own clothes.

우리 학교는 교복 방침을 가지고 있었지만, 지금 우리는 사복을 입을 수 있다.

풀이 과거의 상태를 나타내는 조동사 used to는 '~이었다'로 해석한다.

구문 but: '~지만[하나]'의 뜻으로, 두 개의 절 Our ~ policy와 now ~ clothes를 연결

STEP 3

1 (A) can (B) must (C) have to

Q ①

해석 베이킹을 좋아하시나요? 그렇다면 5월 5일에 있는 제3회 서울 베이커리 축제에 오세요. 여러분은 자신만의 특별한 케이크를 만들어서 그것을 집에 가져갈 수 있습니다. 모든 성인들은 이 특별한 행사에 참여해도 되지만, 어린이들은 5세 이상이어야 합니다. 여러분은 단지 입장권 값으로 15,000원을 내야 합니다. 이 멋진 기회를 놓치지 마세요!

구문해설

1행 Then **come** to the third Seoul Bakery Festival *on May 5*.

▶ come: 주어를 생략하고 동사원형으로 시작하는 명령문(~하라)

▶ on+날짜: ~에

2행 You can make **your own special cake** ~.

▶ one's own+명사: 자기[자신]의 ~

3행 All adults **may** join this special event, ~.

▶ may: ~해도 된다 (허가)

문제해설

1 (A) 가능을 나타내는 조동사 can이 적절하다.

(B) 의무를 나타내는 조동사 must가 적절하다.

(C) 의무를 나타내는 조동사 have to가 적절하다.

Q 직접 케이크를 만들 수 있는 베이커리 축제를 홍보하는 내용이므로, ①이 글의 목적으로 가장 적절하다.

2 (A) babies are able to sense

(B) they had better step outside

해석 (A) 연구에 따르면 아기들은 부모의 감정을 감지할 수 있다. 게다가 화가 난 부모는 그들의 아기들의 정신적 발달에 해를 끼칠 수도 있다. 아기들이 시끄러운 말다툼을 들을 때, 그들은 스트레스를 경험한다. 이 스트레스는 이후 삶에서 그들을 더 불안하게 할 수 있다. 따라서 부모는 목소리를 차분하게 유지해야 한다. (B) 정말 말다툼이 필요할 때, 그들은 밖으로 나가는 것이 낫다.

구문해설

3행 This stress can **make them *more anxious*** later in life.

▶ make+목적어+목적격보어(형용사): 목적어를 ~하게 만들다

▶ more+형용사: 더 ~한 (비교급)

4행 Therefore, parents should **keep their voices calm**.

▶ keep+목적어+목적격보어(형용사): 목적어를 ~하게 유지하다

문제해설

2 (A) '~할 수 있다'라는 의미의 능력을 나타내는 조동사 are able to를 써서, 「주어(babies)+조동사(are able to)+동사원형(sense)」의 순서로 배열한다.

(B) '~하는 것이 낫다'라는 의미의 강한 충고를 나타내는 조동사 had better를 써서, 「주어(they)+조동사(had better)+동사원형(step outside)」의 순서로 배열한다.

Wrap Up

p.54

❶ can ❷ 의무 ❸ used to ❹ 동사원형

1 She must be at least forty years old.

2 You may[can] take my umbrella.

3 He had better listen to his parents' advice.

4 A big maple tree used to stand there.

5 He would[used to] give flowers to me once a month.

6 You must[have to/should] wear your seat belt in the car.

UNIT 06 수식어구의 쓰임

Point 01 형용사와 부사 p.56

228 We want to drink / something cold.
우리는 마시기를 원한다 / 차가운 무언가를
우리는 차가운 무언가를 마시기를 원한다.

229 I'm pretty sure / <that Jessica will forgive you>.
나는 꽤 확신한다 / <Jessica가 너를 용서할 거라고>
나는 Jessica가 너를 용서할 거라고 꽤 확신한다.

230 I'm terribly sorry / about the delay. We won't let this happen / again.
대단히 죄송합니다 / 지연에 대해. 저희는 이런 일이 일어나지 않도록 하겠습니다 / 다시는
지연되어 대단히 죄송합니다. 저희는 이런 일이 다시는 일어나지 않도록 하겠습니다.

231 The baseball team has played / very well / since last season.
그 야구팀은 경기를 해왔다 / 매우 잘 / 지난 시즌 이후로
그 야구팀은 지난 시즌 이후로 경기를 매우 잘해 왔다.

232 A tiger suddenly / attacked a man. Fortunately, / he wasn't seriously hurt.
호랑이 한 마리가 갑자기 / 한 남자를 공격했다. 다행히도, / 그는 심하게 다치지 않았다.

233 The teacher smiled kindly / at the students / and praised their nice drawings.
선생님은 친절하게 웃으셨다 / 학생들에게 / 그리고 그들의 멋진 그림을 칭찬하셨다
선생님은 학생들에게 친절하게 웃으셨고 그들의 멋진 그림을 칭찬하셨다.

234 Do you know / anyone good at dancing? I really want to learn / to dance.
너는 알고 있니 / 춤을 잘 추는 누군가를? 나는 정말 배우고 싶어 / 춤추는 것을
너는 춤을 잘 추는 누군가를 알고 있니? 나는 정말 춤추는 것을 배우고 싶어.

Point 02 분사와 전치사구 p.57

239 Do you know / the boy <swimming in the pool>?
너는 아니 / 남자아이를 <수영장에서 수영하고 있는>
너는 수영장에서 수영하고 있는 남자아이를 아니?

240 Can I take a seat <next to you>?
자리에 앉아도 되나요 <당신 옆에 있는>
당신 옆 자리에 앉아도 되나요?

241 They ran / towards each other / and hugged tightly.
그들은 달려갔다 / 서로를 향해 / 그리고 꽉 안았다
그들은 서로를 향해 달려가서 꽉 안았다.

242 We gave the police officer / the wallet <found on the bus>.
우리는 경찰관에게 주었다 / 지갑을 <버스에서 발견된>
우리는 경찰관에게 버스에서 발견된 지갑을 주었다.

243 The dishes <served in this restaurant> / are expensive, // but they taste great.
요리들은 <이 식당에서 제공되는> / 비싸다, // 하지만 그것들은 맛이 매우 좋다
이 식당에서 제공되는 요리들은 비싸지만, 그것들은 맛이 매우 좋다.

244 The shocking news <about the war> spread / throughout the world.
충격적인 뉴스는 <그 전쟁에 관한> 퍼져 나갔다 / 전 세계로
그 전쟁에 관한 충격적인 뉴스는 전 세계로 퍼져 나갔다.

245 The trees <outside my window> / block the light. But the birds <singing in the trees> / make me feel good.
나무들은 <내 창문 밖에 있는> / 빛을 차단한다. 하지만 새들은 <그 나무에서 노래하는> / 나를 기분 좋게 만든다
내 창문 밖에 있는 나무들은 빛을 차단한다. 하지만 그 나무에서 노래하는 새들은 나를 기분 좋게 만든다.

Unit Practice pp.58~59

STEP 1

1 We gave the police officer / the wallet / found on the bus.
풀이 과거분사구 found on the bus가 명사 the wallet을 뒤에서 수식하도록 배열한다.
구문 give+간접목적어+직접목적어: ~에게 …을 주다

2 Unfortunately, / Ella spilled[spilt] some coffee / on her new skirt.
풀이 부사 Unfortunately가 문장 맨 앞에서 문장 전체를 수식하고 있다. 전치사구 on her new skirt는 동사 spilled[spilt]를 수식한다.

3 The backpack / with the blue zipper / belongs to

him.

풀이 전치사구 with the blue zipper가 명사 The backpack을 뒤에서 수식한다.

STEP 2

1 I bought a novel written by a famous author.

나는 유명한 작가에 의해 쓰여진 소설을 샀다.

풀이 과거분사구 written ~ author가 명사 a novel을 뒤에서 수식하며, 과거분사는 '~해진/된'으로 해석한다.

2 We saw a beautiful rainbow on our way to school.

우리는 학교로 가는 길에 아름다운 무지개를 보았다.

풀이 전치사구 on our way to school이 동사 saw를 수식한다.

구문 on one's way to: ~로 가는 길[도중]에

3 The sleeping baby must be dreaming of something happy.

자고 있는 그 아기는 행복한 무언가를 꿈꾸고 있는 것이 틀림없다.

풀이 현재분사 sleeping이 명사 baby를 수식하며 현재분사는 '~하는/하고 있는'으로 해석한다. 형용사 happy가 -thing으로 끝나는 대명사 something을 뒤에서 수식한다.

구문 ▶ must: ~임이 틀림없다 (강한 확신)
▶ dream of: ~을 꿈꾸다

4 She has saved so much money over the years.

그녀는 수년 간 정말 많은 돈을 저축해 왔다.

풀이 부사 so가 형용사 much를 수식한다.

구문 have/has+v-ed: ~해 왔다 (현재완료, 계속)

5 My friend told me a story scarier than any horror movie.

내 친구는 내게 다른 어떤 공포영화보다 더 무서운 이야기를 해 주었다.

풀이 비교급 형용사구 scarier ~ movie가 명사 a story를 뒤에서 수식한다.

구문 비교급+than: ~보다 더 …한

6 In the summer, the sun shines brightly for up to fifteen hours.

여름에 태양은 열다섯 시간까지 밝게 빛난다.

풀이 부사 brightly와 전치사구 for up to fifteen hours가 동사 shines를 수식한다.

구문 for+시간: ~ 동안

STEP 3

1 (A) searching (B) found
Q ②

해석 요리하는 것을 좋아하지만 도움이 필요하신가요? 여러분의 문제를 스마트 냉장고로 해결하세요. 그것은 여러분이 필요한 모든 것을 위한 프로그램들을 가지고 있습니다. 조리법 아이디어를 (A)찾는 사람들에게 이 냉장고는 인터넷에서 (B)찾아진 조리법들을 추천해 줍니다. 그리고 냉장고가 그것 안에 있는 음식을 확인한 뒤 여러분의 식료품은 매주 냉장고에 의해 주문됩니다. 얼마나 놀라운가요!

구문해설

2행 It has programs **for all your needs**.
▶ 명사 programs를 수식하는 전치사구

5행 And each week, your groceries **are ordered by the refrigerator** after it reviews the food *inside* ***it***.
▶ am/are/is+v-ed+by+행위자: ~에 의해 …되다 (수동태)
▶ inside it: 명사 the food를 수식하는 전치사구
▶ it: the refrigerator를 가리키는 대명사

7행 **How amazing!**
▶ How+형용사!: 얼마나 ~한가! (감탄문)

문제해설

1 (A) 문맥상 '~하는'이라는 능동의 의미로 대명사 anyone을 수식해야 하므로, 현재분사 searching이 적절하다.
(B) 문맥상 '~해진'이라는 수동의 의미로 명사 recipes를 수식해야 하므로, 과거분사 found가 적절하다.

Q 조리법을 추천하거나 냉장고 안에 있는 식료품을 확인해서 주문해 주지만, 상한 음식을 알려 준다고 하지는 않았으므로, 글의 내용과 일치하지 않는 것은 ②이다.

2 (A) love strange things
(B) from different women covers every wall of the museum

해석 (A)당신은 기묘한 것들을 매우 좋아하는가? 그렇다면 터키에 있는 머리카락 박물관을 방문하라. Chez Galip에 의해 만들어진 그 기묘한 명소는 무서워 보인다. 그 박물관에는 16,000개의 머리카락 표본이 있다. 그곳은 Galip의 도자기 가게 아래에 위치한다. (B)여러 여성들로부터 온 머리카락이 그 박물관의 모든 벽을 뒤덮고 있다.

구문해설

1행 The strange attraction **created by Chez Galip** *looks scary*.
▶ created by Chez Galip: 명사구 The strange attraction을 수식하는 과거분사구
▶ look+형용사: ~하게 보이다

3행 It **is located** *under Galip's pottery shop*.
▶ am/are/is+v-ed: ~되다 (수동태)
▶ under ~ shop: 동사구 is located를 수식하는 전치사구

문제해설

2 (A) 형용사 strange가 things를 앞에서 수식하도록 배열한다.
(B) 전치사구 from different women과 of the museum이 명사 Hair와 명사구 every wall을 각각 뒤에서 수식하도록 배열한다.

Point 03 형용사 역할의 to부정사 p.60

250 The child needs / a toy <to play with>.
그 아이는 필요하다 / 장난감이 <가지고 놀>
그 아이는 가지고 놀 장난감이 필요하다.

251 Matt is building / a house <to live in>.
Matt는 짓고 있다 / 집을 <거주할>
Matt는 거주할 집을 짓고 있다.

252 You can choose / a movie <to watch with me>.
너는 골라도 된다 / 영화 한 편을 <나와 함께 볼>
너는 나와 함께 볼 영화 한 편을 골라도 된다.

253 One way <to lose weight> / is to exercise every day.
한 가지 방법은 <살을 빼는> / 매일 운동하는 것이다
살을 빼는 한 가지 방법은 매일 운동하는 것이다.

254 I spilled sauce / on my hand. I need / a napkin <to clean it off>.
나는 소스를 쏟았다 / 내 손에. 나는 필요하다 / 냅킨이 <그것을 닦아 낼>
나는 내 손에 소스를 쏟았다. 나는 그것을 닦아 낼 냅킨이 필요하다.

255 Joining a club / will give you / a chance <to make new friends>.
동아리에 가입하는 것은 / 너에게 줄 것이다 / 기회를 <새로운 친구들을 사귈>
동아리에 가입하는 것은 너에게 새로운 친구들을 사귈 기회를 줄 것이다.

256 Erica has a baby <to take care of>. So she doesn't have / much time <to sleep> / these days.
Erica는 아기를 가지고 있다 <돌볼>. 그래서 그녀는 가지고 있지 않다 / 많은 시간을 <잠을 잘> / 요즘
Erica는 돌볼 아기가 있다. 그래서 그녀는 요즘 잠을 잘 시간이 많지 않다.

Point 04 부사 역할의 to부정사 p.61

260 We decided / to take a bus / to save money.
우리는 결정했다 / 버스를 타기로 / 돈을 절약하기 위해
우리는 돈을 절약하기 위해 버스를 타기로 결정했다.

261 Sam lived / to have his 101st birthday party.
Sam은 살아서 / 자신의 101번째 생일 파티를 열었다.

262 Kelly must be rich / to buy such an expensive car.
Kelly는 부자임이 틀림없다 / 그 정도의 비싼 차를 사는 걸 보면
그 정도의 비싼 차를 사는 걸 보면 Kelly는 부자임이 틀림없다.

263 I turned on the morning news / to check the weather.
나는 아침 뉴스를 틀었다 / 날씨를 확인하기 위해
나는 날씨를 확인하기 위해 아침 뉴스를 틀었다.

264 Kevin woke up late / in the morning. He ran fast / to catch the bus.
Kevin은 늦잠을 잤다 / 아침에. 그는 빠르게 달렸다 / 버스를 타기 위해
Kevin은 아침에 늦잠을 잤다. 그는 버스를 타기 위해 빠르게 달렸다.

265 I am sorry / to inform you / <that the festival has been canceled>.
유감입니다 / 여러분에게 알려 드리게 되어 / <축제가 취소되었다는 것을>
여러분에게 축제가 취소되었다는 것을 알려 드리게 되어 유감입니다.

266 That boy must be a diligent student / to get such good grades. He will grow up / to be successful.
저 소년은 성실한 학생임이 틀림없다 / 그렇게 좋은 점수를 얻는 것을 보면. 그는 커서 / 성공할 것이다.
그렇게 좋은 점수를 얻는 것을 보면 저 소년은 성실한 학생임이 틀림없다. 그는 커서 성공할 것이다.

Unit Practice pp.62~63

STEP 1

1 Do you have / anything to ask / about the assignment?
풀이 to부정사구 to ask ~ assignment가 대명사 anything을 뒤에서 수식하도록 배열한다.

2 The athlete was happy / to receive a medal.
풀이 감정 형용사 happy의 원인을 나타내는 to부정사구 to receive a medal이 happy 뒤에 오도록 배열한다.

3 She didn't have / time to take a shower / this morning.
풀이 형용사 역할의 to부정사구 to take a shower가 명사 time을 뒤에서 수식하도록 배열한다.

STEP 2

1 Can I have another opportunity to try again?
다시 시도할 또 다른 기회를 가져도 되니?
풀이 to try again은 명사 opportunity를 뒤에서 수식하는 형용

사 역할의 to부정사구로, '~할[하는]'으로 해석한다.

2 He must be busy not to reply to my text message.
그가 내 문자 메시지에 답장을 안 하는 것을 보면 바쁜 것이 틀림없다.
풀이 not to ~ message는 형용사 busy의 판단의 근거를 나타내는 부사 역할의 to부정사구로, '~하다니[하는 것을 보면]'로 해석한다.
구문 ▶ must be: ~임이 틀림없다 (강한 확신)
▶ not to reply: to부정사의 부정형

3 Mason quit his job to start his own business.
Mason은 자신의 사업을 시작하기 위해 직장을 그만뒀다.
풀이 to start ~ business는 동사 quit의 목적을 나타내는 부사 역할의 to부정사구로, '~하기 위해'로 해석한다.

4 I booked a hotel to stay in during our vacation.
나는 우리의 휴가 동안 머무를 호텔을 예약했다.
풀이 to stay ~ vacation은 명사 a hotel을 뒤에서 수식하는 형용사 역할의 to부정사구로, '~할[하는]'로 해석한다.
구문 ▶ a hotel to stay in: 명사 a hotel은 문장의 목적어이면서 동시에 전치사 in의 목적어
▶ during our vacation: 동사구 stay in을 수식하는 전치사구

5 I felt bored because I had nothing to watch on TV.
나는 TV에서 볼 것이 아무것도 없었기 때문에 지루했다.
풀이 to watch on TV는 대명사 nothing을 수식하는 형용사 역할의 to부정사구로 '~할[하는]'로 해석한다.
구문 feel+형용사: ~하게 느끼다

6 Jenny was embarrassed to call her teacher "Mom" by mistake.
Jenny는 그녀의 선생님을 실수로 '엄마'라고 불러서 당황했다.
풀이 to call ~ mistake는 감정 형용사 embarrassed의 원인을 나타내는 부사 역할의 to부정사구로, '~해서[하게 되어서]'로 해석한다.
구문 ▶ call+목적어+목적격보어(명사): 목적어를 ~라고 부르다
▶ by mistake: 실수로

STEP 3

1 ③
Q (1) T (2) F

해석 요즘에는 많은 사람들이 향수를 사용한다. 그러나 그것을 사용한 최초의 사람들은 고대 이집트인들이었다. 그들은 장례식을 위해 향기가 나는 기름을 사용했다. 그 기름은 죽은 이들을 악으로부터 보호하기 위해 시체 위에 발라졌다. 그러나, 향수는 사회적으로 중요한 사람들만을 위한 것이었다. 투탕카멘왕의 무덤이 발견되었을 때, 여러 개의 향수 병이 그것 안에 있었다.

구문해설

1행 But the first people to use it **were** the ancient Egyptians.
▶ 주어가 복수 명사 people이므로 be동사 복수형 were 사용

3행 The oils **were put** onto dead bodies to *protect* them *from* evil.
▶ was/were+v-ed: ~되었다 (과거시제 수동태)
▶ protect A from B: A를 B로부터 보호하다

6행 ~, several bottles of perfume were inside **it**.
▶ the grave of King Tutankhamun을 가리키는 대명사

문제해설

1 ③ to protect는 동사구 were put onto를 수식하는 부사 역할의 to부정사이다.
① to use는 명사구 the first people을 수식하는 형용사 역할의 to부정사
② scented는 명사 oils를 수식하는 형용사 역할의 과거분사
④ of King Tutankhamun은 명사 the grave를 수식하는 형용사 역할의 전치사구

Q (1) 2행 used scented oils for funerals에서 향수가 장례식에서 사용되었음을 알 수 있다.
(2) 4행 perfume was only for socially important people에서 향수는 사회적으로 중요한 사람들만 사용했음을 알 수 있다.

2 Her son was surprised to see only rotten apples.

해석 한 여자의 아들이 몇몇 나쁜 친구들을 사귀었다. 그에게 교훈을 가르치기 위해, 그 여자는 계획을 세웠다. 그들은 함께 열 개의 맛있는 사과와 한 개의 썩은 사과를 자루 안에 넣었다. 나중에 그들은 자루를 열었다. 그녀의 아들은 썩은 사과들만 있는 것을 보고 놀랐다. 그는 썩은 사과 하나가 나머지를 망칠 수 있다는 것을 배웠다.

구문해설

1행 To **teach him a lesson**, the woman made a plan.
▶ teach+간접목적어+직접목적어: ~에게 …을 가르치다

2행 Together, they **put** ten delicious apples and a rotten *one* **into** a bag.
▶ put A into B: A를 B 안에 넣다
▶ one: apple을 가리키는 대명사

3행 He learned **that** one rotten apple can spoil the rest.
▶ that: 동사 learned의 명사절 목적어를 이끄는 접속사

문제해설

2 감정 형용사 surprised 뒤에 감정의 원인을 나타내는 to부정사구 to see ~ apples가 오도록 배열한다.

Wrap Up p.64

❶ 과거분사 ❷ 형용사 ❸ 부사

1 You can[may] bring a book to read.
2 I want to live in a house made of brick.
3 Henry bought me a nice dress.
(=Henry bought a nice dress for me.)
4 The little girl grew up to become a firefighter.
5 A growing child needs plenty of sleep.
6 I called my boyfriend to wake him up.

UNIT 07 비교 표현

Point 01 원급·비교급 구문 p.66

271 Today is as cold / as yesterday.
오늘은 춥다 / 어제만큼
오늘은 어제만큼 춥다.

272 Exercise is as important / as a balanced diet.
운동은 중요하다 / 균형 잡힌 식사만큼
운동은 균형 잡힌 식사만큼 중요하다.

273 Julie arrived at the airport earlier / than her friends.
Julie는 공항에 더 일찍 도착했다 / 그녀의 친구들보다
Julie는 그녀의 친구들보다 더 일찍 공항에 도착했다.

274 Elephants are more intelligent / than most animals.
코끼리가 더 똑똑하다 / 대부분의 동물들보다
코끼리가 대부분의 동물들보다 더 똑똑하다.

275 The baby sleeps as peacefully / as an angel.
그 아기는 평온하게 잔다 / 천사처럼
그 아기는 천사처럼 평온하게 잔다.

276 People say / <that vegetables are a lot healthier / than meat>.
사람들은 말한다 / <채소가 훨씬 더 건강에 좋다고 / 고기보다>
사람들은 채소가 고기보다 훨씬 더 건강에 좋다고 말한다.

277 This couch is more comfortable / than that one. And its design is prettier.
이 소파는 더 편안하다 / 저것보다. 그리고 그것의 디자인이 더 예쁘다.
이 소파는 저것보다 더 편안하다. 그리고 그것의 디자인이 더 예쁘다.

Point 02 원급·비교급 표현 p.67

282 Gia studied as hard / as possible / for the midterm exam.
Gia는 열심히 공부했다 / 가능한 한 / 중간고사를 위해
Gia는 중간고사를 위해 가능한 한 열심히 공부했다.

283 That snake is three times as long / as this snake.
저 뱀은 세 배만큼 길다 / 이 뱀보다
저 뱀은 이 뱀보다 세 배만큼 길다.

284 The earlier you buy the ticket, // the lower the price is.
네가 표를 일찍 구매할수록, // 가격이 더 낮다.

285 Eating out costs two times more / than eating / at home.
외식하는 것은 비용이 두 배는 더 든다 / 먹는 것보다 / 집에서
외식하는 것은 집에서 먹는 것보다 비용이 두 배는 더 든다.

286 Leo is growing taller and taller / every day. Now he is as tall / as his father.
Leo는 점점 더 키가 크고 있다 / 매일. 이제 그는 키가 크다 / 자기 아버지만큼
Leo는 매일 점점 더 키가 크고 있다. 이제 그는 자기 아버지만큼 키가 크다.

287 The more popular a mall becomes, // the more crowded it gets.
쇼핑센터가 인기 있을수록, // 그곳은 더 붐비게 된다.

288 <Since you have prepared for the exam / as much / as you can>, / you will pass it.
<네가 그 시험을 준비했기 때문에 / 많이 / 네가 할 수 있는 한>, / 너는 그것에 합격할 것이다
네가 할 수 있는 한 많이 그 시험을 준비했기 때문에 너는 합격할 것이다.

Unit Practice pp.68~69

STEP ❶

1 The earlier you buy the ticket, / the lower the price is.
풀이 '~할수록 더 …하다'의 비교급 표현은 「the+비교급 ~, the+비교급 ...」으로 표현한다.

2 The new restaurant is far busier / than the old one.

풀이 '~보다 더 …한'이라는 비교급 구문은 「비교급+than」으로 표현한다. 또한 '훨씬'이라는 비교급 강조 부사 far는 비교급 앞에 쓴다.

구문 one: restaurant를 가리키는 대명사

3 That antique watch / is ten times more expensive / than mine.

풀이 '~보다 …배는 ~한'의 비교급 표현은 「배수사+비교급+than」으로 표현한다.

구문 mine: 나의 것 (소유격 대명사)

STEP 2

1 This gold ring is a lot more expensive than the silver one.

이 금반지는 그 은반지보다 훨씬 더 비싸다.

풀이 a lot은 비교급 more expensive를 강조하는 부사이며, '훨씬'으로 해석한다.

구문 one: ring을 가리키는 대명사

2 The package needs to be delivered as soon as possible.

그 소포는 가능한 한 빨리 배달될 필요가 있다.

풀이 「as+부사+as possible」은 원급을 사용한 비교 표현으로 '가능한 한 ~하게'로 해석한다.

구문 ▶ need to-v: ~하는 것이 필요하다
▶ be delivered: 「be v-ed」 ~되다(수동태)

3 The fireworks exploded as loud as thunder in the night sky.

폭죽은 밤 하늘에서 천둥만큼 큰 소리로 터졌다.

풀이 「as+부사+as」는 비교를 표현하는 원급 구문으로 '~만큼 …하게'로 해석한다.

구문 in the night sky: 동사 exploded를 수식하는 전치사구

4 Sometimes taking the stairs is faster than taking the elevator.

가끔은 계단을 이용하는 것이 엘리베이터를 이용하는 것보다 더 빠르다.

풀이 「비교급+than」은 '~보다 더 …한/하게'라는 의미의 비교급 구문이다.

구문 ▶ taking the stairs: 동명사구 주어
▶ taking the elevator: 주어 taking the stairs의 비교 대상으로 쓰인 동명사구

5 The whale is more than five times heavier than the giraffe.

그 고래는 그 기린보다 다섯 배 이상은 더 무겁다.

풀이 「배수사+비교급+than」은 '~보다 …배는 더 ~한/하게'로 해석한다.

구문 more than: ~ 이상(의)

6 The rocket soared higher and higher into the air until it was almost out of sight.

그 로켓은 거의 보이지 않을 때까지 하늘로 점점 더 높이 솟구쳐 올라갔다.

풀이 「비교급+and+비교급」은 '점점 더 ~한/하게'로 해석한다.

구문 until: ~까지

STEP 3

1 ②, ③
Q ②

해석 많은 사람들이 에너지바가 초코바보다 더 건강에 좋다고 생각한다. 그러나 실제로 그것들은 초코바만큼 안 좋다. 그것들은 보통 그 안에 다량의 지방과 당분을 갖고 있다. 따라서 그것들은 열량이 높다. 게다가 그것들은 대개 초코바보다 두 배만큼 비싸다. 그러므로 더 많은 에너지를 얻기 위해, 대신 신선한 과일을 먹어 보라. 그것이 훨씬 더 나은 선택이다.

구문해설

1행 Many people think (**that**) energy bars are *healthier than* candy bars.
▶ (that): 동사 think의 명사절 목적어를 이끄는 접속사가 생략됨
▶ 비교급+than: ~보다 더 …한

2행 **They** *often* have a lot of fat and sugar in them.
▶ They: energy bars를 가리키는 대명사
▶ often: '자주', '종종'이라는 의미의 빈도부사로, 주로 일반동사 앞에 위치

5행 So **to get more energy**, *try* fresh fruit instead.
▶ to ~ energy: 부사 역할의 to부정사구 (목적)
▶ try: ~하라(명령문)

문제해설

1 '~만큼 …한'의 원급 비교 구문은 「as+형용사(원급)+as」로 써야 하므로, 비교급 ②worse를 원급 bad로 고쳐야 한다. 또한 '~배만큼 …한'은 「배수사+as+형용사(원급)+as」로 표현하므로, ③so를 as로 고쳐야 한다.

Q 에너지바는 지방과 당분이 많아 열량이 높으므로 초코바만큼이나 건강에 좋지 않다는 것을 알려 주는 내용이므로, 글의 요지로 가장 적절한 것은 ②이다.

2 The more you lick it, the brighter it becomes.

해석 아이스크림이 어둠 속에서 빛날 수 있을까? 영국인 발명가 Charlie Francis 덕분에, 그것은 정말 가능하다! 그는 해파리로부터 얻은 단백질을 아이스크림에 첨가한다. 이 단백질들은 혀에 닿을 때 작용하기 시작한다. 그래서 당신이 그 아이스크림을 핥을 때 그것은 빛난다. 당신이 그것을 많이 핥을수록 그것은 더 밝아진다. 그것은 대

부분의 아이스크림보다 훨씬 더 비싸지만, 많은 사람들이 그것을 먹어 보고 싶어 한다.

구문해설

2행 He **adds** proteins *from jellyfish* **to** ice cream.

▶ add A to B: A를 B에 첨가하다

▶ from jellyfish: 명사 proteins를 수식하는 전치사구

These proteins **start to work** when they touch the tongue.

▶ start+to-v[v-ing]: ~하기 시작하다

문제해설

2 '~할수록 더 …하다'는 표현은 「the+비교급 ~, the+비교급 ...」으로 나타내므로, 부사 much와 형용사 bright를 비교급 more와 brighter로 바꿔 쓴다. it은 the ice cream을 가리키는 대명사이다.

Point 03 최상급 구문 p.70

293 Kevin gets up the earliest / in his family.
Kevin은 가장 일찍 일어난다 / 그의 가족 중에서
Kevin은 그의 가족 중에서 가장 일찍 일어난다.

294 The roller coaster is / the scariest ride <in this amusement park>.
그 롤러코스터는 ~이다 / 가장 무서운 놀이 기구 <이 놀이공원에서>
그 롤러코스터는 이 놀이공원에서 가장 무서운 놀이 기구이다.

295 Melissa is / by far the most talented / among us.
Melissa는 ~이다 / 단연코 가장 재능이 있는 / 우리 중
Melissa는 단연코 우리 중 가장 재능이 있다.

296 Rome is / one of the most wonderful cities <in the world>.
로마는 ~이다 / 가장 멋진 도시 중 하나 <세계에서>
로마는 세계에서 가장 멋진 도시 중 하나이다.

297 The tornado was / one of the worst disasters <in history>.
그 토네이도는 ~이었다 / 최악의 재난 중 하나 <역사상>
그 토네이도는 역사상 최악의 재난 중 하나였다.

298 This cooking video is / one of the most popular videos <on the website>.
이 요리 영상은 ~이다 / 가장 인기 있는 영상 중 하나 <그 웹사이트에서>
이 요리 영상은 그 웹사이트에서 가장 인기 있는 영상 중 하나이다.

299 That black horse is / the fastest horse <on this farm>. She is also the most beautiful one.
저 검은색 말은 ~이다 / 가장 빠른 말 <이 농장에서>. 그녀는 또한 가장 아름다운 말이다.
저 검은색 말은 이 농장에서 가장 빠른 말이다. 그녀는 또한 가장 아름다운 말이기도 하다.

Point 04 최상급 표현 p.71

304 This test is harder / than any other test.
이 시험은 더 어렵다 / 다른 어떤 시험보다도
이 시험은 다른 어떤 시험보다도 더 어렵다.

305 No player plays tennis better / than Cathy.
어떤 선수도 테니스를 더 잘하지 않는다 / Cathy보다
어떤 선수도 Cathy보다 테니스를 더 잘하지 않는다.

306 My brother is taller / than any other student <in his class>.
내 남동생은 키가 더 크다 / 다른 어떤 학생보다도 <그의 반의>
내 남동생은 그의 반의 다른 어떤 학생보다도 키가 더 크다.

307 No one <in the room> / finished the puzzle as fast / as Howard.
어떤 사람도 <그 방에 있던> / 퍼즐을 빨리 끝내지 않았다 / Howard만큼
그 방에 있던 어떤 사람도 Howard만큼 빨리 퍼즐을 끝내지 않았다.

308 This is not a famous horror movie, // but it's scarier / than any other one.
이것은 유명한 공포 영화는 아니다, // 하지만 그것은 더 무섭다 / 다른 어떤 것보다도
이것은 유명한 공포 영화는 아니지만, 그것은 다른 어떤 것보다도 더 무섭다.

309 Everyone loves Amanda's cookies. No one can make cookies better / than her.
모든 사람이 Amanda의 쿠키를 매우 좋아한다. 어떤 사람도 쿠키를 더 잘 만들 수 없다 / 그녀보다
모든 사람이 Amanda의 쿠키를 매우 좋아한다. 어떤 사람도 그녀보다 쿠키를 더 잘 만들 수 없다.

310 My family is more precious / than any other thing / to me. They always give me / a lot of support.
우리 가족은 더 소중하다 / 다른 어떤 것보다 / 나에게. 그들은 나에게 항상 준다 / 많은 지지를
우리 가족은 나에게 다른 어떤 것보다도 더 소중하다. 그들은 항상 나에게 많은 지지를 준다.

Unit Practice pp.72~73

STEP 1

1 Kevin gets up the earliest / in his family.

풀이 '~ 안에서[중에서] 가장 …하게'는 「the+최상급+of/in/among+비교 범위」로 표현한다.

2 The cheetah runs faster / than any other animal.

풀이 '다른 어떤 ~보다도 더 …하게'라는 최상급 표현은 「비교급+than any other+단수 명사」로 나타낸다.

3 The flu is / one of the most common diseases / these days.

풀이 '가장 ~한 것들 중 하나'는 최상급 구문 「one of the+최상급+복수 명사」로 표현한다.

구문 these days: 요즘에는

STEP 2

1 This was one of the most difficult questions on the exam.

이것이 시험에서 가장 어려운 문제들 중 하나였다.

풀이 「one of the+최상급+복수 명사」는 '가장 ~한 것들 중 하나'로 해석한다.

2 From my experience, no other thing is better than being loved.

내 경험에 비추어 볼 때 어떤 것도 사랑받는 것보다 더 좋지 않다.

풀이 「no (other)+명사+비교급+than A」는 '어떤 ~도 A보다 더 …하지 않은/않게'로 해석한다.

구문 being loved: 전치사 than의 동명사구 목적어

3 Chloe said this book is by far the most interesting one of the series.

Chloe는 이 책이 시리즈 중에서 단연코 가장 흥미로운 책이라고 말했다.

풀이 「the+최상급(+명사)+of ~」는 '~ 중에서 가장 ~한/하게'로 해석한다. 또한 최상급 앞 by far는 최상급 강조 표현으로 '단연코'로 해석한다.

구문 ▶ Chloe said (that) this book ~: 동사 said의 명사절 목적어를 이끄는 접속사가 생략됨

▶ one: book을 가리키는 대명사

4 When I heard her sing, I thought that no singer could sing a song as well as Bella.

내가 그녀의 노래를 들었을 때, 나는 어떤 가수도 Bella만큼 노래를 잘할 수 없다고 생각했다.

풀이 「no (other)+명사+as+부사+as A」는 '어떤 ~도 A만큼 …하지 않게'로 해석한다.

구문 ▶ when: ~할 때

▶ hear+목적어+목적격보어(동사원형): 목적어가 ~하는 것을 듣다

▶ that: 동사 thought의 명사절 목적어를 이끄는 접속사

5 The most delicious dessert among all the ones in the bakery is the chocolate cake.

그 제과점에 있는 모든 것들 중에서 가장 맛있는 디저트는 초콜릿 케이크이다.

풀이 「the+최상급(+명사)+among ~」은 '~ 중에서 가장 …한/하게'로 해석한다.

구문 ▶ among: ~ 중에서

▶ all the+복수 명사: 모든 ~

6 It was reported that New York is more crowded than any other city in America.

뉴욕이 미국의 다른 어떤 도시보다도 더 붐비는 것으로 보고되었다.

풀이 「비교급+than any other+단수 명사」는 '다른 어떤 ~보다도 더 …한/하게'로 해석한다.

구문 ▶ It: 진주어인 that절 that ~ America를 대신하는 가주어

▶ was reported: 「was/were+v-ed」 ~되었다 (과거형 수동태)

▶ in America: 명사구 any other city를 수식하는 전치사구

STEP 3

1 (A) most popular (B) activities (C) latest

Q ②

해석 웹툰을 읽는 것은 오늘날 젊은 사람들 사이에서 가장 인기 있는 온라인 활동 중 하나이다. 웹툰은 왜 그렇게 인기 있을까? 첫째로, 그것들의 대부분이 무료이다. 또한, 웹툰에는 흥미로운 등장인물들이 있다. 마지막으로, 사람들은 가장 최신의 스마트 기기로 그것들에 쉽게 접근할 수 있다. 이런 이유로, 많은 젊은 사람들이 그것들을 읽는 것을 매우 좋아한다.

구문해설

1행 **Reading webtoons** is one of the ~.

▶ Reading webtoons: 동명사구 주어

4행 Finally, people can easily access them **with** the latest smart devices.

▶ with: ~으로, ~을 써서

5행 For these reasons, many young people **love reading** them.

▶ love+v-ing[to-v]: ~하는 것을 매우 좋아하다

문제해설

1 (A), (B) 「one of the+최상급+복수 명사」 표현이므로, (A)는 popular의 최상급인 most popular, (B)는 복수명사 activities가 어법에 맞다.

(C) 형용사 late의 최상급은 the latest이다.

Q 웹툰은 무료이고, 흥미로운 등장인물이 나오며, 접근하기가 쉽기 때문에 인기 있다는 내용의 글이므로, 글의 주제로는 ②'웹툰이 인기 있는 이유'가 가장 적절하다.

① 웹툰을 읽는 것의 문제점
③ 웹툰과 만화책의 차이점

2 it lives longer than any other animal

해석 모든 동물 중에서 어느 동물이 가장 오래 살까? 그것은 코끼리가 아니다. 그것은 거북도 아니다. 그것은 육방해면이다! 어떤 동물도 이 해면보다 더 오래 살지 않는다. 그것은 지구상에서 가장 단순한 동물들 중 하나이다. 그것은 팔, 장기, 심지어 머리도 없다. 그러나 그것은 동물이며, 15,000년 동안 살 수 있다.

육방해면은 지구상에서 가장 단순한 동물 중 하나이고, 그것은 다른 어떤 동물보다도 더 오래 산다.

구문해설

1행 It's not the tortoise **either**.
▶ either: ~도 또한(부정문)

4행 But it's an animal, and it can live **for 15,000 years**.
▶ for+시간: ~ 동안

문제해설

2 '다른 어떤 ~보다도 더 …한/하게'는 「비교급+than any other+단수 명사」로 표현한다.

Wrap Up p.74

❶ as ❷ than ❸ the+비교급 ❹ 복수

1 Dolphins are one of the smartest animals.
2 This building is twice as tall as that building.
3 Ms. Han explains grammar the most clearly.
4 The higher we go up, the colder it gets.
5 This desk is cheaper than that one.
6 Jim is kinder than any other student in my school.
(= No student in my school is as kind as Jim.
= No student in my school is kinder than Jim.)

UNIT 08 관계사

Point 01 주격 관계대명사 p.76

315 I saw / a man <that looked like my father>.
나는 보았다 / 한 남자를 <내 아버지처럼 보이는>
나는 내 아버지처럼 보이는 한 남자를 보았다.

316 People <who always complain> / don't have many friends.
사람들은 <항상 불평하는> / 많은 친구들을 가지고 있지 않다
항상 불평하는 사람들은 친구가 많지 않다.

317 Do you know / a coffee shop <that is open for 24 hours>?
너는 알고 있니 / 커피숍을 <24시간 영업하는>
너는 24시간 영업하는 커피숍을 알고 있니?

318 Anyone <who loves climbing mountains> / can join our club.
누구나 <등산하는 것을 매우 좋아하는> / 우리 동아리에 가입할 수 있다
등산하는 것을 좋아하는 사람은 누구나 우리 동아리에 가입할 수 있다.

319 I will buy / a house <that has a nice garden>, / and grow / flowers <which smell nice>.
나는 살 것이다 / 집을 <멋진 정원을 가진>, / 그리고 기를 것이다 / 꽃들을 <좋은 향이 나는>
나는 멋진 정원이 있는 집을 사서 좋은 향이 나는 꽃들을 기를 것이다.

320 The thief <who stole my bag> / was arrested.
도둑이 <내 가방을 훔친> / 체포되었다
내 가방을 훔친 도둑이 체포되었다.

321 Emma read / an article [about a bear and a man <that live together / in a house>].
Emma는 읽었다 / 기사를 [곰과 남자에 관한 <함께 사는 / 한 집에>]
Emma는 한 집에 함께 사는 곰과 남자에 관한 기사를 읽었다.

Point 02 목적격 관계대명사 p.77

326 Do you have / an adult <who you can consult>?
너는 있니 / 어른이 <네가 상담할 수 있는>
너는 네가 상담할 수 있는 어른이 있니?

327 Is this / the key <which you need / for the door>?
이것이 ~이니 / 열쇠 <네가 필요한 / 그 문을 위해>
이것이 네가 그 문을 열기 위해 필요한 열쇠니?

328 The fish <which we caught / yesterday> / is still alive.
물고기는 <우리가 잡았던 / 어제> / 아직 살아 있다
우리가 어제 잡았던 물고기는 아직 살아 있다.

329 The cook <whom we will meet> / was introduced / on a TV show.

그 요리사는 <우리가 만날> / 소개되었다 / 한 TV 쇼에서

우리가 만날 그 요리사는 한 TV 쇼에서 소개되었다.

330 I read / the book <that you recommended>, // and I found / it enjoyable.

나는 읽었다 / 그 책을 <네가 추천했던>, // 그리고 나는 생각했다 / 그것이 재미있다고

나는 네가 추천했던 책을 읽었고 그것이 재미있다고 생각했다.

331 [Since I know / the man <who the detectives are chasing>], / I was shocked / to hear the news.

[나는 알기 때문에 / 그 남자를 <형사들이 쫓고 있는>], / 나는 충격을 받았다 / 그 뉴스를 듣고

나는 형사들이 쫓고 있는 그 남자를 알기 때문에 그 뉴스를 듣고 충격을 받았다.

332 The farmer has / a son and a sheepdog <that help him / on the farm>.

그 농부는 가지고 있다 / 아들과 양치기 개를 <그를 도와주는 / 농장에서>

그 농부는 농장에서 그를 도와주는 아들과 양치기 개가 있다.

Unit Practice pp.78~79

STEP 1

1 Anyone / who[that] loves climbing mountains / can join our club.

풀이 선행사 Anyone이 사람이고 관계대명사가 관계사절에서 주어 역할이므로, 선행사 Anyone 뒤에 「주격 관계대명사(who[that])+동사(loves)+목적어(climbing mountains) ~」의 순서로 배열한다.

구문 love+v-ing: ~하는 것을 대단히 좋아하다

2 The book / which[that] I borrowed from the library / was very interesting.

풀이 선행사 The book이 사물이고 관계대명사가 관계사절에서 목적어 역할이므로, 선행사 The book 뒤에 「목적격 관계대명사(which[that])+주어(I)+동사(borrowed)+전치사구(from the library) ~」의 순서로 배열한다.

구문 borrow A from B: B로부터 A를 빌리다

3 The salesperson / (who(m)[that]) you asked for help / was friendly.

풀이 선행사 The salesperson이 사람이고 생략된 관계대명사가 관계사절에서 목적어 역할을 하므로, 선행사 The salesperson 뒤에 「주어(you)+동사(asked) ~」의 순서로 배열한다. 목적격 관계대명사 who(m)[that]는 생략이 가능하다.

구문 ask for: ~을 요청하다

STEP 2

1 Have you seen the backpack which has my laptop in it?

안에 내 노트북이 든 배낭을 본 적이 있니?

풀이 주격 관계대명사 which가 이끄는 절이 선행사 the backpack을 수식하는 형태로 해석한다.

구문 Have/Has+주어+v-ed ~?: ~한 적이 있니? (현재완료 의문문)

2 The flight (which[that]) we booked was delayed due to bad weather.

우리가 예약한 항공편이 안 좋은 날씨 때문에 연기되었다.

풀이 목적격 관계대명사 which[that]가 생략된 절이 선행사 The flight를 수식하는 형태로 해석한다.

구문 was/were+v-ed: ~되었다 (과거형 수동태)

3 The concert ticket (which[that]) she bought for me for my birthday was expensive.

그녀가 내 생일을 위해 나에게 사 준 콘서트 티켓은 비쌌다.

풀이 목적격 관계대명사 which[that]가 생략된 절이 선행사 The concert ticket을 수식하는 형태로 해석한다.

4 I saw a man and a dog that were wearing the same kind of shirt in the park.

나는 공원에서 같은 종류의 셔츠를 입고 있는 남자와 개를 보았다.

풀이 주격 관계대명사 that이 이끄는 절이 선행사 a man and a dog를 수식하는 형태로 해석한다. 선행사가 사람과 동물이므로 관계대명사 that을 쓴다.

구문 was/were+v-ing: ~하고 있었다 (과거진행)

5 Phillip met an old friend whom he had not seen in years at the grocery store.

Phillip은 몇 년간 보지 못했던 오래된 친구를 식료품점에서 만났다.

풀이 목적격 관계대명사 whom이 이끄는 절이 선행사 an old friend를 수식하는 형태로 해석한다.

구문 had v-ed: ~했었다 (과거완료)

6 Daisy heard that the teacher who taught her English would retire this year.

Daisy는 그녀에게 영어를 가르쳤던 선생님께서 올해에 은퇴하실 것이라는 것을 들었다.

풀이 주격 관계대명사 who가 이끄는 절이 선행사 the teacher를 수식하는 형태로 해석한다.

구문 ▶ that: 동사 heard의 명사절 목적어를 이끄는 접속사
▶ teach+간접목적어+직접목적어: ~에게 …을 가르치다

STEP ③

1 ②
Q (1) T (2) F

해석 당신은 사막에 사는 물고기에 대해 들어본 적이 있는가? 그들은 폐어이며, 아프리카에서 발견된다. 가끔, 강물이 건조한 지역으로 범람해서 작은 연못들이 형성된다. 폐어는 그 홍수와 함께 이동하여 그 연못 속에서 산다. 그 물이 마르면, 폐어는 진흙 속에 숨는다. 그러고 나서 그들은 몸 안에 저장해 둔 영양분들로 수개월 동안 그곳에서 산다.

구문해설

1행 **Have you *heard of*** fish which[that] live in the desert?
▶ Have/Has+주어+v-ed ~?: ~한 적이 있는가? (현재완료 의문문)
▶ hear of: ~에 대해 듣다

They're lungfish, and they **are found** in Africa.
▶ am/are/is+v-ed: ~되다 (수동태)

4행 Then they live **there** for months on nutrients which[that] they *have saved* inside their body.
▶ there: in the mud를 가리키는 부사
▶ have/has+v-ed: ~했다 (현재완료)

문제해설

1 (A)에는 동물(fish) 선행사 뒤에 올 수 있는 관계대명사 which나 that을 써야 한다. 이때 which나 that은 관계사절 안에서 주어 역할을 하므로 주격 관계대명사이다.
(B)에는 사물(nutrients) 선행사 뒤에 올 수 있는 관계대명사 which나 that을 써야 한다. 이때 which나 that은 관계사절 안에서 목적어 역할을 하므로 목적격 관계대명사이다.

Q (1) 폐어는 연못의 물이 마르면 진흙에 숨어서 몸에 저장해 둔 영양분으로 수개월은 산다고 했으므로, 물 없이도 몇 달을 살 수 있음을 알 수 있다.
(2) 폐어는 물이 범람할 때 그 물과 함께 건조한 지역으로 이동한다고 했으나, 사막에서 태어나는지의 여부는 글에서 알 수 없다.

2 He was a politician who[that] had great wealth.

해석 크리스마스 이야기 *A Christmas Carol*은 스크루지라고 이름 지어진 한 인색한 남자에 관한 내용이다. 사실, 18세기에 진짜 스크루지가 있었다. 그의 이름은 John Elwes였다. 그는 엄청난 재산을 가진 정치인이었다. 하지만 그는 그것을 쓰는 것을 거부했다. 그는 주인이 없는 낡고 더러운 집에서 살았다. 그는 또한 돈을 절약하기 위해 썩은 음식들을 먹었다.

구문해설

2행 In fact, **there was** a real Scrooge in the eighteenth century.
▶ there was+단수 명사: ~이 있었다

3행 However, he **refused to spend** it.
▶ refuse+to-v: ~하기를 거부하다

4행 He also ate rotten food **to save money**.
▶ 부사 역할의 to부정사구 (목적)

문제해설

2 선행사 a politician이 사람이고 관계대명사가 관계사절에서 주어 역할을 하므로, 선행사 a politician 뒤에 「주격 관계대명사(who[that])+동사(had)+목적어(great wealth)」의 순서로 배열한다.

Point 03 소유격 관계대명사 p.80

337 Christina gave me / a skirt <whose size was big / for her>.
Christina는 나에게 주었다 / 치마를 <그것의 치수가 큰 / 그녀에게>
Christina는 그녀에게 치수가 큰 치마를 나에게 주었다.

338 The pen <whose cap is missing> / is Andy's.
그 펜은 <그것의 뚜껑이 없는> / Andy의 것이다
뚜껑이 없는 그 펜은 Andy의 것이다.

339 A man <whose hair was blond> / asked my name.
한 남자가 <그의 머리카락이 금발인> / 내 이름을 물었다
머리카락이 금발인 한 남자가 내 이름을 물었다.

340 She is / a writer <whose book has sold / millions of copies>.
그녀는 ~이다 / 작가 <그녀의 책이 팔린 / 수백만 부가>
그녀는 자신의 책이 수백만 부가 팔린 작가이다.

341 I saw / a movie <whose reviews were good>, // but to me / it was boring.
나는 봤다 / 영화를 <그것의 평가가 좋았던>, // 하지만 내게 / 그 영화는 지루했다
나는 평가가 좋았던 영화를 봤지만, 내게 그 영화는 지루했다.

342 There is / a friend <whose name is the same as mine> / in my class.
있다 / 친구가 <그의 이름이 나와 같은> / 우리 반에
우리 반에는 이름이 나와 같은 친구가 있다.

343 This is / a café <whose owner is a famous actor>. So people <who want to see him> / often come / here.
이곳은 ~이다 / 카페 <그곳의 주인이 유명한 배우인>. 그래서 사람들이 <그를 만나고 싶은> / 종종 온다 / 이곳에

이곳은 주인이 유명한 배우인 카페이다. 그래서 그를 만나고 싶은 사람들이 종종 이곳에 온다.

Point 04 관계부사 p. 81

347 The doctors explained / <how they cured the patient>.

그 의사들은 설명했다 / <어떻게 그들이 그 환자를 치료했는지를>

그 의사들은 어떻게 그들이 그 환자를 치료했는지를 설명했다.

348 Peter wondered / the reason <why Helen didn't call him>.

Peter는 궁금했다 / 이유가 <Helen이 그에게 전화하지 않은>

Peter는 Helen이 그에게 전화하지 않은 이유가 궁금했다.

349 I live / in a town <where I can see many stars / at night>.

나는 산다 / 마을에 <많은 별들을 볼 수 있는 / 밤에>

나는 밤에 많은 별들을 볼 수 있는 마을에 산다.

350 The date <when the movie was released> / was March 24.

날짜는 <그 영화가 개봉된> / 3월 24일이었다

그 영화가 개봉된 날짜는 3월 24일이었다.

351 Spring is / a time <when many people like / to go hiking / in the mountains>.

봄은 ~이다 / 시기 <많은 사람들이 즐기는 / 하이킹을 가는 것을 / 산으로>

봄은 많은 사람들이 산으로 하이킹 가는 것을 즐기는 시기이다.

352 Do you know / the reason <why he was absent from school / yesterday>?

너는 아니 / 이유를 <그가 학교에 결석한 / 어제>

너는 그가 어제 학교에 결석한 이유를 아니?

353 She showed me / the way <she solved the math problem> / step by step.

그녀는 내게 보여 주었다 / 방법을 <그녀가 그 수학 문제를 풀었던> / 차근차근

그녀는 내게 그녀가 그 수학 문제를 풀었던 방법을 차근차근 보여 주었다.

Unit Practice pp.82~83

STEP 1

1 The book whose cover is torn / belongs to Sarah.

풀이 선행사 The book과 명사 cover가 소유의 관계이므로 절 안에서 소유격 대명사 역할을 할 소유격 관계대명사가 와야 한다. 따라서 The book 뒤에 「소유격 관계대명사(whose)+명사(cover)+동사(is torn) ~」의 순서로 배열한다.

구문 am/are/is+v-ed: ~되다 (수동태)

2 Do you remember the station / where we have to get off?

풀이 장소를 나타내는 선행사 the station을 관계부사 where가 이끄는 절이 수식하고 있으므로, 선행사 the station 뒤에 「관계부사(where)+주어(we)+동사(have to get off)」의 순서로 배열한다.

구문 have to: ~해야 한다 (의무)

3 Let me know the reason / why you are feeling stressed / lately.

풀이 이유를 나타내는 선행사 the reason을 관계부사 why가 이끄는 절이 수식하고 있으므로, 선행사 the reason 뒤에 「관계부사(why)+주어(you)+동사(are feeling) ~」의 순서로 배열한다.

구문 ▶ let+목적어+목적격보어(동사원형): 목적어가 ~하도록 허용[허락]하다

▶ am/are/is+v-ing: ~하고 있다 (현재진행)

▶ feel+형용사: ~하게 느끼다

STEP 2

1 I will refund a jacket whose sleeves are too long for me.

나는 내게 소매가 너무 긴 재킷을 환불할 것이다.

풀이 선행사 a jacket과 명사 sleeves는 소유의 관계에 있고 whose는 절 안에서 소유격 대명사의 역할을 하는 소유격 관계대명사이다.

구문 too: 너무 ~한

2 The chef never tells us the way he makes his secret sauce.

그 요리사는 그의 비밀 소스를 만드는 방법을 우리에게 절대로 말하지 않는다.

풀이 관계부사절 he makes ~ sauce가 선행사 the way를 수식하고 있으며, '~한 방법[방식]'으로 해석한다. 관계부사 how와 선행사 the way는 함께 쓰지 않고, 둘 중 하나만 쓴다.

구문 tell+간접목적어+직접목적어: ~에게 …을 말하다

3 Isabella has a son whose birthday is the same as mine.

Isabella는 생일이 나와 같은 아들이 있다.

풀이 선행사 a son과 명사 birthday는 소유의 관계에 있고 whose는 절 안에서 소유격 대명사의 역할을 하는 소유격 관계대명사이다.

구문 mine: I의 소유격 대명사 (= my birthday)

4 There must be a reason why he isn't answering his phone.

그가 계속 전화를 받지 않는 이유가 있는 것임이 틀림없다.

풀이 이유를 나타내는 선행사 a reason을 관계부사절 why ~ phone이 수식하고 있으며, '~한 이유'로 해석한다.

구문 must: ~임이 틀림없다 (강한 확신)

5 I was there at the time when Ethan performed in the school play.

Ethan이 학교 연극에서 공연할 때 나는 그곳에 있었다.

풀이 시간을 나타내는 선행사 the time을 관계부사절 when ~ play가 수식하고 있으며, '~할 때[시간]'로 해석한다.

구문 in the school play: 동사 performed를 수식하는 전치사구

6 The teacher explained to the students how plants adapt to their environment.

선생님은 학생들에게 식물이 어떻게 그들의 환경에 적응하는지를 설명해 주셨다.

풀이 관계부사절 how ~ environment는 '~한 방법[방식]'으로 해석한다. 선행사 the way와 관계부사 how는 둘 중 하나만 쓴다.

STEP 3

1 (A) whose (B) where

Q ③

해석 어느 추운 밤, 옷이 닳고 닳은 한 여자가 법정에 불려 왔다. 그녀는 아이들을 위해 빵을 훔쳤었다. 그녀는 불쌍해 보였지만, 판사는 "법에는 예외가 없습니다. 나는 당신에게 10달러의 벌금을 부과합니다."라고 말했다. 그러고 나서 그는 자기 지갑에서 10달러를 꺼내 그녀의 벌금을 지불했다. 그는 "사람이 살기 위해 빵을 훔쳐야 하는 도시에 살고 있기 때문에 저는 이곳에 있는 모두에게도 1달러씩의 벌금을 부과합니다."라고 말했다.

구문해설

1행 One cold night, a woman ~ **was brought** to court.

▶ was/were+v-ed: ~되었다 (과거형 수동태)

2행 She **had stolen** bread for her children.

▶ had v-ed: ~했었다 (과거완료)

5행 He said, "I also fine everyone here $1 **for living** in a town where people *have to* steal bread **to live**."

▶ for+v-ing: ~ 때문에

▶ have to: ~해야 한다

▶ to live: 부사 역할의 to부정사 (목적)

문제해설

1 (A) 선행사 a woman과 명사 clothes는 소유의 관계에 있으므로, 빈칸에는 소유격 관계대명사 whose가 적절하다.

(B) 선행사가 장소를 나타내는 a town이고, 관계사가 절 안에서 부사 역할을 하므로, 빈칸에는 관계부사 where가 적절하다.

Q 불쌍한 여인을 위해 벌금을 대신 내주고 마을 사람들에게도 교훈 차원으로 벌금을 내린 것을 통해 판사의 사려 깊은 성격을 짐작할 수 있다. 따라서 판사를 묘사하는 말로는 ③'사려 깊은'이 가장 적절하다.

① 탐욕스러운 ② 정직한

2 ① which → whose

② when → why

해석 남아메리카에는 부리가 자기 몸통보다 더 긴 새가 있다. 그것은 칼부리벌새이다. 그것의 부리가 그렇게 긴 이유가 있다. 그것은 후크시아 같은 깊은 꽃에서 (나오는 것을) 먹는 것을 즐긴다. 그렇게 하기 위해, 시간이 흐르면서 칼부리벌새는 긴 부리를 발달시켰다.

구문해설

2행 There is a reason **why** its bill is so long.

▶ a reason을 선행사로 하는 관계부사

It **enjoys eating** from deep flowers, *like* fuchsia.

▶ enjoy+v-ing: ~하는 것을 즐기다

▶ like: ~같은

3행 **To do so**, the sword-billed ~.:

▶ 부사 역할의 to부정사구(목적)

문제해설

2 ① 선행사 a bird와 명사 bill은 소유의 관계이므로 절 안에서 소유격 대명사 역할을 할 소유격 관계대명사가 필요하다. 따라서 which를 whose로 고쳐야 한다.

② 앞에 이유를 나타내는 선행사 a reason이 있으므로, 관계부사 why로 고쳐야 한다.

③ 동사 enjoy는 동명사 eating을 목적어로 씀

④ To do는 목적을 나타내는 부사 역할의 to부정사구

Wrap Up p.84

❶ that ❷ which ❸ whose ❹ how

1 We visited the place where we first met.

2 I like people who[that] keep their promises.

3 The cat that[which] has white fur is my pet.

4 They live in a house whose door is painted red.

5 The dream (that[which]) I had last night was strange.

6 This is how[the way] the machine works.

UNIT 09

접속사와 분사구문

Point 01 시간 접속사 p.86

358 <As I got off the bus>, / I saw my father / at the stop.
<버스에서 내렸을 때>, / 나는 아버지를 보았다 / 정류장에서
버스에서 내렸을 때 나는 정류장에서 아버지를 보았다.

359 The boys played soccer / <until the sun went down>.
그 소년들은 축구를 했다 / <해가 질 때까지>
그 소년들은 해가 질 때까지 축구를 했다.

360 <While I was / in the hospital>, / I kept a diary / every day.
<내가 있던 동안 / 병원에>, / 나는 일기를 썼다 / 매일
나는 병원에 있는 동안 매일 일기를 썼다.

361 You must fasten your seat belt / <before you drive>.
당신은 안전벨트를 매야 한다 / <당신이 운전하기 전에>
당신은 운전하기 전에 안전벨트를 매야 한다.

362 The dog has been / in her family / <since it was just a puppy>.
그 개는 있었다 / 그녀의 가족에게 / <그것이 강아지였을 때부터>
그 개는 강아지였을 때부터 그녀의 가족에게 있었다.

363 <While I was hiking / up a mountain>, / I twisted my ankle.
<내가 하이킹하던 중에 / 산으로>, / 나는 발목을 삐었다
산을 오르던 중에 나는 발목을 삐었다.

364 Paul took the bus / <after school was over>. <When he got home>, / he realized / <that he had left his bag / on the bus>.
Paul은 버스를 탔다 / <학교가 끝난 뒤에>. <그가 집에 도착했을 때>, / 그는 알아차렸다 / <그가 그의 가방을 두고 온 것을 / 버스에>
Paul은 학교가 끝난 뒤에 버스를 탔다. 그가 집에 도착했을 때 그는 그의 가방을 버스에 두고 온 것을 알아차렸다.

Point 02 이유·조건 접속사 p.87

369 She wore a coat / <since it was quite cold / that evening>.
그녀는 코트를 입었다 / <꽤 추웠기 때문에 / 그날 저녁에>
그날 저녁에 꽤 추웠기 때문에 그녀는 코트를 입었다.

370 You can't enter the museum / <unless you buy a ticket>.
너는 박물관에 들어갈 수 없다 / <네가 표를 사지 않으면>
너는 표를 사지 않으면 박물관에 들어갈 수 없다.

371 <As I didn't have breakfast / this morning>, / I feel really hungry / now.
<나는 아침 식사를 하지 않아서 / 오늘 아침에>, / 정말 배가 고프다 / 지금
나는 오늘 아침에 아침 식사를 하지 않아서 지금 정말 배가 고프다.

372 Ricky was happy / <because his parents threw him / a surprise party>.
Ricky는 행복했다 / <그의 부모님이 그에게 열어 주셨기 때문에 / 깜짝 파티를>
그의 부모님이 그에게 깜짝 파티를 열어 주셨기 때문에 Ricky는 행복했다.

373 <Since Becky and I don't like / crowded places>, / we won't go to the beach.
<Becky와 나는 좋아하지 않기 때문에 / 붐비는 장소를>, / 우리는 해변에 가지 않을 것이다
Becky와 나는 붐비는 장소를 좋아하지 않기 때문에 우리는 해변에 가지 않을 것이다.

374 He couldn't get on the plane / <because he left his passport / at home>.
그는 비행기에 탈 수 없었다 / <그가 여권을 두고 왔기 때문에 / 집에>
그는 여권을 집에 두고 왔기 때문에 비행기에 탈 수 없었다.

375 <Unless you are missing / the receipt>, / you can return the item / to us. But you can't get a refund / <if you removed / the price tag>.
<당신이 빠뜨리지 않는다면 / 영수증을>, / 당신은 그 물품을 반품해도 됩니다 / 우리에게. 하지만 당신은 환불받을 수 없습니다 / <당신이 제거했다면 / 가격표를>
당신이 영수증을 빠뜨리지 않는다면 당신은 그 물품을 우리에게 반품해도 됩니다. 하지만 가격표를 제거했다면 당신은 환불받을 수 없습니다.

Unit Practice pp.88~89

STEP 1

1 Kate stayed / at home / until her mother came.
풀이 '~(할 때)까지'는 시간 접속사 until로 표현한다.

2 They couldn't sleep / last night / because[since/as] it was too hot.

풀이 '~하기 때문에'는 이유 접속사 because[since/as]로 표현한다.

구문 it: 비인칭 주어 (날씨)

3 If you don't take care of your plants, / they will die.

풀이 '(만약) ~하지 않으면'은 조건 접속사 if ~ not 또는 unless로 표현할 수 있는데, 빈칸 개수에 따라 if ~ not을 쓴다.

STEP 2

1 Please turn off your cell phone before the performance begins.

공연이 시작되기 전에 휴대폰을 꺼주세요.

풀이 before는 시간 부사절을 이끄는 접속사로, '~하기 전에'로 해석한다.

2 David hasn't eaten ice cream since he started his diet.

David는 다이어트를 시작한 이후로 아이스크림을 먹지 않았다.

풀이 since는 시간 부사절을 이끄는 접속사로, '~한 이후로'로 해석한다.

구문 have/has+v-ed: ~했다 (현재완료)

3 When I catch a cold, my mom makes hot tea with honey.

내가 감기에 걸릴 때 엄마는 따뜻한 꿀차를 만드신다.

풀이 when은 시간 부사절을 이끄는 접속사로, '~할 때'로 해석한다.

4 I couldn't focus on the exam because I stayed up all night.

나는 밤을 샜기 때문에 시험에 집중할 수 없었다.

풀이 because는 이유 부사절을 이끄는 접속사로, '~하기 때문에'로 해석한다.

5 You can't go into the swimming pool unless you wear a swimming cap.

네가 수영 모자를 쓰지 않으면 수영장에 들어갈 수 없다.

풀이 unless는 조건 부사절을 이끄는 접속사로, '(만약) ~하지 않으면'으로 해석한다.

6 Harper enjoys chatting with her friends while she is having lunch at school.

Harper는 학교에서 점심을 먹는 동안 그녀의 친구들과 수다를 떠는 것을 즐긴다.

풀이 while은 시간 부사절을 이끄는 접속사로, '~하는 동안'으로 해석한다.

구문 ▶ enjoy+v-ing: ~하는 것을 즐기다

▶ am/are/is+v-ing: ~하고 있다 (현재진행)

STEP 3

1 (A) if (B) because

문장 해석은 아래 해석 참조

Q ③

해석 다른 동물들처럼, 고양이들은 날씨의 변화를 감지할 수 있다. 예를 들어, (A) 당신의 고양이가 재채기를 많이 한다면, 아마도 곧 비가 내릴 것이다. 그리고 당신의 고양이가 코를 골거나 오랫동안 (바닥에) 등을 댄 채 누워 있을 때, 그것은 좋지 않은 소식이다. 눈 장화를 준비하라, (B) 아마도 날씨가 더 나빠질 것이기 때문이다!

구문해설

1행 **Like** other animals, cats can sense changes in weather.

▶ like+명사: ~처럼

2행 ~, **it** will probably rain soon.

▶ it: 비인칭 주어 (날씨)

3행 Get your snow boots ready, because the weather will probably **get worse**!

▶ get+형용사: ~해지다

문제해설

1 (A) 문맥상 조건 접속사 if(~한다면)가 적절하다.

(B) 문맥상 이유 접속사 because(~하기 때문에)가 적절하다.

Q 빈칸 뒤 예시를 통해 고양이의 행동에 따라 날씨 예측이 가능함을 알 수 있으므로, 빈칸에 들어갈 말로는 ③ '날씨의 변화를 감지하다'가 가장 적절하다.

① 하루 종일 자다

② 쉽게 감기에 걸리다

2 if you plan to live there with your dog

해석 만약 당신이 당신의 개와 함께 네덜란드에 살 계획이라면, 이것을 기억하라. 네덜란드에 있는 대부분의 도시는 개 세금을 부과한다. 당신이 도착했을 때, 당신의 개를 현지 시청에 등록해야 한다. 세금 총액은 당신이 데리고 있는 개의 수에 의해 결정된다. 금액은 도시마다 다르기 때문에, 당신은 당신의 반려동물을 데리고 가기로 결심하기 전에 확인해야 한다.

> 네덜란드에서는, 대부분의 도시가 개 세금을 부과한다. 그래서 만약 당신이 당신의 개와 함께 그곳에 살 계획이라면, 당신은 당신이 살고 싶은 도시의 구체적인 세금 액수를 확인해야 한다.

구문해설

1행 **If** you *plan to live* in the Netherlands with your dog, remember this: most cities **in the Netherlands** charge a dog tax.

▶ if: (만약) ~한다면

▶ plan+to-v: ~할 계획이다
▶ in the Netherlands: 명사구 most cities를 수식하는 전치사구

2행 When you arrive, you **must** *register* your dogs *with* the local city hall.
▶ must: ~해야 한다
▶ register A with B: A를 B에 등록하다

4행 As prices vary **from city to city**, you should check before you *decide to bring* your pet.
▶ from city to city: 도시마다
▶ decide+to-v: ~하기로 결심하다

문제해설

2 '만약 ~한다면'은 조건 접속사 if로 표현하고 '~할 계획이다'는 「plan+to-v」로 표현한다. 조건 부사절에서는 현재시제로 미래를 나타낸다.

Point 03 분사구문_동시상황 p.90

379 He lay on the beach, / <watching the sunset>.
그는 해변에 누워 있었다, / <일몰을 보면서>
일몰을 보면서 그는 해변에 누워 있었다.

380 <Holding some flowers>, / Dorothy knocked on the door.
<약간의 꽃을 들고서>, / Dorothy는 문을 두드렸다.

381 <Cleaning his room>, / he talked with his mother / on the phone.
<방을 청소하면서>, / 그는 어머니와 이야기했다 / 전화로
방을 청소하면서 그는 어머니와 통화했다.

382 <Listening to the radio>, / I heard / the weather forecast <for today>.
<라디오를 들으면서>, / 나는 들었다 / 일기 예보를 <오늘의>
라디오를 들으면서 나는 오늘의 일기 예보를 들었다.

383 Jimmy drove down the road, / <singing his favorite song>.
Jimmy는 도로를 운전했다, / <그가 가장 좋아하는 노래를 부르면서>
그가 가장 좋아하는 노래를 부르면서 Jimmy는 도로를 운전했다.

384 <Sitting by the lake>, / Rachel enjoyed / the fresh air and sunshine.
<호숫가에 앉아서>, / Rachel은 즐겼다 / 상쾌한 공기와 햇살을
호숫가에 앉아서 Rachel은 상쾌한 공기와 햇살을 즐겼다.

385 [Handing Joanna / a letter <of apology>], / Dana said / <that she was sorry>.
[Joanna에게 건네면서 / 편지를 <사과의>], / Dana는 말했다 / <그녀가 미안하다고>
Joanna에게 사과의 편지를 건네면서 Dana는 미안하다고 말했다.

Point 04 분사구문_시간, 이유 p.91

390 <Living by the sea>, / I always enjoy fresh seafood.
= <Because I live by the sea>
<바닷가에 살기 때문에>, / 나는 항상 신선한 해산물을 즐긴다.

391 <Being afraid of snakes>, / he didn't even look at / my pet snake.
= <Because he was afraid of snakes>
<뱀을 무서워하기 때문에>, / 그는 쳐다보지도 않았다 / 나의 반려 뱀을
뱀을 무서워하기 때문에 그는 나의 반려 뱀을 쳐다보지도 않았다.

392 <Walking to the store>, / Sarah found some money / on the ground.
= <When she was walking / to the store>
<가게로 걸어갈 때>, / Sarah는 약간의 돈을 발견했다 / 땅바닥에서
가게로 걸어갈 때 Sarah는 땅바닥에서 약간의 돈을 발견했다.

393 <Waking up / in the morning>, / I smelled something delicious.
= <When I woke up / in the morning>
<잠에서 깼을 때 / 아침에>, / 나는 무언가 맛있는 냄새를 맡았다
아침에 잠에서 깼을 때 나는 무언가 맛있는 냄새를 맡았다.

394 <Being ill>, / he was absent from work / for a few days.
= <Since he was ill>
<아팠기 때문에>, / 그는 결근했다 / 며칠간
아팠기 때문에 그는 며칠간 결근했다.

395 [Knowing / <Hazel always keeps a secret>], / I talk about my worries / with her.
[알기 때문에 / <Hazel이 항상 비밀을 지킨다는 것을>], / 나는 나의 걱정거리에 대해 이야기한다 / 그녀와
Hazel이 항상 비밀을 지킨다는 것을 알기 때문에 나는 나의 걱정거리에 대해 그녀와 이야기한다.

396 <Leaving the house>, / she took her jacket / and surveyed herself / in the mirror.
<집을 나설 때>, / 그녀는 그녀의 재킷을 챙겼다 / 그리고 자

기 자신을 살폈다 / 거울로

집을 나설 때 그녀는 그녀의 재킷을 챙겼고 거울로 자기 자신을 살폈다.

Unit Practice pp.92~93

STEP 1

1 Walking to the store, / Sarah found some money / on the ground.

풀이 시간을 나타내는 분사구문이 되도록 동사 walk를 현재분사 Walking으로 바꾸어 쓴다.

2 Lying on my bed, / I read my favorite comic books.

풀이 동시상황을 나타내는 분사구문이 되도록 동사 lie를 현재분사 Lying으로 바꾸어 쓴다.

3 Knowing the answer, / she raised her hand / confidently.

풀이 이유를 나타내는 분사구문이 되도록 동사 know를 현재분사 Knowing으로 바꾸어 쓴다.

구문 confidently: 동사 raised를 수식하는 부사

STEP 2

1 I nodded, saying that I agreed with David's opinion.

나는 David의 의견에 동의한다고 말하면서 고개를 끄덕였다.

풀이 동시상황을 나타내는 분사구문으로, '~하면서'로 해석한다.

구문 ▶ saying that I agreed with David's opinion
(← while[as] I said that I agreed with David's opinion)
▶ that: 동사 saying의 명사절 목적어를 이끄는 접속사

2 Hearing the news, he immediately called his best friend.

그 소식을 들은 뒤 그는 즉시 그의 가장 친한 친구에게 전화했다.

풀이 시간을 나타내는 분사구문으로, '~한 뒤'로 해석한다.

구문 ▶ Hearing the news (← After he heard the news)
▶ immediately: 동사 called를 수식하는 부사

3 Brushing his daughter's hair, Hudson hummed a lullaby.

딸의 머리카락을 빗겨 주면서 Hudson은 자장가를 흥얼거렸다.

풀이 동시상황을 나타내는 분사구문으로, '~하면서'로 해석한다.

구문 Brushing his daughter's hair
(← While[As] he brushed his daughter's hair)

4 Being so busy these days, he must work on weekends.

요즘 너무 바빠서 그는 주말에도 일을 해야 한다.

풀이 이유를 나타내는 분사구문으로, '~하기 때문에'로 해석한다.

구문 Being so busy these days
(← Because[Since/As] he is so busy these days)

5 Entering her room, she was surprised to find a small bug.

그녀의 방에 들어갔을 때 그녀는 작은 벌레를 발견해서 깜짝 놀랐다.

풀이 시간을 나타내는 분사구문으로, '~했을 때'로 해석한다.

구문 ▶ Entering her room
(← When she entered her room)
▶ to find a small bug: 부사 역할의 to부정사구 (감정의 원인)

6 Feeling like challenging ourselves, we planned to go skydiving together.

도전하고 싶었기 때문에 우리는 같이 스카이다이빙을 하러 가기로 계획했다.

풀이 이유를 나타내는 분사구문으로, '~했기 때문에'로 해석한다.

구문 ▶ Feeling like challenging ourselves
(← Because[Since/As] we felt like challenging ourselves)
▶ feel like v-ing: ~하고 싶다
▶ plan+to-v: ~하는 것을[하기로] 계획하다

STEP 3

1 ②
Q ③

해석 (A)식당에 도착했을 때 Mike는 많은 사람들이 기다리고 있는 것을 보았다. "오래 걸릴까요?" 그는 여자 종업원에게 물었다. 그녀는 노트에 계속해서 적고 있었다. (B)답변을 받지 못해서 Mike는 "기다리는 시간이 얼마나 걸릴까요?"라고 물었다. (C)올려다보며 그녀는 대답했다. "15분 걸릴 거예요." 몇 분 후에, 그 종업원은 다가와 "Willette B. Long 씨, 테이블이 준비되었습니다."라고 알려 주었다.

구문해설

1행 ~, Mike saw **that** many people *were waiting*.
▶ that: 동사 saw의 명사절 목적어를 이끄는 접속사
▶ was/were+v-ing: ~하고 있었다 (과거진행)

2행 She **kept writing** in her notebook.
▶ keep+v-ing: 계속해서 ~하다

3행 ~, Mike asked, "**How long** is the wait?"
▶ How long: 얼마나 오래

문제해설

1 문맥상 (A)는 '~할 때'라는 의미의 시간을 나타내는 분사구문, (B)는 '~하기 때문에'라는 이유를 나타내는 분사구문, (C)는 '~하면서'라는 동시상황을 나타내는 분사구문이다.

Q 여자 종업원은 Mike의 첫 물음을 그의 이름으로 착각하여 대기 손님 명단에 그의 이름으로 적고 있었다. 따라서 여자 종업원이 대답하지 않은 이유는 ③임을 알 수 있다.

2 (A) Having nothing else to do
(B) Turning over the pages
[Turning the pages over]

해석 비행기에서 내 좌석에 앉은 채 나는 주위를 둘러보기 시작했다. (A)달리 할 일이 없었기 때문에 나는 좌석 주머니에서 항공사 잡지를 꺼냈다. (B)페이지를 넘기면서 나는 무언가 흥미로운 것을 찾으려고 애썼다. 하지만, 그것은 대부분 광고로 가득할 뿐이었다. 나는 잡지를 내려놓고 창밖을 응시했다.

구문해설

1행 **Sitting in my seat on the airplane**, I *started to look* around.

▶ Sitting ~ airplane: 동시상황을 나타내는 분사구문
(← While[As] I sat in my seat ~.)
▶ start+to-v[v-ing]: ~하기 시작하다

Having nothing else *to do*, I **took** the airline magazine **out of** the seat pocket.

▶ Having nothing else to do: 이유를 나타내는 분사구문
(← Because[Since/As] I had nothing else to do)
▶ to do: 대명사 nothing을 수식하는 형용사 역할의 to부정사
▶ take A out of B: B에서 A를 꺼내다

2행 **Turning over the pages**, I *tried to find* something **interesting**.

▶ Turning over the pages: 동시상황을 나타내는 분사구문
(← While[As] I turned over the pages)
▶ try+to-v: ~하려고 애쓰다
▶ interesting: -thing으로 끝나는 대명사 something을 형용사 interesting이 뒤에서 수식

문제해설

2 문맥상 (A)는 이유를 나타내는 분사구문이 되도록 동사 have를 Having으로 바꿔 쓴다. 문맥상 (B)는 동시상황을 나타내는 분사구문이 되도록 동사 turn을 Turning으로 바꿔 쓴다. 동사구 turn over는 명사가 목적어일 경우, 「turn+목적어+over」 또는 「turn over+목적어」 둘 다로 쓸 수 있다.

Wrap Up p.94

❶ 동사 ❷ 동사-ing ❸ 동시상황

1 If Steve trusts you, he'll tell you everything.
2 Being tired, I drank a cup of coffee.
(Because [Since/As] I was tired, ~.)
3 Eric will wait until I return.
4 When I hear the sound of rain, I feel relaxed.
5 Waving his hand, he said hello.
(As [While] he waved his hand, ~.)

UNIT 10 가정법

Point 01 가정법 과거 p.96

401 <If I had a sister>, / I could go shopping / with her.
<만약 나에게 자매가 있다면>, / 나는 쇼핑을 갈 수 있을 텐데 / 그녀와 함께
만약 나에게 자매가 있다면 나는 그녀와 함께 쇼핑을 갈 수 있을 텐데.

402 <If you studied / harder>, / you might get better grades.
<만약 네가 공부한다면 / 더 열심히>, / 너는 더 좋은 성적을 받을지도 모를 텐데
만약 네가 더 열심히 공부한다면 너는 더 좋은 성적을 받을지도 모를 텐데.

403 We could play baseball / <if it were not raining>.
우리는 야구를 할 수 있을 텐데 / <만약 비가 오고 있지 않다면>
만약 비가 오고 있지 않다면 우리는 야구를 할 수 있을 텐데.

404 <If I met God>, / I would ask him / to give me a nice voice.
<만약 내가 신을 만난다면>, / 나는 그에게 부탁할 텐데 / 나에게 멋진 목소리를 달라고
만약 내가 신을 만난다면 나에게 멋진 목소리를 달라고 그에게 부탁할 텐데.

405 <If Charles won the lottery>, / he would travel around the world / with his family.
<만약 Charles가 복권에 당첨된다면>, / 그는 전 세계를 여행할 텐데 / 그의 가족과
만약 Charles가 복권에 당첨된다면 그는 그의 가족과 전 세계를 여행할 텐데.

406 It would be so cool / <if it were snowing / right now>.
정말 시원할 텐데 / <만약 눈이 내린다면 / 바로 지금>
만약 바로 지금 눈이 내린다면 정말 시원할 텐데.

407 <If they worked / together>, / they might solve the problem / more effectively.
<만약 그들이 일한다면 / 함께>, / 그들은 그 문제를 해결할지도 모를 텐데 / 더 효과적으로
만약 그들이 함께 일한다면 그 문제를 더 효과적으로 해결할지도 모를 텐데.

Point 02 가정법 과거완료 p.97

412 <If I had listened to you>, / I might not have lost my friends.

<만약 내가 너의 말을 들었더라면>, / 나는 내 친구들을 잃지 않았을지도 모를 텐데.

만약 내가 너의 말을 들었더라면 나는 내 친구들을 잃지 않았을지도 모를 텐데.

413 You could have exchanged your jacket / <if you had had your receipt>.

너는 네 자켓을 교환할 수 있었을 텐데 / <만약 네가 영수증을 가지고 있었더라면>

만약 네가 영수증을 가지고 있었더라면 네 자켓을 교환할 수 있었을 텐데.

414 Ken wouldn't have been stuck / in traffic / <if he had gotten up early>.

Ken은 갇혀 있지 않았을 텐데 / 교통 체증에 / <만약 그가 일찍 일어났더라면>

만약 Ken이 일찍 일어났더라면 교통 체증에 갇혀 있지 않았을 텐데.

415 <If she had been at home / at that time>, / she could have helped her mother.

<만약 그녀가 집에 있었더라면 / 그때>, / 그녀는 그녀의 어머니를 도울 수 있었을 텐데

만약 그때 그녀가 집에 있었더라면 그녀의 어머니를 도울 수 있었을 텐데.

416 [If I had known / <it was his birthday>], / I would have given a birthday gift / to him.

[만약 내가 알았더라면 / <그의 생일이라는 것을>], / 나는 생일 선물을 주었을 텐데 / 그에게

만약 내가 그의 생일인 줄 알았더라면 나는 그에게 생일 선물을 주었을 텐데.

417 <If my father had allowed / me to go out>, / I could have played / with my friends.

<만약 아버지가 허락하셨더라면 / 내가 나가는 것을>, / 나는 놀 수 있었을 텐데 / 친구들과

만약 아버지가 내가 나가는 것을 허락하셨더라면 나는 친구들과 놀 수 있었을 텐데.

418 <If Peter had not been tired>, / he might not have dozed off / during the class.

<만약 Peter가 피곤하지 않았더라면>, / 그는 졸지 않았을지도 모를 텐데 / 수업 시간 동안

만약 Peter가 피곤하지 않았더라면 그는 수업 시간 동안 졸지 않았을지도 모를 텐데.

Unit Practice pp.98~99

STEP 1

1 My wishes would come true / if I had a magic wand.

풀이 일어날 가능성이 거의 없는 일을 가정하는 가정법 과거로, 「주어+조동사 과거형+동사원형 ~ if+주어+동사의 과거형 ...」의 순서로 배열한다.

2 If Gavin were not afraid of heights, / he could go bungee jumping.

풀이 현재 사실과 반대되는 일을 가정하는 가정법 과거로, 「If+주어+동사의 과거형 ~, 주어+조동사 과거형+동사원형 ...」의 순서로 배열한다.

3 If you had read the book, / you could have understood the movie / better.

풀이 과거 사실과 반대되는 일을 가정하는 가정법 과거완료로 「If+주어+had+과거분사 ~, 주어+조동사 과거형+have+과거분사 ...」의 순서로 배열한다.

구문 better: 더 잘 (well의 비교급)

STEP 2

1 If they had taken the highway, they could have avoided the traffic jam.

그들이 고속도로를 탔더라면 교통 체증을 피할 수 있었을 텐데.

풀이 과거 사실과 반대되는 일을 가정하는 가정법 과거완료이고 조동사 과거형 could가 쓰였으므로, '(만약) ~했더라면 …할 수 있었을 텐데'로 해석한다.

2 If you gave up this opportunity, you might regret it for the rest of your life.

네가 이 기회를 포기한다면 너는 남은 네 인생 동안 그것을 후회할지도 모를 텐데.

풀이 현재 사실과 반대되는 일을 가정하는 가정법 과거이고, 조동사 과거형 might가 쓰였으므로, '(만약) ~하다면[라면] …할지도 모를 텐데'로 해석한다.

구문 ▶ it: you gave up this opportunity를 가리키는 대명사
▶ for+기간: ~ 동안
▶ of your life: 명사 the rest를 수식하는 전치사구

3 We would have brought umbrellas if we had checked the weather forecast.

우리가 일기 예보를 확인했더라면 우산을 가져왔을 텐데.

풀이 과거 사실과 반대되는 일을 가정하는 가정법 과거완료이고 조동사 과거형 would가 쓰였으므로, '(만약) ~했더라면 …했을 텐데'로 해석한다.

4 If I were a time traveler, I would witness some of the greatest moments in history.

내가 시간 여행자라면 역사에서 가장 위대한 순간들 중 몇몇을 목격할 텐데.

풀이 일어날 가능성이 거의 없는 일을 가정하는 가정법 과거이고 조동사 과거형 would가 쓰였으므로, '(만약) ~하다면[라면] …할 텐데'로 해석한다.

구문 ▶ the greatest ~ histrory: 「the+최상급+명사+in ~」 (~ 안에서[중에서] 가장 …한)

▶ in history: 명사구 the greatest moments를 수식하는 전치사구

5 If Heidi weren't busy, she could come with us to the party tonight.

Heidi가 바쁘지 않다면 그녀는 오늘밤 우리와 함께 파티에 갈 수 있을 텐데.

풀이 현재 사실과 반대되는 일을 가정하는 가정법 과거이고 조동사 과거형 could가 쓰였으므로, '(만약) ~하다면[라면] …할 수 있을 텐데'로 해석한다.

6 If we had booked the tickets earlier, we might have gotten better seats.

우리가 표를 더 일찍 예약했더라면 우리는 더 좋은 자리를 얻었을지도 모를 텐데.

풀이 과거 사실과 반대되는 일을 가정하는 가정법 과거완료이고 조동사 과거형 might가 쓰였으므로, '(만약) ~했더라면 …했을지도 모를 텐데'로 해석한다.

구문 ▶ earlier: 더 일찍 (early의 비교급)

▶ better: 더 좋은[나은] (good의 비교급)

STEP 3

1 문장 해석은 아래 해석 참조

Q ③

해석 지난 주말에, 나는 한 가게에 갔다. 집으로 돌아오는 길에, 나는 점원이 나에게 너무 많은 거스름돈을 주었다는 것을 깨달았다. 나는 그것을 가지는 것에 대해 생각해 봤지만, 곧 그것을 돌려주기로 결심했다. 만약 내가 그 돈을 가졌더라면 나는 약간의 간식을 살 수 있었을 것이다. 그러나 나는 그것을 돌려준 것을 후회하지 않는다. 나는 정직한 것에 기분이 좋다.

구문해설

2행 ~, I realized **that** the clerk *had **given*** **me too much change**.

▶ that: 동사 realized의 명사절 목적어를 이끄는 접속사

▶ had v-ed: ~했었다 (과거완료)

▶ give+간접목적어+직접목적어: ~에게 …을 주다

3행 I thought about **keeping it**, but I soon *decided to return* it.

▶ keeping it: 전치사 about의 동명사구 목적어

▶ decide+to-v: ~하기로 결심하다

5행 However, I don't **regret giving** it back.

▶ regret+v-ing: ~한 것을 후회하다

문제해설

1 과거 사실과 반대되는 일을 가정하는 가정법 과거완료이고 조동사 과거형 could가 쓰였으므로, '(만약) ~했더라면 …할 수 있었을 텐데'로 해석한다.

Q 가게 점원의 실수로 더 많은 거스름돈을 받았고, 이것을 가질지 돌려줄지 잠시 혼란스러웠지만(confused), 돌려주기로 결심하였고 자신이 정직한 것에 대해 기분이 좋다(pleased)고 했다.

2 ② would have floated → would float

③ has doubled → doubled

해석 중력이 사라진다면 어떤 일이 일어날까? 우리를 지구에 붙드는 힘이 없다면 모든 것이 떠다닐 것이다. 그러나 중력이 갑자기 두 배가 된다면 그것 또한 안 좋을 것이다. 모든 것이 갑자기 훨씬 더 무거워질지도 모르고, 많은 건물들이 무너질지도 모른다.

구문해설

2행 ~ if there were no force **holding us to the earth**.

▶ 명사 force를 수식하는 현재분사구

3행 Everything might suddenly become **much** heavier, *and* ~.

▶ much: 훨씬 (비교급 강조)

▶ and: if절(if gravity suddenly doubled)이 생략된 두 개의 절 Everything ~ heavier과 many ~ collapse 연결

문제해설

2 ② if절의 동사가 과거형(were)인 것으로 보아 가정법 과거 문장이므로, 주절의 동사는 「조동사 과거형(would)+동사원형(float)」이 되어야 한다.

③ 주절의 동사가 「조동사 과거형(would)+동사원형(be)」인 것으로 보아 가정법 과거 문장이므로, if절 동사는 동사의 과거형(doubled)이 되어야 한다.

Wrap Up

p.100

❶ 과거 ❷ 동사원형 ❸ 과거완료 ❹ had

1 If I had saved my money, I could have bought the house.

2 If I had known (that) you were coming, I would have prepared dinner.

3 You might have become a violinist if you had practiced harder.

4 If Mary loved me, I would be happy.

5 If I were a child, I could play all day.

중학

천문장

LEVEL 2

「구문이 독해로 연결되는 해석 공식」